"THE MOST EXCITING, ENRICHING AND ENTERTAINING BOOK I HAVE READ IN SOME LITTLE WHILE . . .

"This is the true story of an art acquisition, written —quite justifiably—in the style of a thriller.

"It is a fine short course in art connoisseurship, a dazzling demonstration of the urbanely cut-throat world of museum politics and international museum competition, an unvarnished portrait of the young man as a single-mindedly ambitious curator on the rise, and an astonishing proof that a first-rate suspense story can be constructed with neither sex nor violence . . .

"It is, indeed, one further thing: a love story, finally obsessive, between a man and a beautiful and glorious object of man's art . . . it is the fascination of the chase and the revelations about the world of fine art that, beyond the denouement, make this such a mesmerizing work."

Los Angeles Times

KING
OF THE
CONFESSORS

THOMAS HOVING

BALLANTINE BOOKS • NEW YORK

TO MY WIFE,
NANCY

Library of Congress Catalog Card Number: 81-9050.

ISBN 0-345-30370-9

This edition published by arrangement with
Simon and Schuster

Manufactured in the United States of America

First Ballantine Books Edition: August 1982

All photographs of the Bury St. Edmunds Cross are courtesy
of the Metropolitan Museum of Art. The Cloister Collection,
1963. Photographs of the Bury Saint Edmunds Bible are courtesy of Corpus Christi College, Cambridge, England.

Contents

The excitement of the chase is properly our quarry; we are not to be pardoned if we carry it on badly or foolishly. To fail to seize the prey is a different matter. We are born to search after the truth; to possess it belongs to a greater power.

—MONTAIGNE

In the Beginning . . .

IN THE SPRING OF 1955, after eight centuries of silence, a mysterious work of art, one of the most beautiful and enigmatic ever created in world history, suddenly turned up in the hands of a strange and secretive collector.

At the very moment the collector discreetly announced he might sell the object, there began a quiet, bitter contest for possession among some of the world's most powerful art museums. Since nothing was known about the work of art, a competition arose to find out where and when the object had been made, where and how it had been hidden for so long, and what its true significance was.

In time, those who had joined the struggle to gain possession and deeper knowledge realized that the work was incomparable in importance and value. In fact, were one to choose a monument from all the world's collections that would most perfectly typify the art, the politics, the religious thought and ferment of one of the most exciting and turbulent periods of Western history, one could do little better than to select this particular work of art. It typifies the spirit and essence of its times.

Yet the object turned out to be even more. Those who came into contact with it found that it profoundly affected their lives. The story is true. It is called King of the Confessors.

CHAPTER ONE

The Waiting Game

THE VAST HALLS of the Metropolitan Museum of Art were awesomely still. The bustling crowds had left hours before; the night guards were far from my department, patrolling galleries blocks away. My office door was wide open, and I could look out and see into a hall filled with a hundred or more suits of medieval armor. God, how beautiful they were! I stopped my nervous pacing for a minute and stood there, just leaning against the doorjamb, captivated by the shimmering reflections darting off the sharp polished-metal carcasses. I listened impatiently for the footsteps of my superior, Margaret Freeman, curator of The Cloisters, who would be returning any minute to tell me I had won. Why was she taking so much time? Where was she? It was already seven-thirty. Jesus, I said to myself, take it easy. Don't be so edgy. I would win.

Winning would give my career a vital boost. At that time—it was the tenth of January, 1960—I was on the bottom rung of the professional ladder at the museum, a fledgling curator in medieval art assigned to The Cloisters, the medieval branch of the Metropolitan situated in Fort

Tryon Park. My official title, curatorial assistant, was the lowest you could have, so lowly that I was listed only once a year in the museum's monthly bulletin. My salary wasn't so lofty, either. Five thousand dollars a year. Even in 1960 that sum didn't go very far.

I yearned to get moving; my nimble feet were ready to race up that long ladder to success. But I knew I had to be patient. I had been working at the Metropolitan for only five months. Patience was one of the hallmarks of the institution. I had heard this from a feisty colleague the day after I arrived at the place.

"There's an anecdote which sums up this business, Hoving, which you ought to know right away," he had said dryly but with gusto. "In the middle of a vast and desolate plain in Mexico, by the side of the long road stretching from Mérida to Chichén Itzá, stands a lonely, dead tree. Right at that tree, the road takes a bend—for the first time in perhaps fifty miles. Nothing much happens. Every once in a while a burro or a cow ambles across the road, just under the tree. Every week or so—even more infrequently—a car will come zooming down the road; the driver will hit the brakes and just make the unexpected corner. Accidents are rare. But day and night, perched in the dried-out branches of that tree, are half a dozen vultures, just waiting for something to happen. You see, Hoving, art collecting is primarily a waiting game. Most of the time, you have to let the play come to you, like the vultures. And face it, a lot of curators are really nothing but creatures of carrion, picking over the leavings of creative artists."

I laughed out loud in the deserted office, picturing those patient old birds out there, waiting for the chance to strike. But it was a bit uncharitable to call curators vultures. A great art curator could be brilliantly creative in his choice of what works of art to chase and collect. I had decided I would become a great curator.

I walked away from the door, sat down at my desk, got up and strode nervously around the darkened room, running my fingers along the table up to the keys of the beaten-up typewriter. It was eight o'clock. Where *was* she? I forced myself to calm down again. I could wait. I was at the threshold of my career. At twenty-eight years of age I had discovered and presented to the museum for purchase a truly important work of art. My first. I was confident I would win it. Yet I couldn't dispel a few lingering doubts. Should I have held out and tried to bargain a bit longer with the dealer? Had I pushed my director too far? I shook off these feelings of apprehension. No! Everything would turn out fine.

The more I reflected, the more confident I became. I had handled it right. I had not been looking for the cross, but when it appeared by chance, I recognized it to be a treasure and quickly pounced upon it. My actions accorded precisely with my philosophy of opportunism.

At that point in my life I did not believe *anything* was either preordained or constant. Even if there were a God, which I didn't believe, he could not possibly have structured his universe so rigidly. In my view, the entire cosmos—galaxies, planets, atoms and neutrons, as well as ideas, opportunities and events—was without plan. There was no purpose. The pieces were simply there, a vast inventory of ideas and impending events—billions of them —arrayed at random. If you tried to grab onto them, you couldn't. They would spurt away like motes of dust glinting in a sunbeam. But if you waited, some of those motes, those impending events, those ideas, would stop flickering around and would eventually nestle against you. And then, if you weren't too abrupt, you could take hold of them and shape and manipulate them in your hands. Yet encountering them was almost always pure chance.

In those days I felt that almost everything I had ever deliberately planned to pursue in my life had gone wrong. Virtually everything that had come my way by luck, unannounced, had turned out great.

I had become interested in the study of art history by chance. It had happened halfway through my calamitous sophomore year at college. Freshman year had been easy, and I had performed adequately. My preparatory education had been superior, and so I could coast along, getting by. But halfway through the second year, disaster struck like a summer squall. I was put on academic probation and was within a single percentage point of being tossed out. To salvage the second term and any college career, I searched for "guts," the easiest courses offered in the curriculum.

"Oh, it's simple, Hoving," one of my roommates told me in exasperation. "Get smart, like me. For Christ's sake, get into art history, a *real* gut. The lectures are terrific. A second after they start, the lights go out. You can get to sleep right away. Art history is easy to pick up, just catchwords. Memorize the slides and photographs, bullshit your way through, and you've got it."

At once I signed up for the only art course in the semester, Art 207. A real "gut," I figured. But within a few days I learned that the course was medieval art and was generally considered one of the dullest and most difficult courses of the university. It was conducted by a famously demanding professor by the name of Kurt Weitzmann.

The moment Kurt Weitzmann stalked down the aisle of the auditorium toward the lectern, his face set into a scowl, I groaned to myself. He started speaking as if he were in the middle of some sentence he hadn't quite finished the semester before. He spoke with a thick German accent, singsong, at a near-falsetto punctuated at times by a barking cough that made part of what he said incomprehensible. But I became fascinated by the man and his words. As I listened, inexplicably I had a deep urge to learn. Something within me, something I had no idea was there, simply ignited. Later on, years later, I came to realize that what had occurred was akin to religious experience. From that unlikely moment on, I knew I wanted to become an art historian.

I thrived on Medieval Art 207 and adored it. I received one of the highest marks in the class. The course proved to be the salvation of my university career. Eventually I chose the history of art and archaeology as my undergraduate major, and under Kurt Weitzmann's careful tutelage I graduated summa cum laude. Then, after a stint in the Marine Corps, I returned to graduate school to receive, eventually, a Master of Fine Arts degree and a doctorate of philosophy.

In the true German scholarly tradition, Weitzmann had inherited the unfinished work of his mentor and professor, a renowned art historian named Adolph Goldschmidt, the preeminent authority on medieval ivory carvings. It was strongly implied that I might, in time, assume the same mantle from my own professor, Weitzmann, and spend my life carrying on the monumental study of the ivories of the Middle Ages. Under Weitzmann I had completed a scholarly and turgidly written doctoral thesis analyzing the antique sources of a group of ivories made for Emperor Charlemagne, and had thus obtained my Ph.D.

But far more important than the doctorate, I gradually learned through Weitzmann the refinements of my chosen profession and became profoundly excited by all its complexities—the methods of research, the secrets of how to identify and date artistic styles, and the lore of iconography. I learned how to look at a work of art, not just *see* it. How to probe, examine and peel a work of art like an onion, stripping its multiple layers right down to the very core of its meaning. From Weitzmann, too, I received my introduction to the most fascinating aspect of art history: how to distinguish between real and fake, truth and forgery. Watching Weitzmann, whose eyes and fingers seemed capable of stroking inner secrets from a mute medieval work of art, I soaked up connoisseurship, gradually learning how to recognize artistic quality in all its subtle gradations.

In graduate school at Princeton it never occurred to me that I might land a job in the largest, richest, most prestigious—and powerful—art museum in the United States. I did know what I would definitely *not* do: become a university professor. The closed-in society of academe had become anathema to me. I was repelled by the thought of a life of cloying repetition—the same round of lectures, year after year, the same base student mentality, only the faces changing.

I began to search for a career where I could combine curiosity and expertise with excitement and action. And so I decided to become an art dealer. In art dealing, I believed, I could combine scholarship with the diplomacy and activity of the marketplace. Through my father, a high executive in the retailing business and a man who wielded considerable influence in the social life of New York, I secured an interview with a vice-president of the finest old-master painting gallery in the world, Wildenstein and Company. A few days before the meeting I was elated to learn that I would be interviewed by the patriarch of the firm himself, Georges Wildenstein, or

"Mr. Georges" as he was reverently called by his employees.

Georges Wildenstein was a reticent, fat little man who looked ill-equipped to run the foremost art gallery in the world. But the unimpressive looks concealed a host of brilliant talents. "Mr. Georges" had an infallible eye for masterpieces and a soft, polite, almost apologetic manner of negotiating which was, in truth, steely and cutthroat. The story making the art circles was that Wildenstein in his late sixties had begun to draw away from the intense and virtually mandatory dinner-party circuit surrounding the art trade and had become virtually a recluse. It was said he preferred to retire early each evening and, ensconced in a massive antique bed, leaf pleasurably through hundreds of photographs at random—of paintings, drawings, sculptures, pieces of furniture, carpets, golden snuffboxes, bibelots, illuminated manuscript pages, reliquaries, monstrances, faience plates—spanning centuries of time and dozens of civilizations, keeping his gifted eyes turned to perfection. What a marvelous man!

I had entered the imposing headquarters of Wildenstein and Company, at Sixty-fourth Street and Madison Avenue, tense with expectation, positive I would be hired the same day. Why else would "Mr. Georges" himself have consented to the interview? I was ushered by an elegant functionary into a chamber covered from floor to ceiling with green velvet. The room, sumptuously carpeted also in green, was vacant but for an easel and two chairs upholstered in velvet situated side by side, facing away from each other.

The appointment had been set for three o'clock. On the dot, "Mr. Georges" was announced. He entered the room, looked once at me, shook my hand limply and nodded. I had the disquieting impression the older man was examining not a human being but an art object—one he found of only routine significance. We sat down. Georges Wildenstein never looked in my direction, never uttered a word. Nervously, I described by background and training and my desire "to gain employment in the most prestigious art gallery of the world." Through it all, "Mr. Georges" maintained silence. He took a position in his plush chair and looked directly away from me. He cupped his hands together in such a way that he could rub one thumb along the side of the other. The gesture became hypnotic and excruciating. I could see that the area of one thumb had become worn, almost translucent. Lamely, I struggled through my presentation, talking faster the more nervous I became, trying to articulate my wish to forge a career with Wildenstein by combining scholarship, a sense of history, and zeal to locate great masterpieces. Finally I stuttered into silence.

Several minutes seemed to pass. Then Georges Wildenstein leaned forward to raise himself from his chair and very softly said, "The combination of interests you describe will not be fruitful in a commercial art gallery. Why do you not choose to work for your father? In my business, sons work for their fathers. Or perhaps you should seek employment in a museum." With that, Wildenstein disappeared.

I still blush when I recall the incident. How humiliating it was! But how fortunate! If it had not been for what I thought at the time was Georges Wildenstein's deliberately rude treatment, I would never have come to the Metropolitan Museum of Art. And, for sure, I would never have been waiting that evening in January of 1960, yearning to hear the decision of the Board of Trustees about—of all things—Wildenstein's personal altar cross!

The Wildenstein cross was a superior piece dating to the early thirteenth century, made originally in Belgium. Although I dared not tell my colleagues, secretly I thought it might have been created by a gifted silversmith known as Hugo d'Oignies. If true, that would be a great discovery. I had come upon the treasure by chance a month or so after I joined the Metropolitan. An art historian from Munich had told me about the object, and described the cross as being hidden away in one of the storerooms at Wildenstein and Company. The information at first seemed unlikely to me, for the firm dealt primarily in paintings. Then I thought, Why not? The company cast its collecting nets worldwide and had offices in New York, London and Paris with powerful contacts in Zurich, the capital city of the art world, where one had utter freedom from import and export restrictions. So I took up the quest.

When I first inquired at Wildenstein's about the mysterious cross, no one seemed to want to talk about its existence. Finally I was informed the cross was not officially a part of the firm's holdings. It had been deposited for years in what was described as the "private chapel" in Georges Wildenstein's luxurious residence adjacent to his gallery.

The story gave me wry pleasure. The image of Wildenstein, the foremost Jewish art dealer on earth, kneeling each day on a prie-dieu in his own chapel before the cross leaped immediately to my mind. It would explain why "Mr. Georges" was so "deeply reluctant to part with the piece," as one of his aides had put it. The tale also admirably supported the price of the object, a phenomenal two hundred thousand dollars.

In time I managed to examine Georges Wildenstein's cross. Instantly I recognized it to be a superior work of art, highly desirable for the collection of The Cloisters. It was covered with thick, precisely tooled and chased plates of highly polished silver. The terminals of the cross were decorated with beautiful inlays of lustrous black niello, depicting the figures of saints. As soon as I had taken the altar cross in my hands, I experienced deep pleasure. The museum had to have it, no question about that. Over some weeks I managed to haggle the astronomical price of two hundred thousand down to "one-fifty." My colleagues in the Medieval Department had inspected it, and liked it. So had the director of the museum, who had given every indication that he would support the acquisition.

But what did the director *really* think about the silver cross, its high price, its desirability? I had no inkling, despite his assurances. He was one of the most enigmatic, quixotic, secretive, deliberately indecisive human beings I had ever encountered.

What happened the day I met him was a mirror of his whole being.

It was a bright spring day, shortly after my encounter with Georges Wildenstein and his velvet chairs, and I was preparing for a chilling ritual that was staged each May by a group of Ivy League colleges and universities, for specially chosen graduate students in art history and archaeology—an annual meeting in New York at which the elite students presented short lectures to the distinguished faculties of these choice institutions. We students called it the "meat market," and it was terrifying. The absolute rule was that you could not, under any circumstances, speak for a fraction of a second over twenty minutes or under eighteen. A mandatory question period followed. As regularly as the spring equinox, one particular inquisitor would show up to toy for a while with each speaker and then demolish every one with a scathing criticism of a part or all of the presentation. This inquisitor was an elderly art historian, Erica Tietze-Conrad, who seemed to most of us to be dedicated to one aim in life: the dismantling of budding scholarly careers.

I had made feverish preparations for weeks before the event. I practiced my speech each day for hours before a bathroom mirror, paced the floor, reread the text and timed myself again and again with a stopwatch. I arranged and rearranged my lantern slides, checking them dozens of times to be sure they were in perfect order. As the day approached, my confidence sapped. At night I would toss sleeplessly and conjure up horrors—being utterly unable to speak, or dropping the slides on the floor and shattering them as I walked to the lectern. That had actually happened to a student years before, or at least so it was said. The poor fellow had passed out cold on top of the chairman of the Art Department of Harvard, his career finished before it had begun.

I was proud of my speech, and was convinced that my material constituted a minor scholarly breakthrough in a field plumbed by established experts for years. Yet, as the grim day of the "meat market" drew near, I became less sure.

I had made my discovery by accident in a graduate seminar on the life and times of an early-seventeeth-century Italian painter, Annibale Carracci, an eclectic artist who worked in a highly classical style. My professor had assigned me the task of tracking down the specific Roman antiquities Annibale had copied to produce a famous series of frescos he had painted in the *Galleria*, or great hall, of the Farnese Palace in Rome. The frescos were totally classical in subject matter and in style. Scholars had always known that one fresco had been copied line for line from a classical scene carved, in Roman times, on the surface of a tiny gem once in the collection of Alessandro Farnese, the patriarch of the noble family and the man who had commissioned the frescos. From that it had been assumed that Annibale Carracci must have borrowed extensively from sculptures, paintings or engraved gems of classical antiquity. Yet no scholar had ever discovered any other example of this.

For weeks I searched Farnese documents and histories. I found nothing. I pored over hundreds of photographs of Greek and Roman sculptures, trying to match one of them to at least one figure on the painted ceiling of the Farnese *Galleria*. I drew a blank. With ten days left before my seminar report, which by tradition had to go on for three hours, I had worked myself into a panic. What in Christ's name would I do? I couldn't talk for so long, saying little more than that I had found nothing, or merely that I was edging toward the suspicion that Annibale Carracci might not have given a damn about classical antiquity.

And then it happened. For a different seminar, on Pompeiian wall paintings, I was leafing desultorily through the pages of a book on Roman sculptures and other antiquities in the Naples Museum. I happened to pause for a few seconds over a striking photograph, taken as though the photographer had hung himself by his heels from the dome of an enormous rotunda filled with ancient Roman statuary. The photograph was a tour de force, but of little use to me. I was about to turn to the next page when I detected something that made me rise out of my chair and laugh aloud in the quietude of the dingy graduate study room. Suddenly I had it—a gimmick!

It wasn't just *any* gimmick; it was the ultimate gimmick. One of Annibale's figures, the god Mercury, portrayed as if he were flying straight out of the wall, was exactly the same as one of the Roman sculptures in the dramatic photo of the rotunda. Only the angle of the head had been changed. Could it be that that very sculpture had been deliberately copied by Annibale from an odd angle? In a minute I had proof! I had in my research material an engraving of the interior of the Farnese *Galleria*, made just after Annibale had completed his frescos. The interior was punctuated by a number of spacious niches in which Alessandro Farnese had proudly placed his very favorite ancient sculptures, dug from ancient sites all over Rome. And there, in one niche, stood the very sculpture that had been photographed so dramatically in the Naples Museum.

In a day I had learned that every one of Alessandro's hundred or so antiquities had ended up in the Naples Museum. Within a few days more I had figured out that approximately half of the figures in Annibale's fresco had been directly copied from antique sculptures in his patron's private collections, many of them displayed in those niches. Each one had been ingeniously disguised by Annibale, who had sketched them from wholly unexpected angles. And before me no one but Alessandro and Annibale had ever known about the pun.

I had breezed through my seminar, but now I faced the far shorter "meat market" presentation with trepidation. But I needn't have worried in the least. My voice was slightly strangled at the start, and the palms of my hands remained moist throughout, but my technique was smooth and my aplomb consistently maintained. I even dared to play with my audience, pretending to be pedantic, going on at some length about the "considerable significance of the cut gem" and how, because of it, "Annibale had always been thought of as felicitously intrigued by the lure of the classical past." Then, when I gauged that the experts in the audience had sized me up as a clod merely repeating what was commonly known, I hit them.

I punched my lantern slides on the screen, side by side—first a figure from Annibale's frescos and then, lightning fast, a photograph of one of the antique sculptures in the Naples Museum which had inspired it. With each pair—a dozen or so—I cited the year Alessandro Farnese had excavated the work of art. For the grand finale, I showed a slide of Alessandro's beloved Roman sculptures on display in the niches of the Farnese *Galleria*.

When I was through, Erica Tietze-Conrad rose briskly to her feet. I faced her eagerly. I was looking forward to blasting her if she raised a single objection. She gave me a hard and penetrating look and then proclaimed in a sibilant, Teutonic accent, "I am convinced. I congratulate you." There was a bit of clapping, and then the audience rushed for the exit to go to lunch.

I stayed behind to retrieve my slides, savoring the little victory. I was about to cry out loud, "Hoving, you clever bastard!" but didn't because at the last second I saw a man standing quietly before me. He was of medium height, sort of portly, dressed in a dark well-tailored suit, impeccable except for a rumpled shirt which poked out incongruously from the bottom of his vest. His hair, thinning, was jet black, plastered to his orblike head. His eyes were disturbingly intense. He seemed to be in his late fifties.

"Good report," he said in a deep, carefully measured voice while he examined my face without blinking. He paused and then suddenly asked, "May I, ah, ask . . . did you find any references, in your research on the Farnese Palace, to a table—a massive table with carved marble legs and a top richly decorated with intarsia?"

"A what? An antique table?" I burst out, confused by his questioning, flustered by his riveting gaze.

"Not *classical* antique," the man answered. "It would be sixteenth century and must have been commissioned, I expect, by Alessandro Farnese."

"I don't recall," I replied lamely. "The only table I ran remember in one of Annibale's frescos is not copied from anything antique. No. Sorry." I smiled politely and turned to gather up my material.

"Perhaps you would care to glance at the table I'm talking about," he said. "It's only a few minutes away. Come for just a moment. Perhaps seeing it will refresh your memory."

He was an art dealer, I figured at first. Then I knew I was wrong, because he went on, "My table is over at the Metropolitan, just three blocks away. I'd deeply appreciate your opinion of it."

I had no idea who he was. But he seemed to know me and he had taken it for granted that I recognized him. There was no way I could get out of going with him; and although I felt ill at ease, I realized I didn't really want to avoid the opportunity. I had become intrigued and caught up by a sense of adventure. I was also filled with pride. No one in my life had ever asked me to give advice on a work of art.

CHAPTER TWO

The Game Is Joined

WE WALKED THREE BLOCKS from the lecture hall to the museum. The man said nothing until we had reached the bottom flight of stairs leading to the main entrance of the imposing structure.

"Since you're a medievalist, this must be your second home," he stated casually.

I was startled and a little anxious. How did this oblique individual know I had been specializing in medieval art? What curious game was he playing with me?

I had visited the Metropolitan Museum only two times in the preceding ten years, so I lied, smoothly and amiably. I chatted on about how much I adored the place; how I came as frequently as I could, knew the medieval collection *very* well, wished I could come more often. It was easy; in those days, I had always been able to lie convincingly without any hesitation.

The man walked swiftly through the main hall of the museum into a spacious corridor lined with a profusion of glass cases jammed with a bewildering number of early Christian and Byzantine works of art—objects of my

13

particular field. Thank God he didn't stop to talk about them. I had never bothered to study them closely.

We came to the end of the corridor. He casually removed a chain suspended across an ill-lit stairway and plunged down the narrow steps. We descended two long flights and at the bottom proceeded rapidly along a narrow passageway in the depths of the art museum. The passage was a maze to me, seeming to twist back upon itself once or twice. Eventually we entered a cavernous underground chamber, perhaps one hundred feet long by fifty feet wide, with a ceiling that seemed to me to be three stories high. At the far end of the room was an enormous steel door, sealed shut. And there, set off to one side of the door, was a wooden crate half the size of a railroad boxcar. Standing in front of the crate was the table. It was magnificent, more a piece of sculpture than a table, really. Its two stout marble pedestals were carved into a pair of ferocious griffins which supported a massive stone slab, fully six inches thick and inlaid with thousands of colored stones—a ravishing mosaic of white, iridescent blacks, pearls, ivories, russets, palm green and lapis lazuli, surrounded by a blood-red border—fashioned into swags of flowers forming the opulent coat of arms of the Farnese family.

"My table," the man said with a wave of his hand. "Did you ever come across *this* in your research?" he softly demanded. "It is, I believe, the very table ordered by Alessandro Farnese for his *Galleria*. Yet, so far, I've not found a specific reference to it."

"It *is* incredibly beautiful," I told him. "But no, I have never heard of it before. You must realize that I was only looking hurriedly, even frantically, for classical material Annibale might have been trying to copy."

"Yes, of course," he replied, "and you found an impressive number." He turned to me, fixing me with his deep-black eyes. "Come to my office, would you? I want to discuss a certain matter with you. I hope you have the time to join me. We can have a sandwich at my desk and talk—not about the table, but about your future."

I could not have been more astonished had he slapped me in the face. My mind was churning with anticipation. We retraced our steps, passed through the great central hall of the museum, walked for what seemed a quarter of a mile to a small flight of stairs and up to a door marked "Executive Offices." The man unlocked the door. We entered a series of secretarial cubicles, all empty; it was Saturday. As the man busied himself with the lock on an impressive oak door, I began to panic. Stealthily I glanced at a nearby desk where a batch of mail was neatly stacked. The letter on top was addressed to "James J. Rorimer, Director, The Metropolitan Museum of Art, New York City."

The office was a large square room illuminated by three low arched windows which offered a curiously truncated view of Fifth Avenue. An empty round walnut table surrounded by half a dozen chairs dominated the room. The walls were bare, covered over by a faded green grasscloth. Strange, I thought, that the director of the most prestigious art museum in America would not have a single painting hanging on the walls. One of the few pieces of furniture was a nondescript highboy with a cluster of books and periodicals stacked on it in disorganized fashion. In the corner of the room near the windows was a stolid desk, its top bare except for two telephones. The man I urgently hoped would indeed be James J. Rorimer, Director, slumped heavily into a cracked-leather chair and propped his feet, clad incongruously in brown army boots, upon the desk. He reached back for a pipe from a well-filled rack set on a shelf and motioned me to sit down. He studied my face intently as he packed the pipe from a tin can of tobacco, lit it with a series of frantic puffs and immediately set it aside.

I gathered up my courage and said, "Mr. . . . *Rorimer*, I hope you don't mind my saying I find all this to be a bit mysterious."

"I like mystery," Rorimer retorted with a grave expression. Then a smile enlivened his round impassive face, illuminating it with a startling brightness, crinkling the corners of his eyes. Abruptly, James Rorimer was no longer the forbidding individual of seconds before. Although I still felt I was about to be ambushed, I had to relax at the sudden human warmth which exuded from him.

"I rarely bother to come to the meat market," he spoke out, picking up his pipe. "But I am pleased I went this time. Roland Redmond, the president of the Metropolitan, informed me you would be speaking. Your father happened to tell Redmond about the symposium at a dinner party."

I drew back in surprise. Had I . . . ? Yes, I guess I had mentioned something, in passing, to my father.

Noting my reaction, Rorimer added with a smile, "The art world obtains information from everywhere." He paused again to flame up his pipe, looking at me unwaveringly from under his bushy eyebrows. His eyes glimmered with pleasure. "Your presentation was good," he intoned, "but it was not appreciated by everyone in the audience. You might want to know that a certain professor from Yale sitting next to me—I cannot reveal his name—was livid that you, a mere graduate student, and from *Princeton*, had discovered what he had apparently been looking for for years."

Rorimer laughed and sucked on his dead pipe. His face became serious and he began to speak slowly, searching for each word carefully. "Kurt Weitzmann and I have had a long discussion about your career. You are one of his most promising students. He feels you might be best suited for curatorial activity. He believes you might be one of those rare individuals who can deal with both the theoretical and the physical reality of art."

I listened in amazement as James Rorimer reeled off the titles of some seminars I had taken, grades I had received and detailed information regarding my dissertation, which I had not even completed.

"You might be interested to know I also had a talk about you with Georges Wildenstein. So you are interested in art dealing? Young man, do you mind if I give you a piece of advice?"

I nodded dumbly.

"If you ever enter into art dealing, you will never, *never*, be able to work in an art museum. The prejudices are that strong. If, however, you work in an art museum, and you find you do not like it, you can always become an art dealer and a far better one at that."

There are few times in one's life when one is struck by advice so bluntly delivered, so lucidly expressed, that one recognizes the undeniable logic of it. This was one of those times. It took me a hundredth of a second to make up my mind. From that moment on, I wanted to work in the Metropolitan. And I told him so.

But then James Rorimer backed off. He didn't offer me a job right away, although he alluded obliquely to the possibility. He took great pleasure in drawing out the affair. Over several weeks, I was called to come to New York three or four times to have a "friendly chat about the future," as he put it. Two months after we met in July 1959, he finally made a formal proposal: the position of curatorial assistant, assigned to the Medieval Department and The Cloisters. I accepted at once and began my duties a month later.

During the period of friendly chats, I had dug discreetly into James Rorimer's background. The standard references told me of his birth in 1905 and his graduation from Harvard in the class of 1927, and the fact—astonishing, I thought—that he had never obtained an advanced degree. I learned of his long involvement in the building and development of The Cloisters, the superb branch museum of the Metropolitan situated on the northernmost end of Manhattan Island and devoted to medieval art. He had become director of the Metropolitan in 1955.

From several people who knew him or had worked for him, I absorbed much more.

"Jim Rorimer, or Jimsie, is absolutely brilliant as a collector of art," one informant who had worked with him, never *for* him, told me. "He knows objects better than anyone else in the museum profession, but he can be sloppy sometimes. He's been fooled and has collected a few fakes like all great collectors. Rorimer is a clever manipulator of people. He can handle his trustees, he can raise money like no one else. But, deep down, he's a bit scared of them. If he likes you—if you are one of his boys —he will see that you go far, fast. Remember, however, Rorimer wants all the credit for himself. Another thing you ought to know—he's secretive as hell, yet *he's* the first one to spill secrets."

"Rorimer is a pompous, stuffy, arrogant, jealous, conniving man," said another, who had worked under him. "But, what the hell, he's extremely gifted. Even with his faults, I admire him a great deal. Not many people know that he's Jewish. His father, I think it was his father, was a big-time interior decorator from Cleveland, and he changed the family name to Rorimer from Rohrheimer. Once an uncle, who had kept the name, came to the museum and cried out to someone at the information desk that he wanted to see his nephew, Jim Rohrheimer. When the person called Rorimer, poor Jim didn't leave his office. There aren't many Jews in the museum world. I suppose that's why he has this inferiority complex. But, no matter, he's the best museum man in America."

Within a month of starting at the Metropolitan Museum, I had charted my goals. I would become curator of the Medieval Department and The Cloisters. And then, in time, I would succeed Jim Rorimer himself. Arrogant, dreamlike as it sounds, I never had any real doubt that eventually I would become director of the Metropolitan. I recognized I had winning, if not particularly winsome, assets. I knew I could be quick, disciplined, tough, sensitive and ruthless. I also recognized I had the ability to disguise my worst traits to most people. I too could be devious without qualms. I was devoted to hard work. And I was blessed with a one-track mind.

There were just five people ahead of me in the Medieval Department and The Cloisters. They were capable yet placid people; admirable but listless professionals. I was relieved when I realized I wouldn't have to crush anyone in my climb to the upper levels. Well, perhaps one, an eager young chap who had arrived at the museum to work in the Medieval Department the very week I had. He was also an assistant curator but had no doctorate. Rorimer had hired him without saying a word to me. But the threat didn't last long. The first impression the fellow made in the snobbish Metropolitan proved indelible. He walked in boyishly, full of cheer, with a crew cut, wearing bright-red short socks with a pale-blue suit. That did it forever. From then on, his most distinguishing feature was a perpetual look of embarrassment. He soon disappeared.

Within two months of joining the museum, I had fathomed the two fundamental secrets of getting ahead: rooting out great works of art on the international art market and winning at James Rorimer's favorite administrative game, which was to pit a number of staff members against each other. The trick was to win without making lasting enemies.

Of course I had made a few enemies at the museum. In such a complex bureaucracy, you always do. But I practiced the art of being friendly and accommodating to everyone at the same time. Even the skeptics and the enemies were lulled. The dean of the curators, an arrogant and brilliant individual, had become deeply suspicious of me. It was reported that during the coffee hours, where he held sway trading rumors, he had said I was "too active" to be a curator. And I found myself wondering if he was right.

Another senior curator had said I was "a marionette, moving fluidly at times, gyrating and jiggling wildly at others; but a puppet with a difference—Hoving controls his own strings!" Again, I wondered if he was right. At least he had also remarked that I had an eye and a deep love for works of art. But sometimes that love could turn into an obsession for pure acquisition. Everyone in the museum gossiped about the time, during an international conference on medieval art, when I had rushed to the podium at the end of a lecture presented by a distinguished French professor on the recent discovery of dozens of spectacular early Gothic sculptures embedded for hundreds of years, forgotten, in a farmhouse wall at Châlons-sur-Marne. I had not been interested in a point of scholarship. I wanted to know if any of the pieces might be for sale.

From my first months at the Metropolitan, I pursued art with a tenacity that can only accompany the high ambition of youth. I personally inspected every single object in the Medieval Department and The Cloisters—some fifteen thousand of them. I hounded art dealers, auction houses and private collectors. I studied advertisements for art sales throughout the world. I assembled lists of where *anything* of quality or desirability might be hidden anywhere. No one told me to do it. I simply immersed myself, and within five months Rorimer designated me his chief liaison for collecting in both the Medieval Department and The Cloisters. Not that I was the sole voice in determining what would be brought to Rorimer's attention as a likely purchase—my colleagues were of critical importance—but gradually my associates became accustomed to telling me what works of art they thought the museum should buy. In time, I became the sole conduit of information to James Rorimer. The financial dimensions were unique. The Cloisters alone received annually from its endowment over half a million dollars just for the purchase of works of art.

Partly with Rorimer's help but mostly on my own, I formulated a personal philosophy and a special technique for examining works of art. It became a kind of gospel to me, more powerful than any religion.

The mainstay of my philosophy was the realization that the lifeblood of the great Metropolitan was collecting. Pure and simple. Every other function of the institution—conservation, exhibition, scholarship, teaching—evolved from that basic act. It was chase and capture, one of the most invigorating endeavors in life, dramatic, emotional, and fulfilling as a love affair. It was, I decided, an act of passion, a tense, visceral, intellectual, highly serious, yet amusing act of passion. But I also knew that the passion had to be exercised with detachment, with control.

The endeavor required hard work—foot-slogging, gumshoe detective work. To become a truly exalted collector I had to make myself into a professional connoisseur—an "eye," as they say in the museum business—someone who can recognize quality among all works of art in all fields and in subtle gradations. What would it take? Saturation, the one constant ingredient common to the training of all accomplished connoisseurs. And that's why I studied and restudied all those works of art in the Medieval Department and The Cloisters. Only by touching, feeling, peering at, sometimes even tasting, every work of art under my stewardship could I begin to comprehend what quality was all about. But I wasn't cocky enough to think that just saturation would automatically make me a connoisseur. One required also an undefinable, near-mystical, inborn talent for detecting the best. There were plenty of art experts in the world of museums and especially in universities who were not connoisseurs and who would never be. They were merely experts, stuffed full of facts and book knowledge, with no instinct for quality. The French had a term for what I was after, *grand goût*, an extra-fine sense of taste. I hoped I had that.

In time I invented a checklist to help me examine a work of art I was thinking of buying, a step-by-step process to force me to probe deeply. First and most important, I'd write down *quickly* my initial, split-second reaction to the thing. I wouldn't dress up or edit or ponder my words. I would capture the spirit of my eye's absolutely instant impression. Something like "warm, good, strong" or "blue, electric, thin." I became convinced that noting my spontaneous impression was crucial. I had already seen how a doubting phrase or an apparently meaningless word later spotlighted a flaw in a piece, dimly perceived at first glance but definitely there.

Then I found it valuable to scribble a detailed, pedantic description of the thing. By plodding through such a description I forced myself to touch and feel and weigh the work of art. It got me to drag my eyes over every millimeter, as if my eyes could touch the surface. At the same time I'd try to examine the work from all angles and from various distances—very close, using my magifying glass, and then from across the room.

After that I'd ask, What's the physical condition of this thing? Does it show wear? Age? I would describe that wear to myself and try to date each bump, crack and abrasion. I took note of all visible repairs. Were they old or were they really modern repairs made to look old? I fast discovered that forgers sometimes added an "ancient" repair to make one think the work of art had to be old to have been repaired in antiquity.

I would also try to analyze the basic elements of corrosion if the object was metal. Every metal but gold corrodes, and even gold if it happens to be an alloy. I memorized the basic stratifications of the corrosion of those metals customarily used during medieval times. Ancient bronze has, for example, a distinctive sandwich: on top, a green surface of cupric oxide, which lies over a brown patina of cupric chloride. Old silver invariably turns dark purple in thin, flaking layers.

If I couldn't find those standard characteristics, a warning bell would go off in my mind. But one of my colleagues added a complication to the formula by telling me that sometimes a genuine corroded ancient bronze will have been cleaned down to the bronze and then painted green to make it look old again. And if one rejected the thing because it had a "modern" surface, one could in that rare case condemn a true and excellent work of art.

I would also ask whether this work of art had a use. Until modern times almost all works, even paintings, had a specific purpose. After I established the fact that the piece had a use I would determine whether the pattern of wear fit that usage.

Next, I'd move on to style. Did the thing have an identifiable, datable style? Was the style consistent with the period in which the work of art was said to have been made? Was the style consistent throughout? Were there signs of several styles? If so, why? Was it that I was dealing with something made during a transitional period, when the artist had been influenced by more than one stylistic element? Or was I looking at a work by a young artist, an experimental artist?

After style I'd identify the subject matter of the piece and find comparisons. No subject was unique.

Then I would analyze the "iconography," the term art historians employ to describe the precise way a particular subject matter is treated. Iconography cannot date a work of art or localize it, but it can be of help in determining authenticity.

I would then delve into the documentation. Was my object documented right back to the moment of its origin? I'd be sure to authenticate the documents themselves. The faking of them was not unheard of. I would carefully search out every book or article where the thing had been published. Occasionally I would seek outside verification, when I thought I could trust a colleague in another institution.

Before my examination came to a close, I would subject the work of art to a range of scientific instruments in the museum laboratory: X ray, infrared, ultraviolet, microscopic sections, spectrographic analysis, neutron activation, thermoluminescence, carbon 14. All of which was great stuff but didn't amount to a black box with its magic needle pointing to REAL or FAKE. The "eye" was still the boss. And obviously I couldn't haul all those instruments around as I visited dealers and galleries. To make up for the lack, I invented a scientific portable field kit. Easily affordable, mine contained a small flashlight, a magnifying glass with three power lenses, a

Swiss Army knife (the model with the scissors, the plastic toothpick and the file), a small bottle of xylene—a mild and quick universal solvent for varnishes and gunk—a couple of cotton ear swabs and a miniature ultraviolet lamp. If the vendor turned his back for even a few minutes I managed a lot of instant cleaning and probing.

That completed my checklist. When I had followed it all, I would go back to see if what I had found conformed with my first instinctive impression. Was it a piece of *quality?* Did it *grow,* become more beautiful? Did it penetrate the very recesses of my heart? Was my passion aroused? Did that passion increase, making me incapable of stopping myself from reaching out to touch the work, caressing it as if it were a woman? Did I ache to possess it? If so, then I'd go for the thing.

But most times I would begin to hatch doubts. And if I did, if I discovered that my first reaction contained suspicious words, or if flaws were revealed after my study, then I'd start what I called a "doubts list." And I would start the examination all over again.

When I thought I might be dealing with a forgery, which was about thirty percent of the time, I would try to find solid proof for the surmise. I had been told by James Rorimer that although it was a mistake to collect a fake, an error every adventurous connoisseur had made, *it was an absolute sin to brand as a forgery an authentic work of art!*

Kurt Weitzmann had taught me that all fakes fall into a few simple categories. Knowing this took away some of the awesome fear of stumbling into buying a forgery.

The simplest category of fakes was the near-perfect copy. That was easy to detect: from saturation, one knew the original. Next was the clever pastiche, a paste-up job in which the faker took elements from a number of known pieces and brought them together out of context. That too offered no great difficulty. The final category, the most difficult fake to detect, was the truly creative "original" in which the forger concocted what must have existed in an artist's work, say in a youthful period, but had not managed to survive.

I had been told that all forgeries collapsed in time. Even the most superb did not last much longer than a generation. No matter how perfectly and stealthily a forger might have recreated the style of a bygone period, his *own* style was embedded there and would in time stand out more clearly than that of the period in which it was supposed to have been made

But I hoped I would buy few forgeries in my career. I dedicated myself to strive for quality, go after the best examples possible in every area, works that summed up their epoch or the artist, works that had exerted strong influences throughout time. That was my ideal, and I had found it in Georges Wildenstein's great silver cross.

As I waited in the quiet of the evening for Margaret Freeman to return from making the presentation to the Purchase Committee, I thought painfully about the only responsibility I had not managed to gain. Rorimer had not allowed me to appear in person before that select committee of the Board of Trustees to make the presentation myself. I consoled myself with the realization that in six months' time at most I would face the trustees and plead my own cases. At this moment with the great silver cross it didn't much matter. Rorimer certainly knew I had found and recommended the piece. I was positive he would inform the trustees of my accomplishments.

I heard her coming. There were the faint sounds of footsteps clicking on the terrazzo of the great hall. She was in the narrow gallery leading to the office. Wasn't she walking a little slowly? I wondered why she hadn't called from Rorimer's office. I figured she wanted the pleasure of telling me the good news face to face. I balled my fists tightly in my lap and stiffened my shoulders. I could scarcely breathe. What a moment in my career! I conjured up a little false anxiety just to add to my pleasure.

Peg Freeman entered the office and sat down heavily. She looked tired, drawn. She gave a quick shrug and said, "Well, we lost it."

For a flash of a second, I couldn't believe it.

"James turned me down flat," Peg exclaimed listlessly. "He told me that he had made up his mind days before the meeting. So all my arguments were a waste of time. The trustees knew he wasn't going to support the piece. Could he have done it to humiliate me? I had to wait so long before I could go into the meeting. Oh, no, that's foolish. Tom, I'm so sorry. I know how much you counted on getting the cross."

That son-of-a-bitch Rorimer, I said to myself, and I wondered how damaging to my career the rejection of the cross would be. How stupid did I appear to Rorimer and the trustees—my God, the trustees!—for having *insisted* that we buy the object?

"I'm truly sorry," Peg said lamely. "I tried my best. Perhaps *you* could have convinced them—"

"Listen, tell me," I interjected harshly, "what was his reason? What exactly did Rorimer say?"

"Nothing, really." Peg waved her hand aimlessly and paused, then stared firmly at me. "You might as well know. James told the trustees that the cross was interesting enough for them to have a quick look at it, but that after reflection he had come to the conclusion that a certain young curatorial assistant in the Medieval Department had been a bit exuberant in pressing so forcefully for an outrageously expensive object. And that was that."

"Did he mention me by *name?*"

"You know, I cannot remember. I don't believe he did," she answered, pondering the question and me.

I walked out of the museum like an automaton, striding through the subterranean passageways, north to the great hall of the receiving entrance where I had seen Rorimer's table months before, and out into the parking lot. I brutalized my little foreign car, viciously stamping on the pedals, impelling it through the tangled traffic. I sped down Broadway to Commerce Street in Greenwich Village, dumping the automobile at the gas station across from the brick-front house where I lived. I threw open the door and ran up the narrow stairs to the upper floor of the crowded apartment, startling my wife, Nancy.

"I need a drink," I growled.

"What in God's name has happened?" she asked, looking at me astonished.

"Rorimer! He saw to it that we—I was turned down, turned *out* on the silver cross! Apparently he never wanted the thing and was playing some perverse game with me, putting me in my place." I recounted vehemently what Peg Freeman had told me.

"Are you convinced the cross was so very important?" Nancy queried.

"Losing it is a monumental disaster. There won't ever be anything like it on the market again," I cried out. "And, my God, what's going to happen to my career?"

"Oh, you'll be all right. Anyway, it seems to me that there are so many works of art coming up for purchase. I suppose you can't get them all."

"Goddammit," I shouted, "this was an important one, perhaps the most important of my life."

"I *am* sorry. I think I know how you feel," she observed thoughtfully. "But try to calm down. You tried your best."

"My career!" I lamented.

"Nothing will happen," my wife said sweetly. "You can get emotional and you do exaggerate. Sometimes I wonder if you're so taken by an individual work of art itself or by the art of getting it—like a trophy."

I stared at her for a few seconds. Nancy Melissa Bell, Vassar girl, a beautiful girl with a pleasing full figure, a pretty face, nice blond hair, perfect white teeth—and an intelligent girl too, gifted with a lightning sense of judgment. As usual she had hit the nail on the head.

I had a couple of drinks, retreated into the chamber I used for my study and began to type my daily journal. I had kept it for years. It was my foxhole in the war of life.

I am depressed—so depressed—because I am not getting anywhere. As usual I do not *think* enough. I am, once again, closing in on myself and am locking petty worries into a false and hypocritical melancholy. I have such ambitions, yet I yearn to break out of the confining capsule of the museum career—that very capsule in which I deliberately placed myself. But could it be true that I don't want to escape, after all?

What do my colleagues see in me? Someone happy? Someone with visions of grandeur? Someone unsure, too? So my colleagues must say: there goes Hoving, the thin-faced, angular, stooped-over fellow, who searches for the clever and who knows how to impress the right people at the right time—smart, but not wise—crafty and quick, but perhaps completely superficial.

The conclusion of that journal entry of January 10, 1960, became a swamp of self-pity into which I sank, without struggling. I typed onward.

I want nothing more than success. But what I'm really doing is to strive after the very abstractness of success. Just how it comes, and where, makes little difference. Success, adulation—notice—are my primary wishes. Can I be serious? Life is not like that. I believe I deserve success, yet I feel I am doomed never to find it.

I stumbled up the stairs and fell into bed. It was nearly one o'clock, and my head and my stomach were caught up in the sickening whirls of drunkenness. I began to plummet and swoop through an infinity of nausea. I hated that more than anything else, and I would do anything to avoid it. So, in the dead of the night, I dressed and walked for hours along the docks of the West Side, desperately filling my lungs with great drafts of the biting, cold air.

I got home just before dawn fairly sober. Teetering around a bit and not too quietly, I slipped into bed beside my wife and after a few moments of paralysis, finally snuggled up against her splendidly warm body. She stirred.

"You are a *one*," she whispered. "And I really am sorry about your lost cross."

CHAPTER THREE

The Quest Commences

THE NEXT MORNING a light, cold rain glistened on the cobblestones of a quiet Seventh Avenue South. The sky was moody gray, the perfect atmosphere for contemplation. My pangs of guilt over getting drunk and cursing Rorimer, my benefactor, disappeared by midday. A lingering embarrassment hovered in the recesses of my mind for a while. Soon that too faded away as I forged ahead with new plans for the future.

"What are you writing, a letter of resignation or a poison pen?" Nancy jokingly asked when she observed me scribbling away on a yellow pad propped upon my knee as I leaned back in a chair, soaking up the heat from the radiator.

I laughed. "No, I'm just trying to figure out where I screwed up with the silver cross. I was too quick, too aggressive, too confident and too cocky. I made the mistake of believing the silver cross would talk for itself. I didn't prepare a persuasive enough set of arguments. And I didn't work hard enough on Rorimer to explain why the cross was important for us to have. And how right you were! Damn you! I did treat the cross like a trophy, a personal victory, rather than the splendid work of art it is."

The telephone rang. It was James Rorimer. He started talking in a slow, husky voice, without any salutation at all.

"You might want to know the real reason for the decision at the board meeting last evening. It's a confidential matter, especially to Peg Freeman, who must never know." There was a pause and sucking sounds as he lit his pipe. "The silver cross is a commendable work of art. You were right in wanting to have it. I suppose you feel I made a great mistake in not buying it."

"Oh, not really," I lied, abandoning all courage. "I pushed it because I thought it was part of my job to let you know anything of interest, anything that might be of quality."

There was another pause from Rorimer.

"Too bad you couldn't have made the presentation yourself. Peg Freeman is primarily responsible. She's to blame for losing the cross. Got flustered. Never could perform before the committee. The key members were not sanguine."

I didn't utter a word. Who was telling the truth, Freeman or Rorimer?

"Perhaps if *you* had been there . . ." Rorimer went on. "Well, perhaps we should talk seriously about, ah, seeing that your appearance before the committee comes about sooner than I had planned."

My God, I thought, was Rorimer about to make a definite decision?

"But, of course," he went on smoothly, "I shall have to discuss it with Roland Redmond. We wouldn't want you to be advanced too rapidly."

Rorimer had hinted several times before that I might become the active representative before the Purchase Committee for all acquisitions of medieval art. But since nothing had happened, I guessed Redmond had blocked the opportunity. Even though he had brought me to the attention of Rorimer, I was convinced he disliked me.

"I do like the silver cross," Rorimer rambled on. "You know, I examined it many times over the years."

Another lie? I was sure he had not heard of the object before I told him.

"Impressive." He stopped for several seconds. "But I, ah, find the price difficult. Seventy-five would be the right price. In time I shall offer Wildenstein that amount, and we shall settle for one hundred, which is still far too much, but I suppose worth it. Let Georges stew in it for a while; he'll settle. I think it likely that he'll throw in the cross with the purchase of a certain painting. I can't talk about it. Highest security. But in a month or two there may be, ah, an extraordinarily important painting offered by Wildenstein. I may be able to arrange a special price for both. Anyway, I wanted to tell you *not* to be disappointed. You should be congratulated for bringing the cross forward. No one else in the department would have done that. I admire your persistence. That's why I took a chance and hired you, and that is why we shall soon make certain changes in the Medieval Department beneficial to you. Good job."

The line went dead. That was all. Cryptic, oblique, suggestive, yet nothing really said. It was typical James Rorimer. And it was typical of me too to have lost heart and failed to let him know how I actually felt. Thinking over his words, I was elated to know that no damage whatever had been done to my career.

"So he's a hero again," Nancy muttered sarcastically when I told her that Rorimer was already thinking of allowing me to appear before the trustees. "Take care," she added. "Remember that Dick and Pooh Randall are coming for dinner tonight. Maybe you'll end up like Dick, once Rorimer's fair-haired boy and then *out*. Did you ever find out why he quit The Cloisters?"

"Never really." I said gloomily, "I'd guess the two just didn't get along. Dick was a talented curator. But he never became an expert in medieval art and certainly never an avid hunter. Dick almost deliberately did *not* join the mandatory game of playing up to Jim's ego. He wasn't much of a politician. He's a wry, wise-cracking Yankee who always reminds me of a cocky bantam rooster, and he's also something of a cynic."

"So how is it working with James J. Rorimer?" Dick Randall asked that evening while we were having drinks before dinner.

"The first real blow came yesterday," I told him. "After

seeming to support it at first, he mysteriously rejected a magnificent silver cross, school of Hugo d'Oignies. I don't really know exactly why. The price maybe. It was one-fifty."

"Oh, *that* cross," Randall cut in.

"You *know* about it?" I exclaimed. "I had been told I was the first person in America to see it."

"Of course I know about it. It was being offered to everyone."

"Wildenstein showed it to *you!*"

"Sure. The world-famous silver cross, which nobody wants. Didn't you know? God, Hoving, I expected more from you. Wildenstein was flogging the piece to every museum across the United States. We were offered it at Boston. But at fifty thousand I thought it was outrageous."

"What!" I cried. "Whatta you mean? *Fifty?*"

"Hey, take it easy. Actually I never heard of it," Randall said, and then he leaned back and brayed with laughter. "Was it really good?"

"Yes, it's fabulous! Get serious, Dick."

"I'll bet James didn't buy it because you were the one who found it and wanted it. That happened to me once or twice. It's a shame. But no use brooding about it. And now I suppose you'll be going after the great . . . Well, let me put it this way. There *are* other silver crosses. But there is only one ivory cross."

"What's this?" I asked warily.

"But surely you must know about the ivory—*you*, the truffle hound of The Cloisters." Randall seemed to have become honestly serious. "There is only one cross on the world art market you should be concerned about. Only one up to the high level of the collections of The Cloisters."

Randall spoke quietly, with intense feeling. Convinced he was finally being sincere, I leaned forward.

"Here's the story. There is nothing like it in the world. The ivory cross is about two feet tall, completely covered with dozens of carved figures. Each one is only about half an inch in height. And the cross is decorated with an incredible number of inscriptions, one for virtually each figure, carved on a series of ribbon-like scrolls in

Latin, Greek, even Hebrew. The object is absolutely remarkable!"

I shook my head in wonder.

"It's true. A large altar cross sumptuously carved in walrus ivory was available for purchase not too many years ago. And it probably still is. The owner was convinced it was Anglo-Saxon, definitely English, around 1050. I recall he claimed it had been made just before the Norman Conquest."

"Has this cross been published?" I asked. "I sure don't remember it in Goldschmidt."

"Oh, no. Definitely never published."

"Seems peculiar Adolph Goldschmidt didn't know of it," I mused. "Dick, are you kidding me about this cross?"

"Nope. There is, I assure you, an incredible two-foot-high ivory cross, loaded with figures and inscriptions—a unique piece—probably for sale right now."

"Where is this thing?"

"Underground."

"*What?*"

"Sure. It's in a vault deep in a bank in Zurich."

"Dick, who's the owner?"

"A most interesting character. A Yugoslav by birth, Austrian by citizenship, lives in Tangier and keeps most of his fantastic collection in this walk-in bank vault in Zurich. I have been told that he is a wealthy arms dealer."

"That's comforting," I replied. "What's his name?"

"I remember he calls himself Topic Matutin Mimara or some such. He doesn't have just one name. There are two, three, perhaps more. It all depends on where he happens to be living or whom he is talking to. He's in the files at The Cloisters. Look under Topic, pronounced 'Topeech,' or Mimara or Matutin. His full name is, I remember, Ante Topic Mimara Matutin."

"How much was Topic Mimara, or whatever was his name, asking for this cross? Did you really have a good look at it? What was it like? How does it compare to the other ivory crosses surviving from the Middle Ages? King Ferdinand's cross in Madrid? Queen Gunhild's cross in Copenhagen? Where can I contact Mr. Topic?"

"So many questions. Let's see, I had a very good chance to examine it. Two or three hours. Do you have

something I can draw on? I'll show you what it looks
like. It has a tall, thin bottom shaft, slightly curving; and
a crossbar with a circular ivory in the center and—the
most distinctive feature—square blocks on the ends.
And . . .

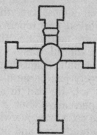

just above the center, a sort of ledge, jutting out, which
was a bit curious. I recall there was a bronze crucifix
attached to the ivory, rather poorly. The crucifix didn't
look authentic to me. After a while I think Topic told
me he had put the bronze figure of Christ there himself.
The cross, to answer another of your questions, I would
say, is . . . incomparable. The price? Somewhat high.
Topic Mimara was asking a mere two million dollars for
his treasure."

"That's absolutely crazy!"

"That's what Topic wanted. Anyway, you ought to get
in touch with him. There should be a number of his
addresses in The Cloisters' file. I'm not positive he is the
owner. I believe Topic may be middleman for someone
else. He's a little mysterious. What do I really think of
the cross? Well, that is where we have a slightly delicate
situation."

"What's so delicate?" I muttered, confused.

Dick Randall hunched over the dining-room table, took
a slow sip of his wine, put his face close to mine and
whispered, "I believe that the ivory cross—the unique,
the fantastic, the spectacular cross—is the best forgery I
have ever seen in my life." Then he roared with laughter.

I stared at him dumbfounded.

"Now, why am I telling you this? To sharpen your
eye. So that you can be better at authenticating treasures.
You owe it to yourself to see this cross. Ask James to
buy you a round-trip ticket to Zurich and take a look.

Topic Mimara has the most marvelous collection of fakes
ever assembled by anyone in history. You'll love it!"

I felt abused and told Randall so acidly. As a defense
to my embarrassment and annoyance I harshly demanded
why he thought the ivory was such an obvious forgery.
Randall explained that almost everything Topic Mimara
had was fake or reworked and repainted. "If he actually
believes his objects are authentic, then he's the most
addleheaded collector of all time."

I pounced upon Randall, dismissing his logic that the
cross had to be a forgery just because it lay among a host
of spurious works of art. He had to admit that guilt by
association was not persuasive. But it didn't matter. Internal evidence in the cross was overwhelming. The figure
style was utterly unprecedented and not medieval in style
at all. The cross was too rich, too ornate, too ambitious.
And there was one crowning argument. The placard, the
ivory ledge jutting out prominently over the head of
Christ, was *not* inscribed "Jesus of Nazareth, King of the
Jews," the only inscription possible which appeared on
virtually every cross in Christendom. The inscription on
Topic Mimara's was something impossible. The placard
on his cross proclaimed: "Jesus of Nazareth, King of the
Confessors." *Confessors!*

Had Dick Randall really seen a cross, or was his entire
story a fabrication? I couldn't be sure. Did the object
exist at all? I was determined to find out. So, on the
day after hearing Randall's story, I decided to search
through the files in The Cloisters.

I drove up Eighth Avenue, empty on a Sunday morning, and over to Riverside Drive, past the Soldier's and
Sailors' Monument, unkempt and deteriorating, covered
with graffiti. I swept by Grant's Tomb, which was re-
markably pristine. God knows why General Grant has
been spared. Was it some sense of political awe—some
sense of conservation, buried in the hearts of even the
most determined New York City vandals—which had
spared Ulysses Grant? Or was there actually a division
of riflemen hidden within to keep the General safe forever? I turned onto the Henry Hudson Parkway and
drove rapidly past the Esso station just before the George
Washington Bridge and proceeded north to The Cloisters

turnoff. I cut a sharp right up a steep, winding road under a rough-hewn granite bridge which looked like a miniature Pont-du-Gard. I made a very sharp left and drove slowly up the cobblestone private drive of The Cloisters, twisting and narrow, barely wide enough for even my diminutive car. I stopped at the massive wood-and-steel portcullis gate, the entrance to the employees' parking area. Two quick honks on the horn. Within minutes a guard came out, saw me and waved, and activated the electric key. With a shuddering clatter the huge gate rose.

I parked in the courtyard laid with Belgian blocks, glanced at the ramparts surrounding the court and ran into the entrance hall, easily catching the bunch of keys the guard tossed me.

To view The Cloisters across the Hudson from the Palisades or from the battlements of Fort Tryon just to the south you would think you were looking at the walled city of Carcassonne or a monastery looming up in the distance. Not at all. The Cloisters is a modern museum opened in 1938, enclosing one of the richest collections in Romanesque and Gothic architecture outside of Europe. One can find most of a cloister of the early twelfth century plucked from a monastic church nestling in the village of San Michel de Cuxa in the Pyrenees. Next to that a columned chapter house from Langon in central France stands alongside a series of modern galleries carefully made to look medieval.

To culture snobs, The Cloisters is disgusting. To them it's nothing more than a hodgepodge of ancient European architectural history, ripped out of context, pasted together to form a dreamlike but haphazard ensemble. Once, a short-tempered French scholar of medieval history whom I was conducting through the place on his first—and final—visit turned to me with a sour look and asked, "Please tell me, if you will, just *who* conceived this . . . oh so *romantic* place?"

I missed the acid flavor of his question and amiably told him that a lusty American sculptor of the turn of the century, George Grey Barnard, had been originally responsible. Barnard was the very image of the supermasculine creator. He seemed to adore posing for photos on top of a precarious scaffolding, bare-chested, wearing

trousers and a leather apron, tapping delicately with a
chisel at the blunt point of an exquisitely formed nipple
of a lush marble beauty in one of his overblown masterpieces entitled *The Ages of Woman* or suchlike. Barnard
was also a collector, one who had worked on a global
scale. He had traveled throughout France, Spain and
Italy around 1900, buying up every medieval work of
art or architecture he could lay his hands on. He sent
home entire cloisters, sculptured portals, whole chapels,
a hundred capitals, two hundred columns, a host of
plinths, a dozen tomb effigies, myriad corbels, and lintels,
fonts, arches, arcades, colonnades, carved stone coats of
arms and kilometers of odd stonework. He purchased all
that from abbots, priests and monks who were casual, to
say the least, about their architectural heritage. George
Grey Barnard preserved antiquity forever by dispensing
cash on the spot. To his credit, he did have a gifted
eye. A mediocre sculptor he might have been, but he
was an excellent collector. In all, Barnard was a far more
gifted collector than his contemporary plunderer of ecclesiastic European property, William Randolph Hearst.

I told the French visitor how Barnard gathered the
fragments together at his studio on 114th Street and
Amsterdam Avenue and how the assemblage had become
the sensation of the city and the world of art around
1915. After that Barnard, or his estate, sold his enormous
quantities of architecture and sculpture to the philanthro-
pist John D. Rockefeller, Jr., who had purchased what
was known as the Bliss estate, private property with a
mansion, on the north end of Manhattan. Rockefeller
had given the property to the city for a park, calling it
Fort Tryon Park, but retained the acreage where he built
The Cloisters as an architectural highlight for the green
space. Eventually Rockefeller gave the institution an endowment, incredible for those days, of no less than ten
million dollars, and such world-famous treasures as the
Unicorn Tapestries. In time, under James Rorimer's lead-
ership, The Cloisters became a distinguished museum
and one of the greatest repositories of medieval art anywhere in the world.

The Frenchman took it all in, groaning with distaste
from time to time as I proudly showed him another piece
of architecture which Barnard had lifted off the map of

37

Europe and which Jim Rorimer had set cleverly into the ensemble. As the professor departed he thanked me crisply and added, "It is an American miracle, is it not? And where are the monks?"

I didn't dare tell my distinguished guest that for several years after the opening of the establishment, certain members of the security force actually had worn monastic garb.

I had fallen in love with The Cloisters the moment I walked into the place, and I still have the deepest affection for it today. If you dream a little, you can float through time to the eleventh century in southern France, through twelfth-century Spain and all the way to the beginning of the sixteenth century in Germany. And that route will take you past some of the most dazzling works of art in all of Christendom. Cheers for George Grey Barnard and John D. Rockefeller, Jr.!

On that brisk Sunday morning in January 1960, I made a quick tour of the deserted galleries, noting that all the treasures were safe. With a special few I lingered a few minutes, mystified by the awesome power that seemed to surge forth in tangible waves. Certain works of art in The Cloisters—the Mérode Altarpiece; the silver chalice from Antioch, said to have been the Lord's cup at the Last Supper, but in reality created five centuries later; the diminutive Book of Hours once held lovingly by the Queen of France, Jeanne d'Évreux, throughout her prayer hours in the late fourteenth century—were veritable magnets to my eyes and mind. Electric energy seemed to flow from them. How could mere human beings have made these magical objects!

I made my way by a tiny private elevator, the interior of which was iron strapped and studded—the only "medieval" elevator in the world—to the top of the lofty tower, a unique eagle's nest overlooking the city. The spacious room was illegal, at least according to the Building Code. Back in 1937 the architects had, thank God, ignored the regulation that undivided interior space could not have windows on all four sides.

The cross, the fake ivory. Where would I find it in the files? "Purchases Offered and Declined." I went first to the subheading "Cross"; then to "Ivory." Not a damned thing. Next I searched for Topic, Ante and Mimara and

Matutin. All combinations. Again nothing. Randall had probably made up the entire tale. But eventually I con-concluded that he couldn't have invented it. Even he didn't have the imagination to concoct such a name and a yarn.

There weren't so many files, only about two hundred. Gradually I worked my way through every single folder marked "Purchases Declined" from the year 1940 forward. Most of them contained photographs and glowing letters from dealers around the world extolling the "uniqueness" or "superiority" or "the exceptional value" of whatever it was. I chuckled at some of the purple prose and the similarity of it all, as if one writer had composed the lot. What rubbish the institution had been offered over the years! I was amused to see a dozen photographs of obvious forgeries peddled, innocently or not, by dealers.

After several hours of shuffling through material, I found what I was looking for. It was buried in a file marked "Parsons, Harold." Stapled to the outside was a business card printed in German Gothic letters with the name Ante Topic Mimara and another name, Matutin, added in pen. The handwriting was strange, cautious but free. The file contained letters, memos and several tattered pages of notes.

I picked up the file and a note pad and made myself comfortable on a smoothly polished marble slab in one of the windows overlooking the Hudson River. I gazed for several minutes down at the majestic river, dotted with ice floes, and to the Palisades, shining in the sunlight. What would I unearth?

The first document was a letter to James Rorimer dated May 20, 1956, from a certain Harold Woodbury Parsons, Via Sistina 59, Rome. I'd never heard of the man, but I knew the street, having lived in Rome for most of a year during 1956 and 1957 when I took a break from graduate school. The address was near the church of Santa Trinitá dei Monti, close to the Spanish Steps and not far from the German library, called the Hertziana, where I had spent long hours studying. I must have walked by Parsons' house a dozen times.

The letter to Rorimer brimmed with flattery.

Knowing your passion for your beloved Cloisters and your dedication to acquire for it the finest works of art available in the world, I have the pleasure of informing you that a little known but wealthy collector who keeps most of his objects and paintings in Zurich has in the past week come to consult me on "placing" various masterpieces of medieval art with the truly appropriate institution.

I was already enthralled by the man's style.

Let me elaborate the sequence of events. Through my dear friend Fritz Volbach, whom I believe you know, a wealthy art collector, A. Topic Mimara, learned I was a retired American art museum consultant and advisor to one or two private collections. He recently came to my residence in Rome to make my acquaintance. He was travelling with his collaborator, Dr. Wiltrud Mersmann, a scholar of renown in the field of medieval art. . . .

I put the letter aside for a moment to think. Professor Fritz Volbach—I knew of *him*. He was a scholar of early Christian ivories, the author of a slim and exceedingly dull catalogue of the material. Was Volbach also an art dealer on the side? If so, it wouldn't be the first time. Professors and museum curators in Europe often supplemented their meager incomes by dealing in art or by writing expertises for dealers. I made a note to check further on Fritz Volbach through Kurt Weitzmann at Princeton. But *who* was Wiltrud Mersmann? I had never heard of the individual as an art scholar in any field. I reminded myself to search through the catalogue cards in the library to see if Mersmann had published anything. The unfamiliar name and Parsons' description of Mersmann as renowned made me suspicious. The most godawful junk was invariably served up in a package that contained at least one *curriculum vita* of a "renowned" art historian, connoisseur or expert who had never been heard of before or since. Intrigued, I returned to Harold Parsons' letter.

Mr. Topic Mimara invited me to come to Zurich to examine his extensive collection of paintings and "objets d'art." Although I have not yet had the opportunity to do so, I have examined a number of photographs and have found a host of medieval objects which I sincerely believe would be of the greatest interest to you and your splendid Cloisters. One of them, however, is *incomparable*, a medieval cross, the masterpiece of all known Winchester ivories. . . .

I leaned back again from my reading. So the cross was supposed to come from Winchester Cathedral! Not a bad locality at all. Just the best. The only problem was that virtually no scholar had ever been able to prove beyond a doubt that any one of the two dozen surviving English medieval ivory carvings dating from the tenth through the twelfth centuries had actually been created in Winchester, which was particularly known for a glorious group of illuminated manuscripts. Nonetheless, I made the notation on my pad: "Cross, Winchester."

Parsons continued:

You owe it to yourself to examine this masterpiece, personally, as soon as possible. I have been able to obtain, from Mr. Topic Mimara, a temporary option for you. But this exclusivity can only be maintained through the summer. Best personal wishes,

HAROLD

Jim Rorimer had answered promptly and coldly, saying that his schedule prevented his examining Topic Mimara's holdings. Rorimer had informed Parsons he would assign his "able assistant, Richard H. Randall, Jr.," to look into the object, and closed by asking for photographs and the price of the "incomparable" Winchester cross.

Harold Parsons responded within the week and attempted to change Rorimer's mind, using skills of persuasion worthy of a diplomat.

Although I am convinced that one of your hand-picked associates would appreciate the importance of the majestic cross from Winchester Cathedral and another one of Topic Mimara's masterworks, a splendid reliquary glass decorated with typical "Winchester" initial and floral designs in colored enamel, I wish you would find time to go yourself. Only your experienced eye, which so very often has discovered the unusual treasure, can understand these unique pieces.

What was this glass? What had Topic done, I wondered—miraculously unearthed the entire contents of ancient Winchester Cathedral?

Parsons had really laid it on. "The cross is unknown by anyone else and unpublished," he wrote; "it resides in Zurich with no exportation restrictions at all. Only you, with your unsurpassed courage to make the grand effort, will be able to act decisively."

Eagerly I searched ahead through the file for photographs of the amazing cross. But there were to be no photographs. According to Parsons, "Topic Mimara will not let them out of his hands, for he had made a promise to a great European art museum not to part with them. But I am certain," Parsons assured the director of the Metropolitan Museum, "that he will cede you a set upon your personal visitation."

That was annoying but clever of Mr. Ante Topic Mimara, I thought. He knew well enough not to jeopardize a potential deal by shipping off photos, which *never* give the full impression of a work of art. And I also had to admire the deft way Parsons had cast in his mention of a European museum. Parsons might be sugar sweet, but he was crafty. Now, what about the price?

But the price was unquoted. Parsons had used the standard ploy.

The price, I must tell you candidly, is high, in the area that a fine painting would command. But Topic Mimara argues that the price is correct for such a unique survival of English Medieval art, where, as you know, there are precious few survivors after the depredations of Henry VIII and Oliver Cromwell.

Parsons did point out that the price was "discussable." And speaking of finances, he had hastened to let Rorimer know "whatever fee the owner will pay me for my services, will be completely separate from any ultimate monetary arrangement he makes with The Cloisters or the museum ultimately to acquire the masterpiece."

James Rorimer had refused to give ground and go himself, which I thought was a little cavalier of him. The greatest medieval ivory cross in existence? My God, there were only two known in the whole world, and *they* were both in museums. Nevertheless, Dick Randall had been dispatched. He had met Topic Mimara at the Hotel Sankt Peter in Zurich. I wrote the name down on my pad. Randall had seen a surprising quantity of objects from Topic's collection. The file contained three pages torn out of his notebook, listing twenty-five works of art, all dating to the Middle Ages. Under "Authentic" he noted a Limoges enamel crucifix of the thirteenth century at five thousand dollars; an ivory carving of a king on horseback, probably twelfth century, possibly Cologne, at ten thousand; and at least a dozen minor objects. Everything else was described by Randall as hopeless in quality or outright fake. He had marked the purported forgeries by the sign "(f)." These included some grandiose objects: an "early Christian gold glass chalice, complete at $200 thousand, (f)"; "a Carolingian glass bowl of modern glass painted with copies of mss. initials in enamel, (f)"; "a walrus ivory cross with inscriptions in Greek and Latin—German bronze crucifix copy on it—*fantastic* work (f), 2 million only."

A month after his unfruitful visit, Dick Randall had sent a glacial letter to Ante Topic Mimara at an address in Tangier, Morocco, 97 Boulevard de Paris. "Dear Monsieur Topic, Thank you for showing me the objects in Zurich. None of them are of interest to the Museum for acquisition."

And that was it! Slam!

This finality had not deterred Harold Parsons. He had written Rorimer again and again, defending the cross and the glass objects. But Randall had crushed Parsons' attempts with a succinct memo to his boss: "This latest letter is hogwash. The cross is one of the worst forgeries (or best) that I have ever seen. Unquestionably wrong. The price was one million dollars, which gives you some idea of Mr. Matutin Mimara's mental arithmetic; everything else was either fake or fussed up. . . ."

Still, Harold Parsons had persisted in his personal crusade to place the cross. In the spring of 1957 he had written directly to Peg Freeman, urging her to come to Europe and examine the great ivory. By this time he had moderated his earlier enthusiasms. The cross was no longer the "finest treasure to have survived medieval time." "Personally, I have seen few of his objects," he wrote, "but William Milliken visited the bank in Switzerland, at my suggestion, and thought the glass especially fine . . . but the big ivory crucifix puzzled him. . . . Volbach, I am told, accepts it beyond question. If genuine, it is certainly an astonishing survival."

So, I said to myself, William Milliken, the director of the Cleveland Museum of Art, had been offered the cross and had gone to see it. He too had been troubled! Milliken had a superb eye. That was not so good for the cross!

Parsons wrote to Peg Freeman that Topic Mimara "lives mostly in Tangier . . . where the bulk of his collection is housed in his villa, and a good deal of the time in Austria of which he is a citizen, having some time ago renounced his Yugo-Slav nationality." Parsons mentioned that some of what he called "the incomparable glass collection" had been published in a highly reputable German scholarly publication, *Pantheon.* I made a note to check the article.

Parsons ended his communication to Peg Freeman by saying that he would try to find out more about Topic's collection, which, he suspected, "has, at some time, been owned by Royalty or some religious institution."

Those were the contents of the file. I replaced them in the cabinet and perused my notes. It sounded intriguing, like the beginning of a detective novel. But would it really be worthwhile to chase after an improbable, unpromising collector and his doubtful ivory cross? I slouched down into an overstuffed leather chair and pondered the matter for a while, suspecting it would be a waste of energy. Dick Randall had probably been right in his evaluation. And the suspicious reaction of old Bill Milliken of Cleveland was a strong argument against the object. Should I drop the whole thing? Probably. Then, languidly, I decided I might as well follow up on the cross just a little longer. Dick Randall was right in one thing: to take at least a passing look at a highly creative forgery could be worthwhile.

In the library I found the volume of *Pantheon* in which an expert had published his opinions of the early Christian glass in Topic Mimara's collection. Instantly, I recognized that the early Christian chalice representing Christ as the Good Shepherd hoisting the Lamb of God to His shoulders was a ridiculous fake. It was clear that the so-called "unique expression of profound faith of the earliest worshippers of Christian faith," as the scholar had phrased it, had been copied line for line from a fragmentary gold glass in the Vatican museum. I got out the standard publication on gold glass in the Christian Museum of the Vatican and made a comparison. I had been right. Topic Mimara's piece was a crude attempt to copy the original. In the Vatican glass, the figure of the Shepherd holding the Lamb across His solid shoulders was stalwart and delineated by a series of energetic lines. In Mr. Topic Mimara's chalice, the figure was a graceless amalgam of man and beast; it looked, in fact, like a glob of gilded marzipan. If Topic's "unique ivory cross" was anything like his gold glass, it would be a disaster.

I left the library and walked slowly around the deserted cloister of San Michel de Cuxa to think things over. How peaceful the cloister was! The imposing arcades of pink stones carved into fantastic images had been protected for the winter by a series of glass partitions. There were dozens of banks of fresh flowers and plants placed throughout the cloister, and they filled my nostrils with the moist odor of verdancy. The courtyard outside was blanketed with snow which had been driven against the black trunks of the four apple trees and had drifted up the side of the limestone font, which over the centuries had calcified into a hue whiter even than the fresh snow. I savored the beauty of the vista.

What should I do? Let it be, I admonished myself. Why should I chase the warped vision of an improbable cross to the ends of the earth? My shaky career couldn't accommodate another mistake with yet another cross. I had lucked out once. This time I wouldn't risk it. The chase had come to an end.

Then I was struck by a most peculiar feeling. It was as if my whole brain had actually shifted deep within my skull. I realized that if Dick Randall had correctly described the peculiar inscription, "King of the Confessors," the ivory cross coud not possibly be a fake. No forger would have been able or would have wanted to make up those unique words, Jesus of Nazareth, King of the Confessors. Fakers wanted to do what everyone else had done. King of the Confessors . . . King of the Confessors.

I repeated the words softly to myself. They were words of triumph and hope. Confessor. A confessor was one of the faithful, in a category just below the martyrs, who had given up everything for the Christian faith—life, possessions, soul. The confessors were those who had taken up the cross through an overpowering love; those who had the courage to reveal their weaknesses and secrets; those who would lay bare the baseness of their pitiful mortal beings; those who could expose their sins. The melancholy yet victorious poetry of the words resounded with truth.

A museum curator, a professional collector, is supposed to react to a work of art dispassionately, analytically. Intuition or the heart should never be allowed to stand in the way of reason. But I urgently wanted the cross to be genuine. I so yearned to discover and acquire one of the greatest treasures existing that I manipulated the mysterious cross in my heart and mind. I could see it standing virtually in front of me. I could almost reach out and take it in my hands. At that moment, for me, the ivory cross became genuine and of triumphant importance.

So I began the quest. I wrote down the key steps in my campaign to find and acquire the cross, if it was still available.

1. Topic Mimara, who is he, where is he?
2. The Cross, where is it? What is it?
3. The competition, who has seen it and who is after it?

I paused and wrote down a fourth step.

4. Rorimer, what will he think?

I reached him by phone at his desk at the museum. He was impressed that I too was busily working away on a Sunday and told me so. He chatted for several minutes, and asked me—rather poignantly, I thought—how his office in the tower of his beloved Cloisters looked. He sighed; it was impossible for him to visit there any more. He had not been able to do so in more than half a year.

I described the correspondence. Rorimer remembered vaguely something about a Topic Mimara and an ivory cross.

"From what you tell me, Thomas, it is hardly worth-while. Perhaps it would be more fruitful to look ahead to fresh triumphs than to try to dredge up the spurned and forgotten," he drawled. "You know, John Rockefeller, being a Baptist, had little interest in packing The Cloisters with crosses, anyway. Of course, that really doesn't matter now, since I have full freedom to decide what I want to buy."

I told Rorimer about Harold Parsons' and Randall's conviction that the cross was a fake. But I countered strongly with my intuition that the piece might be genuine, and great.

"Well, then, look into the thing, if you wish, but don't take too much time. Dick Randall, although *personally* a difficult boy, did have a fairly decent eye. Talk to Kurt Weitzmann. He'll know. But *whatever* happens, do not, under any circumstances, *ever*, contact Harold Woodbury Parsons! He's been mixed up in some pretty peculiar transactions over the years. I don't wish the museum to have anything to do with him."

Within minutes after speaking with Rorimer, I had the concierge of the Hotel Sankt Peter in Zurich on the phone. "No, Herr Topic Mimara is not currently at the hotel. Yes, he comes frequently." But the hotelman did not know when he would next arrive, telling me, "He just appears without advance notice." I was advised to try the Hotel Wolff in Munich. I left a message for Topic Mimara to call me.

I telephoned the Hotel Wolff. No luck. Herr Topic Mimara had not been a guest in at least four months, perhaps more. I left a message there too.

At first it seemed the overseas operator had never heard of Tangier. When the existence of the city had been established, I told her about Ante Topic Mimara Matutin at 97 Boulevard de Paris. After twenty minutes of shouting his name in transatlantic telephone code—Théâtre, Opiot, Pigalle, Issoire, Charlemagne; Marseille, Issoire, Marseille, Argonne, Rouen, Argonne; et cetera—I heard through diverse clickings, clankings and hummings that

Topic Mimara Matutin was unknown. There was no such person, no such address.

I gazed longingly at the name Harold Woodbury Parsons, and more than once my hand reached out for the telephone. How simple it would be to get him on the phone, tell him my name, ask him to contact his client and urge him to call me at home. Rorimer would never know. Or would he? I was about to call, but then I weakened. For *this* cross, I had to be obedient.

Oh, to hell with obedience! I'd take the chance that Parsons would never mention the conversation to James Rorimer. The time was ripe. It would be six hours later in Rome. Maybe Parsons would be home for dinner.

Within a minute, surprisingly, the overseas operator located the number. Soon the phone, so far away, was ringing.

"*Signore, telefono da America,*" the operator said.

"Hallo. Harold Parsons here. Hello? . . . I say, do you hear me? Hallo?"

I froze. Images of Rorimer castigating me flooded my mind. "You *telephoned* Parsons? Minutes after I specifically warned, *ordered,* you not to do so? You're fired!"

"Hello. . . . *Hello.* . . . Who is there?"

Gently, I replaced the receiver.

CHAPTER FOUR

Fakes and Treasures

NOTHING AT ALL worked that January of 1960 in my quest for the Winchester cross. I sent a half-dozen copies of a letter to Topic Mimara at every known address, each one registered, dispatched special delivery. The ones to Europe were returned "Addressee unknown"; the one sent to Tangier simply vanished.

I wrote a cautious letter to Dick Randall in Boston seeking additional leads on reaching Topic. Of course I didn't let him know I had discovered the file on the cross. Despite his apparently firm conviction that the cross was an outrageous fake, I was concerned he might change his mind. Randall was still a potential competitor. When one is smoking out a work which may be great, the cardinal rule, in James Rorimer's book and therefore in mine, is, *never* seek information about the object from a rival.

Randall, typically, sent a joking reply. But when I read his letter I detected an underlying note of seriousness about the Topic collection which he had not imparted before.

DEAR TOM,

Why should I give rivals the addresses of valuable items? Eh? Well, just this once.

I think you will find considerable correspondence in the files . . . There are even some photos, I think. In any case, he always meets one very mysteriously at the Hotel Sankt Peter in Zurich and takes you to the bank to see his junk in a vault. He is a bore and so is most of his material, but then the few good things are worth the wait.

Are you planning a coup? If so, please notify the State Department and Mr. Kennedy before leaving the country for more smuggling opportunities. Wildenstein is under surveillance.

But Randall also revealed that "Hanns" knew about Topic Mimara and had him in his files. That gave me a chill. For Hanns Swarzenski, the curator of decorative arts at Boston's Museum of Fine Art and Dick Randall's superior, was generally acknowledged to be the most gifted connoisseur of medieval and early Renaissance art in the United States. His father, George, had also been an art historian and had brought his son from Germany to America in the 1930s. "Hitler had shaken the tree, and the two best apples of medieval art history had fallen to the ground in Boston," as one observer had put it. Both Swarzenskis, father and son, became in turn curator of decorative arts at the prestigious M.F.A., and the acquisitions they made have seldom been equaled by any other institution.

Hanns Swarzenski was blessed with an uncanny sensitivity for objets d'art and preferred them by far to paintings or large-scale sculptures. He had a special affinity through "vision, touch and taste," as a competitor phrased it, with the physical and even the inner spirituality of the minor arts. He realized that inherent power could possess more monumentality than size alone. To watch him pick up and scrutinize a small bronze enamel or piece of jewelry was to see a man whose fingers, eyes and mind became magically wedded to the artifact. But ask him to expound upon it? Impossible! He was seemingly inarticulate. The fact that he never managed to shuck off his obtuse German accent did not help. To make matters worse, Swarzenski seemed incapable of speaking directly to anyone. He would move his leonine head restlessly

from side to side, anything to avoid direct eye contact.
Sooner or later in a conversation he would press his head
so far down into his barrel chest that his chins, half of
his face and all of his words would disappear. At one
International Congress on Art History, Swarzenski had
been recruited to deliver the keynote lecture on his
speciality, English art of the Romanesque period. He had
thumped to the podium on crutches and impressed a
part of the audience who were convinced he was talking
about art history; others, who knew him better, were
enchanted by his rambling account of how he had broken
his ankle swimming off Cape Cod three weeks earlier.

I wondered whether Swarzenski had ever seen the
cross and, if he had, what he thought of it. Yet, knowing
his tenacity in pursuing masterpieces, I did not dare seek
his opinion.

Although I avoided talking to anyone on the outside
about the cross, I did go to the most gifted—and socially
prominent—curator on the staff of the Metropolitan,
Theodore Rousseau, Jr., who, Rorimer had told me in an
aside, had once, he believed, seen the Topic Mimara
collection.

Ted Rousseau seemed to symbolize everything life was
supposed to mean. He was more handsome than any film
star; yet he ignored his physical appeal, deprecated it,
not by talking down about it, but by an attitude which
indicated in just the right way that the mind weighed far
more on the scale of merit than a mere physical exterior.
Even those who were most envious of him had to admit
he was sincere in that. And the individual in the Metropolitan who was most envious of Theodore Rousseau, Jr.,
was James Rorimer. So I had to be cautious with both of
them.

Rousseau was the curator of the most exalted department of all in the institution, European Paintings. The
best of the best. Rousseau was American, but had been
raised in France and educated at Eton, Oxford and
Harvard. He was independently wealthy and socially a
paragon—in New York, Paris, London, Palm Beach, Madrid. He was brilliant in languages. It was said that in
only a month before he went on his first trip to the Soviet
Union he had mastered Russian well enough to flabber-
gast and enchant his hosts at the Ministry of Culture by

giving an impromptu three-minute toast. Ted Rousseau seemed to many to be the hallmark of the Metropolitan Museum. More than once at a dinner party James Rorimer had been confronted by a socialite seated next to him with the words "Oh, you are at the Metropolitan. Tell me, do you work for the director, my dear friend Ted Rousseau?"

Rousseau's aura of romance was confirmed by accomplishments. He had been with the Office of Strategic Services during World War II, assigned to Lisbon, where he had carried out undercover missions into Vichy France and even, it was rumored, into German-occupied territory. After the war Rousseau had been assigned as one of the interrogators of Hermann Goering. Through his command of the German language and his impeccable manners and charm, he had drawn out from the Reichsmarschall evidence of crimes no one on the tribunal had dreamed of. Although Rousseau was repelled by the deflated, perverted Nazi, he claimed to have been momentarily enchanted when, at dawn in the claustrophobic prison cell, he had initiated several weeks of questions about Goering's looting of European art treasures with the words "And now, Herr Reichsmarschall, I want to deal with the question of culture . . ." Goering perked up, smiled and growled, "Culture! I have always agreed with our poet Hanns Johst who used to say, 'When I hear the word culture, I uncock my revolver's safety catch.'"

"Sometimes I tend to get that feeling myself," Rousseau told me over lunch at the Veau d'Or, a fashionable French restaurant in midtown Manhattan where he reserved a special table daily. "The Metropolitan has become so bureaucratic in recent years. Curators seem inclined to spend most of their time avoiding original works of art." He paused. "So what *are* your acquisition plans for The Cloisters and the Medieval Department?"

"You are presuming I have the power to make those plans," I said, trying a little false humility, which he ignored.

"If you don't, you will," Rousseau said with an engaging smile.

"Instead of simply visiting the dealers to see what they have, reacting to their inventories, I have started with the collections and discussed the weaknesses and the needs. Now I am looking to fill the holes. My best weapon is money, The Cloisters Purchase Fund. I look upon it as some kind of sword which should never be sheathed. To make it work it should be brandished around a bit. I differ from Jim, who swears by the gospel of secrecy. His constant refrain is, Never let an art dealer know you have money. My gospel is different. If you have the money for art, use it. Don't bargain. Accept the quoted price, or walk out, politely. The dealer will learn. Next time you deal with him and gradually throughout the world with other dealers, you will hear something coming after you, and that will be the privilege of first refusal. And *that's* the edge! But perhaps you think I'm peculiar."

But of course I knew Ted did not think I was at all peculiar. He was, or appeared to be, mesmerized, which is what I had intended. I had to enlist him. I needed his sangfroid, his easy access to certain key trustees, his manifold contacts with the luminaries of the labyrinthine art world.

"May I ask you a question?" I said. "What is your system of sizing up a work of art?"

"I study the hands, which to me are the mirrors of true artistic excellence and the artist. And from the hands I try to become fully acquainted with the subject and thus the artist. Or, if I'm looking at a landscape, I seek the temperature, the atmosphere, of clouds, rocks, trees— the *sounds*, if you will, emanating from these elements. Peter Brueghel's *Winter*, in Vienna. The cold is brusque, not brutal, just brusque, and real. Penetrating, implacable, knifelike. The trees crack with the cold. You can almost hear the sap solidifying, snapping the wood as the meager winter sun disappears. The snow rakes across the faces of the hunters returning to the village. All is becoming dark, full of contrasts, black and very white gray."

I nodded and smiled in appreciation.

"A still life is reality," Rousseau continued. "Something so actual the skin of the apple resists your teeth for a second. And the grape sours on your tongue. Or the fish smells a bit rank. All is edible, or at least it was yesterday. Finesse, quality, technique. They are fine. But there is more, much more. Magic, essence, the hidden voice. Those are things I look for. But not always. I too sometimes search for what is merely on the surface—the condition of things, the paint glazes, the layers of varnish, the evidence of restoration, the fixings, cleanings, and repairings made after the master. You know, the meat and potatoes." Rousseau paused and queried, "Tell me, exactly how old *are* you? And what are you up to?"

I laughed. How quickly can a lifelong friendship be hatched.

I told Ted Rousseau about my ambitions, not even leaving out the hope that someday I would become director of the museum. I even told him about my latest dream, the ivory cross, and why I had become so deeply attached to something that I had never seen and that I was not even sure existed.

"The cross exists, don't worry about that," Rousseau interjected, surprising me, "and so does the owner, Topic. I met him two or three years ago, and I found him rather a sympathetic rogue. I had been tipped off by an amusing old bird by the name of Harold Parsons that Topic owned a Rembrandt and a Rubens of superior quality. I met him at some little hotel in Zurich. Then we ambled over to a bank. He told me that his choicest paintings, including a superb Raphael, were in Tangier and tried to persuade me to travel there with him that very day.

"I didn't take him up on that, particularly after seeing the two pictures in the vault. The man seemed to be vulnerable, pathetic, rather lost as far as his judgment about art was concerned. With considerable pride, he showed off a number of terrible drawings of the nineteenth century, calling them Ingres and Delacroix, which they were definitely not. And he trundled out half a dozen Impressionist paintings, appalling daubs. Funny, it was obvious that this Topic was utterly convinced he had gathered together some of the finest pictures in the world. I have never encountered such a self-deluded collector in my years in the profession. After an hour or two I became impatient to get away, but he put his hand on my arm—it was a sad gesture somehow—and begged me to look at one more object. He insisted that I would be the first person in the world to view his greatest treasure from the Middle Ages. I waited, although I was already very late for my luncheon engagement. With a flourish he placed a sizable ivory cross before me on the table.

It seemed to be about two feet high. I did look at it, but not too closely. It isn't my field. And Topic fluttered around it, talking on about how superb it was. My impression, an indelible one, I'm afraid, is that the thing looked like a piece of old yellow soap."

"You mean you thought it was phony?" I said sadly.

"I fear so," Rousseau said, "but I hasten to add I didn't give the thing a great deal of attention. And, of course, medieval is definitely not my speciality. Yes, my reaction was doubtful. I recall that the hands of the little characters carved all over it were exceedingly rigid."

"I wonder why Topic Mimara claimed you were the first person from the Met to look at it," I mused. "Dick Randall saw Topic's collection, and his cross, in the early fall of 1956. He too believed the cross was fake."

"I see. Listen. I must tell you something. Forget about me and my opinions. Don't listen to me, or Randall or anybody else, least of all Jim Rorimer, about this cross. When you have a feeling about a work of art such as you do, allow nothing to stand in your way. Only you can pursue the object. Because of your strong faith, everyone, everything else should become peripheral. When you are driving for a work of art and you are responsible for making the decision to acquire or reject it, you are a thousand miles closer to it than anyone else in the world. The rest of us are mere observers, and probably always will be. Trust your gut, and your eye, but primarily your gut."

"May I count on your help?" I asked. "I may need your assistance, with Rorimer, and I'll need your power with some of the trustees. If I ask, will you help?"

"Count on it." Rousseau smiled. "Nothing would please me more than to have you prove my opinion wrong."

"Ted, who the hell is Parsons and why does Jim hate him?"

"Harold Parsons? He's an elderly aesthete and part-time art commissionaire, a fussy older-generation type. Parsons has been obsessed for years with discovering forgeries. And he *is* deft at detecting them. Perhaps he has unmasked one of Jim's mistakes. Jim prefers to do that himself."

When I returned from lunch I learned that Rorimer had phone my office three times. I called him and he summoned me up to his office. "Where were you? I see, a three-hour lunch with Rousseau. He spends more time at Veau d'Or than at the museum. Don't you fall into that."

I stood waiting for the next blow.

"I have decided to take you to Europe this summer. I'm bringing my family. You may, if you wish, bring Nancy."

I just stood there amazed.

"That's all," Rorimer said. I was headed for the door when he called out again. "Oh, wait, deal with this thing, please," he said gruffly and handed me a manila envelope. Inside was a one-paragraph letter from a certain Harry Sperling and a photograph of a stone relief depicting the Annunciation. The angel and the Virgin Mary were standing in an arcade within a castle decorated with towers and crenellations. The relief seemed to be in good condition except for the lower right-hand corner, which was broken off. The letter said:

DEAR JIM,
This relief is, I am told, Italian and Romanesque and can be obtained for $50,000. Not being acquainted with medieval art I really cannot assure you if it is as purported or if it is any good at all.

"What do you make of it, Jim?" I asked.

Rorimer leaned back in his chair and sighed. "It is beginning to be no longer a question of what *I* think. That's your job now." He motioned for the photograph and studied it closely, flicking his glasses up to his forehead. "It seems to me we ought to turn it down. Seems weak. I never did like early Italian sculpture. Fifty is outrageous."

"Who is Harry Sperling?" I asked.

"Harry's a dealer in paintings and drawings. He's the surviving nephew of a man by the name of Kleinberger who had damned good old masters. Sperling handles good but not great paintings. But I like him for a special reason. He's the world's leading expert in arranging that almost any work of art you have seen, anyplace in the world, suddenly turns up safe and sound in Switzerland, eminently exportable to the United States. He maintains offices in New York, but spends much of his time at the Hotel Piccadilly in London. You'll find him a man dedicated to his unique profession. And he's totally honest too."

I showed the photograph of the Annunciation to Peg Freeman and my other colleagues in the Medieval Department. Their reaction was negative. So I went through the motions only. I spent an hour in the museum's library, trying to find a comparison for the relief in standard reference books on Italian sculpture of the Romanesque period. Finding nothing, I wrote a polite letter to Harry Sperling declining the sculpture. But I didn't return the photograph, which would have been the normal, and courteous, thing to do. I don't know exactly why I did not. A persistent yet muted bell kept ringing in the back of my head. Had I not seen something like the Annunciation once? I wasn't sure. Much as I tried, I couldn't pin it down.

Yet the bell wouldn't stop ringing. So a few days later I reviewed my first reactions upon seeing the photograph of the piece: "Chunky, frank, classic, yet not classic. Italian. Florentine?" I decided to give it one more try.

I have a simple yet effective technique for tracking down the style of a work of art which is not immediately identifiable. I capture in my mind the essential stylistic elements and start searching broadly at first, trying to find comparisons for the object in a general historical period, say the entire Romanesque epoch. Then I attempt to narrow that down to a few decades, a region, a workshop, or a specific artist. I collect as many photographs as possible from books or from the slide and photo archives, and race through them, putting to one side those which bear *any* sort of stylistic relationship, even a hint. Then I cull from that pile, throwing away all but the most pertinent, and start all over again, focusing closer with each search.

In the case of the Annunciation relief there were three basic stylistic elements: the decoration, the architecture and the figures. Each was distinctive, particularly the architecture with its series of heavy arches adorned with a classicizing egg-and-dart motif. The figure style was striking. The angel and the Virgin Mary were stout little creatures with fat faces shaped like lima beans. Their

mouths were sharp, straight incisions jammed up close
to flattened noses. Their bodies were obscured by heavy,
ironed-down draperies terminating in wide trumpet folds.

I buried myself in the basement of the museum library
at an isolated table. I pulled from the stacks all the general books on Italian medieval art, about thirty of them.
They must have contained at least two thousand illustrations! In two days I had sifted through the lot but found
no striking comparisons. I did note that five sculptures
looked generally like the Annunciation relief. Every one of
them had been made in Tuscany, in places like Pisa,
Prato, or Florence. They weren't all that close to the
Annunciation, but they were close enough to lead me to
a more intense examination of Romanesque sculptures in
Tuscany in the twelfth and thirteenth centuries.

From the library catalogue cards I made a list of
books and bound periodicals dealing specifically with
Tuscany. I was surprised to find there were sixty books.
I located each one, carried them all down to my lonely
table and studied what must have been another thousand
illustrations. After three days my mind was numb; my
body ached from carrying the volumes back and forth.
From time to time I had spasms of double vision. My
head throbbed.

Finally I was down to the last three books. In my
search I had flushed out little indeed. The only convincing
stylistic comparison to Sperling's Annunciation was a group
of sculptured square panels embedded in a marble pulpit
of the mid-twelfth century in the Florentine church of
San Miniato al Monte. The decorative elements were
similar to those on the Annunciation, but not exactly.
The pulpit had only one carved figure, a stiff image of
Saint John the Evangelist leaning out of the front of the
pulpit like some figurehead on an old sailing vessel. I
studied the carving with burning eyes, and for a moment
I hallucinated that the face, with its thin mouth under a
squashed nose, and with its almond-shaped eyes each
punctuated with a round black pupil, was identical to the
Virgin's in the Annunciation. But the photo was too in-
distinct for me to be sure.

At one o'clock in the morning, alone in the darkness of
the library and utterly disheartened, I decided to give up.
James Rorimer and my associates had been right after

all. As I cast my eyes over the photograph of the Annunciation I couldn't imagine why I had become attracted
to the damned thing at all. Completely drained, I wearily
paced around the dimly lit table.

At that exact moment I got a breath of second wind.
Why should I give in? What did Rorimer really know?
He hadn't given the Annunciation more than two seconds
of his time. The thing was *my* responsibility. He'd given
that to me! And what the hell did my colleagues know?
The Annunciation was a powerful, primitive work of art.
It deserved one last look. As I glanced through the essay
describing the pulpit of San Miniato, I noticed a footnote
which mentioned an article in a periodical entitled
L'Arte, written in 1906 by a scholar named Odoardo
Giglioli, about a Romanesque pulpit in a church near
Florence I had never heard of—San Leonardo in Arcetri,
a suburb in the hills overlooking Florence. Another book
to hunt down! I was almost ready to forget it, I just
didn't have the strength anymore. And then I saw that the
volume was one of the last three lying on my table.

I thumbed through and found the article. In the middle
of it I came across a minuscule, slightly out-of-focus
photograph showing a pulpit embedded in a wall, a
pulpit decorated with a series of square panels with
figurative reliefs. I knew immediately I had found what
I was looking for. The pulpit of San Leonardo had six
reliefs depicting the life of Christ. The Tree of Jesse,
Nativity, the Three Magi, the Presentation in the Temple,
Baptism, and Deposition, but no scene depicting the
Annunciation! The style fit the Annunciation relief like a
glove. The same draperies, figures, decoration, egg-and-
dart arches, castles, bulbous lima-bean faces, slashed
mouths, squashed pug noses, almond eyes.

I was utterly alert, my headache gone, my eyes gleaming. I devoured the article. The pulpit in San Leonardo
had been crafted in the mid-twelfth century for a Florentine church called San Piero in Scheraggio, which had
been demolished in the sixteenth century to make room
for the famous Uffizi, the offices built for Cosimo de'
Medici by the architect Giorgio Vasari. The reliefs had
been dismantled and stored. Two hundred years or so
later, the last of the Medici, the Grand Duke Pietro
Leopoldo, a man obsessed with the ancient relics of

Florence, had gathered up all the reliefs he could find—just six of them—and had reassembled them in the small parish church up in Arcetri. The seventh relief was missing.

I rushed to my office and cabled Harry Sperling at the Piccadilly Hotel in London:

> DISREGARD MY LETTER ON ANNUNCIATION RELIEF. HOLD FOR
> US AN OPTION TO BUY. WHAT KIND OF STONE? WHAT ARE
> THE MEASUREMENTS?
>
> HOVING

In four days a letter arrived from Sperling:

> I will be delighted to hold the sculpture for The Cloisters.
> I am most intrigued to learn what you discovered about
> it that caused you to change your mind. When we meet
> I hope you will feel free to explain. The stone is marble
> and the measurements are: 26¼ by 24¼ inches.

Perfect! The San Leonardo reliefs measured the same. All I had to do now was figure out just where *our* Annunciation—I had already acquired it in my mind—fit into the original pulpit.

The next day, very casually, I dropped in on Rorimer and showed him the photographs in the article. He examined the evidence and then looked at me with a melancholy expression on his face. He cocked his head to the side and whistled softly to himself. "My God, you've got it. Did any of your colleagues help in this?"

"They told me the piece was insignificant."

"So did I. Well, I am jealous of you," Rorimer said. "Damn jealous! Look at this paperwork. That's all I do anymore. Follow up the Annunciation with Sperling. I'll do the bargaining—no, we'll do that together. But you talk to him first. Where is the sculpture? England? Well, find out. And I just want to let you know, I've made up my mind to promote you this July to assistant curator of both Medieval and Cloisters." I could feel my chest breasting the tape.

Within a fortnight Harry Sperling turned up in New York. He was a short, peppery man with sparse kinky black hair. "What did you manage to find out about the relief to make you send that message?" he asked, his eyes alight with pleasure.

Then I spilled out my story. Sperling strutted with excitement, slapping his hands together in delight.

"Marvelous. I have already obtained a ten percent museum discount from the owner for you. So your discovery will cost only forty-five."

"What if I hadn't told you how important it was?"

"Ah, no. I'm the kind of art dealer—a rare type—who will always make you a better deal when I'm let in on a secret. Listen. After what you just told me, I'll take another two thousand five hundred dollars off the price. And I'll never let Jimsie know you told me."

"Where's the piece now, Harry—England?"

"No. The Annunciation relief is propped up against a broken-down Fiat in a small garage on the outskirts of Genoa."

"Italy!" I cried out. "How can you buy the piece in Italy and get it out?"

"I see no difficulty," Sperling said calmly. "My advice is, go take a look at it. I'll set up an appointment in Genoa. If you like it, I'll arrange its shipment to Switzerland."

"Is that difficult?" I asked him, not really wanting to know, realizing I was being drawn into a conspiracy to smuggle. "How is it done?" I continued, throwing caution aside.

"There are dozens of ways—car, boat, truck. The Italians don't care. Quite a number of people in Italy, very respectable people, make a steady living out of smuggling works of art. One of my favorite techniques is to take a small station wagon, pile the back with mattresses, lay a work of art under them, and rent the services of a small child. On a very hot Sunday afternoon I drive from Venice to the border. So will thousands of other tourists. A few kilometers before customs I stop and buy a large ice-cream cone for the child. By the time I have reached the crowded border and the smartly dressed, white-gloved and harried customs officers, the child has smeared the *gelato* all over his face. The customs man always recoils in horror and orders me to drive through."

Seeing the Annunciation relief in Genoa fit in perfectly with the summer tour Rorimer had arranged. In June,

Nancy and I flew to Europe and teamed up with James Rorimer and his family. Rorimer had shipped over his Chevrolet station wagon for the trek. The plan was to drive from Paris through the Loire Valley to see the châteaux, travel to Spain all the way to the great pilgrimage cathedral of Santiago de Compostela, then back across the Riviera into Italy, and to Genoa.

Liberated from his administrative duties and once again in the France and Spain he adored, James Rorimer was no longer the dour director but a lighthearted and captivating human being who drove us from one monument to another as if we were riding on the back of a hummingbird. He became an inexhaustible font of information and fun. The experiences of his youth, the contents of articles, books, scholarly journals he had read years before, conversations with colleagues about the thousands of works we visited, streamed forth from him endlessly. I had never learned more about art in any two months of my life.

On one occasion our party had become entrapped in a guided tour of a famed château. Facing the prospect of plodding through several dozen period rooms with a tour guide who never seemed to take a breath as he spewed out his misinformation in a nasal monotone, Rorimer finally cried out, "Enough!" In full view of the incredulous guide and an envious group of tourists, we clambered out a window and escaped.

Another time, in the massive cathedral of Salamanca, Rorimer and I had gotten into an argument over a bronze-gilt-and-enamel statue of the Virgin Mary decorating one of the altars.

"Superb," I told him.

"Copy," Rorimer shot back.

"Strong," I fired at him.

"Weak," he said.

"Original," I countered.

"Fake," he bellowed.

"Genuine," I insisted.

The priest who had chanced by grew pale when he saw the two of us, shoes off, squatting on top of the altar, examining the sculpture with our magnifying glasses. He departed, confused but satisfied, after Rorimer explained in fluent Spanish who we were.

"Genuine!" Rorimer exclaimed when we were again alone laughing uproariously. "Just as I said before!"

In Barcelona James Rorimer introduced me to what seemed like a hundred art dealers, a dozen superb restaurants, the "only decent seats in Sol y Sombre" at the bullring, Antonio Gaudi's Parque Güell and his incomplete Art Nouveau cathedral, and the overlook on the great hill looming over the port city christened *Tibi Dabo* —"To Thee I Will Give"—signifying the words the Devil used to entice Christ with the wealth of the world.

Rorimer proudly escorted me to a "secret" collection from which he had purchased, for three hundred and fifty thousand dollars, a painted cross, an altar frontal and a sacristy chest, all late Romanesque. This collection was owned by two eccentric old brothers named Junyer. As we toured the collection in their mansion one of the brothers gaped at us in silence while the other chattered away in Catalan, not a word of which Rorimer or I could understand. The silent brother would stop from time to time to urinate in his pants, his face taking on a look of sheer rapture.

After this bizarre visit we paid a courtesy call to the director of the Catalan Museum, José Gudiol, an amiable and garrulous art historian who, Rorimer instructed me, should not be told a word about the three objects he had bought from the Junyer collection.

Gudiol and Rorimer talked animatedly for a while about the art market. Out of the blue, Gudiol mentioned the Junyer collection and advised Rorimer to examine it.

"But be on guard," he added, "there are a few forgeries there, particularly Catalan painted objects of the late Romanesque period. Around 1900, Catalonia tried to secede from the rest of Spain. Nationalism was rampant. Every wealthy person in Barcelona had to own an example of Catalan art of the early period, for patriotic reasons. Supply could not keep up with demand. Two gifted forgers, Ozo and Ruiz, who by the way was Pablo Picasso's father, churned out excellent fakes, usually by repainting badly damaged originals."

"What kinds of things, José?" Rorimer managed to ask in a strangled voice.

"Oh, such things as frontals, statues, church chests, and crosses. I have an example of one of these fakes right here in my laboratory," Gudiol said casually, motioning to a guard. "I'll have it brought up."

We were standing in a magnificent gallery at least a hundred feet long. A pair of attendants entered at the far end, carrying a three-foot sculpture of the Virgin Mary enthroned. In a flash of a second, Rorimer and I could see—we turned at once to look at each other aghast—that the saints which happened to decorate the side of the wooden throne were fakes identical in style to the figures obviously painted by Ozo and Ruiz for The Cloisters' altar frontal, cross and chest.

Rorimer immediately cabled the museum with instructions to cancel a forthcoming article on the objects, to halt all press releases, and to send the pieces to the conservation lab for a thorough chemical analysis. Afterward we repaired to a beach on the Costa Brava.

"It was all my fault," Rorimer groaned. "I personally insisted we buy them and saw to it they were exported from Spain. Sperling did that for me. I must telegraph Roland Redmond and inform him of this poisonous news. Two lessons learned: Take your time, and never, *never,* rely on what conservators tell you. Everyone who studied those things in conservation—virtually picked them apart —assured me they were just fine!"

Early next morning James Rorimer informed the museum's president by telephone that the purchase he had made for three hundred and fifty thousand dollars was misspent, and courageously swallowed his error.

And then the two of us, leaving our families to return to the United States, went on to Genoa and the Annunciation relief.

"Jim, what do you really feel about being involved with a work of art that, if we like it, will obviously have to be removed from Italy and taken to America?"

"I would never have anything to do with such an unconscionable act," he said piously.

The next morning, in a garage on the outskirts of Genoa, we met a swarthy man, shaped like a fireplug, who uttered one word in the two hours it took us to examine the Annunciation relief. "Here," he grunted, pointing to the sculpture. Then he turned away from us and for the whole time picked at his teeth as fastidiously as though he were conducting an archaeological excavation under the Vatican.

The relief fairly shone in the subdued light of the garage. It was powerful, beautiful and eminently desirable. As we drove out of the town, Rorimer was euphoric. "The price is staggering. But we have to have it."

"Jim," I interrupted him, "let's drive to Florence and look at the stone panels in the pulpit of San Leonardo itself. Maybe we can find proof that the Annunciation once fitted into the rest of the reliefs."

"Wonderful idea!" And as we made our way toward Florence, Rorimer became his conspiratorial best. "Florence will be terribly crowded. The town will be crawling with American art historians. We must be incognito. There must be some way to book into a hotel under false names. Maybe we can find an out-of-the-way *albergo* and speak French."

We headed first for the peaceful suburb of Arcetri in the hills looking down on Florence. The pulpit had been reerected in the left hall of the chapel. We could see even more clearly than by the photographs that our relief obviously belonged with the other six. But we couldn't tell precisely where it might once have fitted in. I noticed a Latin inscription carved along a border beneath the reliefs, which gave brief descriptions of the scenes. Nowhere was there a reference to the Annunciation. When we left, I bought a set of sepia postcards of the pulpit which must have dated to the turn of the century.

We drove toward Florence to search for a modest inn, along a narrow road which twisted down a precipitous incline and merged into an even smaller lane. Suddenly the station wagon became wedged between the walls of what by now had turned into a pedestrian path. After half an hour of shoving and grinding, aided by the inhabitants of the adjacent houses, the car came free. During that time our cover was blown. One of the individuals who had come out to see for himself what kind of fools would try to drive an automobile—and an American station wagon at that—down the *vicolo* was an art historian from Smith College. We abandoned the idea of a modest *albergo*. By the time we had found the last available room in the city, in a small hotel on the Lungarno Acciaiuoli, most of the American colony in Florence knew of the arrival of the distinguished director of the Metropolitan Museum.

We went our separate ways, Rorimer to an elegant dinner someplace, I to link up with some old friends from graduate school who were living in Florence. My party broke up just after midnight. I sauntered back to the hotel in the cool, refreshing evening. I felt mellow. Pleasant memories of the times I had stayed in the beautiful city flowed through my mind. When I reached the Piazza della Repubblica I sat down at a café, ordered a cognac, and took out the sepia postcards of the pulpit in San Leonardo. Suddenly my eye was drawn to the photograph of the Deposition of Christ, and particularly to the inscription. It was ANGELI PENDENTEM DEPONUNT CUNCTA REGENTEM—roughly, "The angels let down the hanging King of Kings." Strange. Because old Nicodemus, not the angels, was lowering the dead body of Christ. The two angels in the scene had no part in the drama. They were hovering in the firmament far above the cross. And something else captured my attention. The letter I at the end of the word ANGELI was unlike all the other I's, but was more like half the letter U. I had to see that pulpit and its inscriptions again.

At dawn I hiked up to Arcetri and watched the sun come up over Florence, seeing its rays cut golden streaks into the blue-gray dome of the cathedral and illuminate the Renaissance palaces, the chapels and the tower of the Palazzo della Repubblica. San Leonardo was open. With my pair of miniature binoculars I studied the pulpit elevated some ten feet above me and tried to pick out the letter I. It seemed to be shaped differently from the others. It was imperative to get up there and have a closer look. There was a little door to the right of the pulpit which I figured must be its entrance. As I began to pull on it, the custodian of the church shuffled out from behind the altar and looked at me with surprise.

"How can I get into the pulpit?" I implored him. "I have to examine a part of it. I am an American scholar. I must look—it's the most important thing in my life."

It was as though a dozen people a day entered his lonely church and requested a visit to the pulpit. The custodian didn't even shrug as he unlocked the door.

I scurried up the narrow stairs, leaned over and shone

my flashlight on the word ANGELI. I could see that a
piece of plaster partly covered the I. I took out my Swiss
Army knife and began to scrape away.

"Hey, *americano,* what are you trying to do?" the
guardian called out.

"It will only take me an hour," I shouted down. "I'm
going to cut two of these sculptures out of here. Okay?
I'm going to take them with me to America."

A great laugh pealed out. "Go ahead. Who would care?
When you're finished getting them out, sweep up." Another bellow of laughter.

The fantasy crept irrepressibly into my brain—cutting
out the reliefs, loading them into James Rorimer's Chevrolet, and driving away.

"Take them," the custodian muttered between guf-
faws. "Better in America."

My suspicions proved to be correct. The I was actually
the letter U. And, of course, ANGELU meant nothing in
Latin. It had to have been the singular, ANGELUS, and
that could only mean the *Angelus Domini,* the Angel
of the Lord at the Annunciation.

Rorimer was delighted when I told him the news.
"Great work. I wondered what you were up to. You came
in late. I think so, at least. And I think you left at dawn.
I slept very soundly. Fine work!"

"Jim," I said, wanting to capitalize on my success, "we
were so lucky in coming to Florence, but there's something else we should do. Let's telephone Harold Parsons,
make an appointment with the owner of the great ivory
cross, and go see it in Zurich before it's too late."

"Young man. No! You have achieved one triumph
today. That is enough. Parsons is a dangerous man involved in something gravely damaging to the museum.
I cannot discuss it. Anyway, we have to get back quickly
to Paris. You must track the owner of the cross on your
own, not through Parsons. *Never.*"

Before Rorimer and I departed from Florence for
Paris, I dropped into the incomparable Uffizi Gallery for
a last, loving glance at my favorite paintings—by Sandro
Botticelli, Hugo van der Goes and Piero della Francesca.
As I walked into the museum, I realized that the narrow
vestibule where I was walking was the former side aisle

of the very church where my Annunciation relief had originally stood, San Piero in Scheraggio.

As I started the long climb up the steps to the galleries, I was struck by an unexpected feeling of remorse. What right had I to rip away from Italy a work of art which had been created within the very bosom of the land? What would the Annunciation really mean, isolated on a lonely pedestal in The Cloisters, so far removed in distance and time from Florence? What were James Rorimer and I doing? What piracy were we about to commit? Suddenly I was shaken. But not for very long. A process of rationalization set in. Collecting meant taking risks. Collecting meant possession. Italy had six reliefs. A seventh would only cause administrative confusion. The pulpit up there in San Leonardo already had enough sculptures. By the time I reached the top of the stairs I had tucked my ridiculous anxieties into the recesses of my mind, never to surface again.

Within two days of my leaving Florence the sculpture had arrived in Geneva addressed to a convenient name supplied by Harry Sperling. Two weeks after that, it was in the storeroom of The Cloisters.

CHAPTER FIVE

"Faupic"

WHEN WE RETURNED from our glorious trip, it was as though I had walked into the middle of a glacier a thousand miles wide and colder than outer space—James Rorimer. Back in the museum, forced once again into administrative duties, the man was peremptory, almost rude.

By late fall, time began to pass slowly for the first time since I had joined the museum. The art market was slim, no dealer had anything worthy of more than a passing glance. I was slogging through the research for an article on the Annunciation relief. The thrill had vanished from the endeavor. By the end of November I began to feel like an old horse with blinders on, nose stuffed into the feed bag, munching away on already half-digested oats. Finally I finished my article and, in the spring of 1961, saw it in print. How thrilling that was! Now I could devote my full attention to the ivory cross.

I never lost hope that I would track down the owner of the cross and actually see it. But there were times when I began to believe that Ante Topic Mimara Matutin had vanished and his mysterious cross with him. I wrote a half-dozen letters but never heard a word.

It is not easy to explain, and perhaps foolish even to attempt it, but at times I actually felt the living, physical presence of the cross out there. Then, just as quickly, I would become convinced the thing was only an illusion. Some days I wanted to find it, but sort of casually, just as I might want to fiddle around with a jigsaw puzzle, and then set it aside. Other days I had lost any desire to track it down, because finding it might destroy my feeling that the object was sacred, something better kept in my mind rather than held in my hand. But then, just as abruptly, the desire to find the cross and its will-o'-the-wisp owner would overwhelm me. I felt impelled by a hidden power, sucked along by a magnetic force I simply could not comprehend.

More often than not my mind would veer away from the thing. Perhaps I was frightened by the cross. Not because Randall had called it a fake—I had no anxiety about being tricked. I was fearful of the cross because I sensed, deep down, I wasn't equipped to deal with it historically or, even more importantly, as a religious object.

The least interest I had in life was religion. I couldn't remember ever being attracted to it. Any hope of being absorbed by the Christian faith, other than studying writings pertaining to medieval art, had been driven out of me a long time ago at school. There the Christian doctrine was dispensed automatically—all formula, rote, repetition. It had been something to chant in unison during weekly chapel services.

Yet I knew that the cross must possess a deep religious significance. Confusing and conflicting emotions surged through me. I simply could not wipe out of my mind the intriguing words "King of the Confessors." I spent a little time researching the phrase—not just the word "Confessor."

One day, on a curious impulse, I picked up the New Testament and perused the Book of John. It was as though something nudged me along to read certain lines: "He was in the world, and the world was made by him, and the world knew him not. . . . And [John the Baptist] confessed, and denied not, but confessed, I am not the

Christ. . . . And looking upon Jesus as he walked, he
said, Behold the Lamb of God!" I found these lines exceedingly strange. The words seemed linked somehow to
the cross.

It was because of that persistent feeling that I broke
the rules, and placed my career in jeopardy. Without saying a word to Rorimer I took the train to Boston, placed
a call to the Fine Arts Museum from the station, and
asked for Hanns Swarzenski. He was surprised and delighted to hear from me. I had to see him at once, I
told him.

"Come on over," he said brightly. "It will be a pleasure
to talk with you. Sure, I'll keep it quiet. From Jim? Sure.
The time of *day* is a secret to him."

When I settled down in the ragged chair in his small
office, I once again pledged him to secrecy. He looked
at me, amused, from beneath his lion's-mane eyebrows.
I asked him directly whether he had ever met Topic
Mimara, seen his collection and the ivory cross, and
whether he was trying to purchase the object.

Hanns Swarzenski threw his shaggy head back and
rumbled with laughter. "Topic! Oh yes. The collection?
Yes, that too. The great unique cross. Ah! Now, *there* is
a story. It started back in the summer of 1957, on my
annual trip to Europe."

He told me the story at length, and I made rapid
notes while he talked so that I would remember it. As he
spoke I grew even more excited.

"With the highest expectations," Swarzenski began,
"I had gone on my usual summer trip to Europe in May
of 1957 to look for objects. But after a few weeks in
Austria, Germany and England I saw the market was
very dry. So I went with my wife to Italy for a week's
vacation and then planned to go to Paris, where I hoped
the search would be more fruitful. After that I had to go
back to Boston.

"It was the stuff spy thrillers are made of. While still
in Rome, I got a frantic phone call from my secretary in
Boston waking me in the dead of the night to say that a
certain Harold Woodbury Parsons urgently wanted to
meet me to discuss the sale of—I shall never forget the
words—'the greatest English early Romanesque monumental carved ivory crucifix existing on earth.'

"Before I dozed off I wondered why the hell my office had wakened *me* and not Parsons. Parsons was in Rome, perhaps just down the street. I had never met the man, but I knew of him. Parsons' reputation was fairly rancid around the museum. But it didn't matter. I had long ago made a personal policy never to make the mistake of failing to go after a work of art simply because someone of questionable character was involved with it. And, besides, my curiosity was piqued by the 'greatest English early Romanesque monumental carved ivory crucifix existing on earth.' That was of course nonsensical, but still . . .

"The next evening Parsons came for me and my wife, Brigitte, in a black Mercedes sedan driven by a driver garbed in dove-gray livery. He swept us off to one of the finest and most expensive restaurants in Rome, the Tre Scalini. I was delighted, for if there's anything I cherish more than art, it is eating well.

"I had expected to get detailed information about his fantastic ivory cross, its price, the provenance, some insights about its owner. But Parsons refused to reveal anything. He sat there looking very pleased with himself and fluttered his hands over the candle like a pair of agitated moths. But he laughingly begged off all business talk. He kept saying everything was too superlative for serious discussion. The evening was too enchanting; the repast too exquisite; Brigitte, far too beautiful. I didn't reveal it, but I was furious that this elderly art dealer was stringing me along about something that appeared to sound better than it actually was. Why else would Parsons carefully avoid any discussion about the cross? All the man would say was that he would arrange a meeting with the owner of the cross, a certain Ante Topic Mimara, whom he described as 'the most peculiar but most compelling art collector I have ever run into.'

"I had an amusing time, nevertheless, with Parsons. I had never run into anything like *him* in my life. He seemed to be entirely composed of perfectly manicured baby fat. His skin was pink and delicate, and seemed to glow from within. Parsons wore a Savile Row double-breasted seersucker suit with a trim vest. *That* I'd never seen before! The man's *accent!* I'd never heard of anything like that either, an efferverscent combination of Boston and Oxford, cadenced in a never-ending chain of skillful pleasantries. Parsons doted upon Brigette. My wife was a well-known film actress in Germany in the early 1930s. Most surprisingly to me, Parsons showed a detailed knowledge about German films.

" 'My dear Hanns,' Parsons said to me when we parted, 'I believe what you will come across in the bank vault will truly amaze you.'

"Two days later at my hotel in Paris, I received a cable. It said something like 'Would be pleased to meet in Zurich. Three days from today. Ten o'clock. At the Union Banque de Suisse. You will recognize me by a white carnation.' I vividly remember the cable was signed 'Faupic.'

"Faupic! Can you imagine such a typographical error! *Faux pic*—you see, 'fake picture.' I wondered if that was to be an omen.

"I went alone to the entrance to the bank on the Bahnhofstrasse and encountered what I can only describe as an outrageous and comic apparition. Standing out incongruously amongst a crowd of dark-suited Swiss bankers and men of affairs was a short, heavyset man dressed in a light-beige suit—it was almost yellowish—and wearing an enormous carnation in his lapel. The man had markedly sloping shoulders. His arms seemed to curve around his body as if they were stitch lines on a punch ball. This strange individual introduced himself formally as Topic Mimara Matutin, art collector and restorer. Then he half embraced me. I was so surprised. The man seemed utterly servile.

"Topic conducted me to a basement of the bank and motioned me to sit at a table set in front of the massive highly polished steel door of a walk-in vault. Assisted by two silent bank attendants, Topic carried five works of art out of the chamber and placed them on the table before me. He edged a leather box about a foot high toward me. It was almost as if he were stalking me with it. Then, with a theatrical flourish, he opened the twin doors of the box.

" 'I found this treasure,' Topic said almost in a chant. I shall never forget his words! 'This is unique. It is *the* most valuable early Christian chalice of all! *I* found it years ago in 1922, near Tivoli. I was painting the ancient ruins of the Villa of Hadrian. It was the height of noon.

The sun was baking down, sending rivers of light through the cypress grove, and I could hear the voices of two peasants singing as they dug away in the hot, cracked soil. Then, my friend, something happened. I was at once alerted. I have special senses. The farmers' voices changed. Oh, they continued their song, but, instead of singing naturally, suddenly they were singing in a way that indicated to me, mysteriously, that they must have found something miraculous in the earth and did not want to alert me to it. I left my easel and walked over, asking them what they had discovered. And the pair were so astonished—they were simple men—that one of them handed me a glass cup caked with dried-out clay. I recognized it instantly to be an ancient chalice. I cleaned the interior surface with a finger and found *this*.'

"With this, Topic Mimara plucked the green goblet out from its container and held it up to my face so that I could look inside. There I saw a representation of Christ portrayed as Good Shepherd. The image was etched in gold leaf captured within two layers of glass. 'Splendid, isn't it?' Topic commented.

"I was struck dumb. I must have grunted aloud. To myself I said, 'Fake, Faupic.'

"In rapid succession Topic moved four more objects alongside the chalice. He would point to each one and boom out the words 'Unique in the world!'

"The first object was a foot-high wooden replica of the famous bronze statue in the right-side aisle of St. Peter's in Rome, representing Peter as pope and teacher. It was wretched, obviously modern, poorly carved, and atrociously painted in dirty white and chocolate brown. It was repellant! But Topic Mimara actually came right out and told me that the piece was *the* original model of the magificent statue of the early thirteenth century.

"After that came two painted wooden heads of warrior saints. Thick, dull visages. Both of them looked highly suspicious to me. These were followed by a roundel in stained glas representing Saint Peter—strangely enough, wearing a beard. Topic proudly pointed out that this stained glass dated to the early twelfth century, came from Chartres Cathedral and was the only example in the world showing Saint Peter with a beard. It too was 'unique.'

"And then suddenly before me I saw a great cross, gleaming in ivory as if it were made of gold. A cross in ivory with the snubbed-off branches of the Tree of Life carved on the upright and crossbar of the front. It was a highly memorable shape. The ends were square blocks, and the center, the crossing, was a perfect roundel bursting with tiny, beautifully carved figures. The back was almost totally composed of little half or full-length figures in windows or niches. Another roundel dominated the back, as did some exceptionally powerful Evangelist symbols.

"I remained glued to that glorious object for more than two hours. At my very first glance I was thrilled. I must have jumped out of my chair a half-dozen times or more to walk around the table, to examine the cross from yet another angle. From time to time I would reach out so I could stroke a part of the yellow, glistening ivory. But I do remember I did so tentatively, almost as if I half expected to receive an electric shock. It was truly the most amazing work of art I have encountered.

"I was initially attracted by a large, beautifully written inscription, or series of them actually, which ran from top to bottom just along the edges of the sprouting buds of the Tree of Life which formed the substance of this ivory cross. The inscription started off: TERRA TREMIT MORS VICTA . . . , 'Earth trembles, death vanquished . . .,' but I didn't write any more down and I cannot remember now what the rest of it said. I do have the keen feeling that *this* inscription, particularly, will offer a clue to the history of the object. It was that I was in a hurry and also too excited for research. Anyway, the phrases seemed to be a reference to the earthquake at the precise moment of Christ's death on the cross *and* a reference to Christ's having vanquished the power of death over human beings by *His* death. Much as I wanted to write down the large inscriptions on the front—and I seem to recall there were also other large ones on the upright sides— I just didn't have the time. Later on, I regretted my action profoundly.

"I next directed my attention to the central roundel on the front of the cross. Remember, the cross is made of square ends and a marvelous round carved medallion of ivory in the middle. The medallion is spectacular. It bursts with figures and is supported on the outside by four flying angels. It seemed to be a reference to the Wheel of Life. The scene depicted a sinuous snake hanging on the forked stick. This is obviously the Brazen Serpent raised up in the desert by Moses before a crowd of fearful Israelites.

"The story is in the Book of Numbers. And it tells of a dreaded serpent, sent by God, which struck down the Israelites with its venom. But soon the victims were healed, after Moses made a brass reptile and stuck it up on a pole. The sight of the thing restored the stricken Israelites to life. Life! You see, the sign of Christ on the cross would restore life to all men. And, of course, the Brazen Serpent is the symbol of the Crucifixion taken from the Old Testament. Right away I recognized the cross to be a typology, using quotations or scenes, or both, from the Old Testament as specific predictions and prefigurations of the teachings and actions of Christ.

"The back was more beautiful even than the front. Up and down the entire length of the upright were windows with a bust-length figure in each one. I thought the figures *must* be prophets. Each was identified by name. The top four were, I recall, David, Solomon, Obadiah, Hosea. Each held a scroll with a quotation from his book. David's saying from the Psalms was: 'They pierced my hands and my feet . . .' It was the classic typology, or prefiguration, for the Crucifixion. I cannot remember anything else. It was marvelous, I thought. I grew more and more enthralled as I investigated the near-secret writings. I wished I could stay for days and unravel every message. But that was, of course, impossible.

"I went back to the front and tried to identify the scenes carved there. On the right square block was the Descent from the Cross, with Mary and John lamenting, surrounded by the Roman centurion and a crowd of the faithful. Below was the shrouded corpse of Christ stretched out upon a great stone. At His feet, a figure was anointing Him. Other figures, represented only by tiny faces seeming to float on the surface of the ivory, were weeping bitterly.

"The block on the left side was the most poetic representation of the Holy Women at the Tomb I had ever seen. I was amazed at the depth of emotion imparted to the diminutive women. And I could see Christ, on the left, carrying the cross of Resurrection, jumping up and out of the tomb, up toward a kind of ledge which looked like the placard over the head of Christ, but it was a curious shape.

"And on the ledge there were some figures. I tried to identify them. But I could not."

For the first time in his hypnotizing talk, I dared to interrupt Hanns Swarzenski. "Did you see an inscription on that ledge or placard saying 'Jesus of Nazareth, King of the Confessors'? Or did Topic Mimara say anything about it?"

"No. Very curious. He didn't. That's a strange inscription."

"Would you think the cross could be a forgery?"

"Bah. Ridiculous!"

"Would a forger have written 'Confessors'?"

"Bah. Nonsense." He paused for only a moment. "The top block of the cross was the Ascension of Christ, with the body of the Savior rocketing into heaven so quickly that half His body is impelled into a bank of clouds. That indicates, at least to me, the undoubted presence of an English artist. I believe that this curious motif was invented by an English artist of the eleventh century and was used and reused for hundreds of years afterward. You seldom find it in works of art produced elsewhere.

"There was so much to learn about the cross. A world. Virtually the significance of the Old and New Testaments. I couldn't do more. It is unlike any cross in all the thousands I have ever seen.

"After those hours of looking I simply fell back into my chair drained, thrilled to the depths of my soul. The cross is unbelievable! It has to be one of the most ambitious and most beautiful crosses to have survived the entire Middle Ages!

"Where was it made? England. It has to have been. Or, on the off chance, Germany—Westphalia under strong English influence. The date? Probably the first half of the twelfth century and probably closer to 1120 than 1150. All the stylistic facts will come in time. All the information on where it was made and even possibly by whom will surely come to light! I asked myself if it would be possible for Boston to acquire it. Topic Mimara had been sitting quietly, observing me from across the table. He

spoke up, seeing that I had paused in my examination.
"He said, 'What do you think, Dr. Swarzenski?'

"I told him I was much intrigued. I asked, 'Is the
cross for sale?' He was strange in what he told me. 'It is.
Yes, of course. Absolutely. The cross, the entire collection,
must go to Boston—only to Boston. Your museum would
be the best place for my treasures. Only you, Doctor,
can truly comprehend the greatness of these objects.'

"I was taken aback by the rush of words. I asked if he
had any information about it, any idea what it was. The
man said very firmly, 'The cross is English. I am convinced that it was made around the year 960, at Winchester—*Winchester!* Don't you agree?'

"Well, I was so astonished at that patently ridiculous
statement on the date, I simply gaped at Topic Mimara.

"*'Tenth* century, *tenth* century,' Topic Mimara kept
saying. 'There is little information about the cross. My
collaborator, the art historian Frau Doktor Wiltrud Mersmann, has prepared a study for a scholarly journal. I can
give you a copy of it. But only for you. Never show it to
anyone, no one. Promise?'

"I had never heard of any Mersmann, but I nodded
eagerly. Were there photographs of the cross? Large
photos? No, there weren't. But the man told me I'd find
some photostats among the pages of the unpublished
manuscript. I pored through the unbound sheets. Not
much. The pictures would hardly suffice for a serious
examination of the cross. But Topic told me that was all
he would permit me. Perhaps later he would give a full
set."

Once more I interrupted Swarzenski. "Do you still have
this article?"

"No. Sorry. I believe I lost it."

"Damn!" I said.

"Yes," Swarzenski sighed. "Well, I pointed out to him
that the captions for the illustration all ascribed the cross
to England in the mid-eleventh century, not the tenth.
And Topic Mimara grew disturbed, saying, 'Ah, but she
is wrong, don't you agree? I have forbidden her to publish
the theory. I seek the truth. The truth!' His voice rose on
the word 'truth.' He told me that Boston should purchase
his entire collection of 'unique works' of art. And I asked
the price for the cross. He said, 'It is too early to discuss

such a thing as price. I want you to think about buying all six pieces.'

"Then I asked him where he obtained the cross. His reaction was unusual. He hunched his body down into his chair and shot me a look that was both wary and forbidding.

"He said, 'I am a man of honor, Dr. Swarzenski. I am pledged never to tell a soul where I found the cross. I will never reveal the secret. I will resist till the end. If I were standing on the edge of the highest mountain and someone were to say, "Tell or be pushed," I would gladly fall to my death. But where it comes from doesn't matter. I want to sell the cross and its companion pieces to you, to Boston. It is the collection or nothing. Surely we can make an arrangement.'

"I had to know the price, I told him rather impatiently. I tried to tell him I had directors and trustees to convince. How in God's name could I do that without a firm price?

"He said, 'Don't be difficult. Do not ask for such things. Make an arrangement now, in principle. Say you will purchase the group for the Boston Museum. Then we will work out the details.'

"It was impossible, and I told him so. I had tried to reason with him, but he would have none of it.

"'Take the manuscript,' he told me. 'Think it over. I can be accommodating. I shall talk to you tomorrow morning.'

"I told him I had to leave early for a plane. I left as quickly as I could. I was infuriated by the man's irrational behavior.

"At seven the next morning, Topic Mimara telephoned to inform me he was downstairs waiting at the hotel entrance. And when my wife and I left the hotel to walk the two blocks to the airport bus, Topic Mimara was out front, like some kind of lackey. Topic insisted he accompany us to the railroad station. He even tipped the hotel porter carrying the luggage.

"'Make an arrangement in principle for Boston,' the man kept pleading. 'Only *you* can do it.'

"I told him I could *not*. What he asked was crazy. Without a price, without photos, I could do nothing. I said he should name his price. But only for the cross. What was the price?

"Topic said only, 'We will talk about that later, Dr. Swarzenski.' Then he lowered his voice and whispered into my ear, 'Make a deal. Now! I will guarantee that you will have a share—you understand, you know, huh? A personal share, a good share.'

" 'Goodbye, Herr Topic.' I spat the words in contempt as I boarded the bus. I never saw him again. A bribe. Imagine! And anyway, later on I heard that he was asking something between seven hundred fifty thousand and a million. I talked to my director. We agreed we didn't have the money. But the cross is great!"

It was a relief to know Boston wasn't pursuing the cross. I fully trusted Hanns. The cross was obviously a world masterpiece and authentic. He had told me a great deal, but he had no information on where the man was to be found or how I could reach him now. Would I ever track him down?

Not long after my meeting with Swarzenski, that information fell into my hands. Rorimer had asked me to make a list of promising works of art in Europe for his forthcoming trip during June and July. This time I would not accompany him but would go later, on my own for the first time, to search throughout England, Switzerland, Italy, France and Spain for likely acquisitions and to visit a landmark exhibition on Romanesque art to be held in Barcelona in October.

I instructed the secretary of the Medieval Department, Marjorie Baucom, to send out, once again, a letter to Topic Mimara at every known address, saying that Rorimer wanted to see his cross and would be in Zurich at the end of June. She typed the letters up and handed them over to me to sign. On top of the pile was a letter in German addressed to the chief of Austrian police in Vienna, requesting that the letter be forwarded as urgently as possible to Ante Topic Mimara or Topic Matutin.

"Why this?" I asked.

"Something occurred to me," she replied. "I remembered that Topic Mimara is supposed to be an Austrian citizen. I think that's what you told me at one point."

"Right."

"So I called the embassy in Washington and found out that those tidy Austrians keep tabs on all their citizens, no matter where they may be living, even in other countries. Perhaps it will work."

Weeks went by, and not a word from anywhere. Rorimer flew off to Europe. Cool, buoyant June turned into the moist, heavy heat of July. One morning, sapped by the oppressive weather, I dragged myself to the office, hours late. Marj Baucom's normally quiet manner had vanished.

"Here it is," she said, excitedly waving a letter. "For goodness' sake, open it quickly. *Look!* It's from Topic from Tangier."

The letter was in German, and I translated it quickly.

DEAR MR. HOVING,
I thank you for your letter of May 18, which I have received a few days ago from the Police Direction in Vienna. I regret very much that I was not able to meet Mr. Rorimer to render him the service of showing the cross in Zurich, but I was sick and convalescent in a hospital in Munich, so that I was for the first time here in Tangier in months. In Tangier I found your other letter. I shall be here till the end of September. In case you have the wish, you can reach me in Tangier. Only if you do wish to write me, please send your letter special delivery, for there is no guarantee otherwise that your letter will arrive. And please know that in the future it is not necessary to communicate through the Austrian police. I wish you all the best and the highest, fullest attention to your wishes.

A. TOPIC MIMARA

"Oh, my God!" I shouted, "I'm off the starting blocks. Finally off!"

I dashed to the telephone and called Rorimer's office to find out where he was in Europe. It was just possible I could still engineer a meeting between him and A. Topic Mimara. But, to my chagrin, I learned that Rorimer had already returned from Europe and was in Ohio on his farm. That was bad. If only he had been overseas he might have been able to probe into the situation. Then I could have clinched the deal.

Where before there had been silence, suddenly there

seemed to be a cacophony. I dashed off a letter of thanks to Topic. Rorimer received a letter from Harold Parsons dated July 24 and written on stationery of the Hotel Cipriani in Venice. Rorimer's office sent a copy of it to me.

It was incredible. According to Parsons, Topic had just been in Rome to consult with him about "placing his great Winchester ivory." Topic, Parsons wrote, was in "absolutely no hurry to sell the cross because he is rich and knows quite well it could only be bought by one of three or four museums in the world. He is utterly convinced he will easily be able to sell the masterpiece at the staggering price he is asking for it."

Parsons emphasized that the fee he would receive from Topic had no bearing on the price the owner was asking, "a price which he will surely ultimately obtain." Topic, he claimed, "had paid an enormous sum for the object years before" and had made "great personal sacrifices to secure it on the installment plan." In those days Topic was not as wealthy as he had become since. According to Parsons, Topic was studying the piece in collaboration with Dr. Wiltrud Mersmann, whom Parsons described as "a scholar of some renown in the field of Medieval Art, and the woman Topic has lately married."

Parsons enclosed a list of all the people who had been alerted to the cross over the years. Some of the names I knew—Milliken, Randall, Swarzenski. But Parsons mentioned other people as well. When I saw their names I got the chills: Pope-Hennessy of the Victoria and Albert Museum, London; Sherman Lee, director of Cleveland; William Wixom, the curator of Medieval Art at Cleveland; and Ruppert Bruce-Mitford, the curator of the British and Medieval Antiquities of the British Museum.

Bruce-Mitford, whom I didn't know and would have to check out thoroughly, had gone to Zurich in recent weeks, according to Parsons, and had stayed for five full days, fully equipped with reference books and photographs. He had "spent *all* of those days in the vaults . . . studying the cross." Parsons lamented the fact that "our American Museum men, as is their wont, had only a brief time to spend: we have so little time in America, alas!" Except for Wixom from Cleveland, who had stayed a full day. I knew Bill Wixom to be a tenacious collector. He frightened me.

"All the Americans had been enthusiastic," Parsons wrote. "All were staggered, and still are, by Mr. Topic Mimara's valuation. The price was half a million dollars for Cleveland, last year, when he had undergone a serious spinal operation and thought his days were numbered."

I dropped the letter on my desk and stared sourly for a few minutes out the window into the courtyard. Five hundred thousand dollars! It was a terrifying price. But at least Topic had come partly to his senses. At least he had backed off from the price of one or even two million dollars he had casually quoted years before to Dick Randall.

As I digested the rest of Parsons' letter, further anxieties swept over me. "Now Topic has recovered from his illness and the price to England is 200,000 pounds." I calculated the pound at $2.82. That would make Topic's price much more than half a million. It would be approximately $564,000. Would his price ever stop jumping around?

Parsons begged Rorimer to see the ivory and buy it.

Personally, I hope to see the cross permanently housed in Cleveland or The Cloisters. Have the courage to charge for it, as you have for other battles you have won. Such things will never come again, for it is one of the greatest masterpieces of art extant. The inscription alone is one of the greatest interest and significance.

What the hell did *that* mean? Was he referring to the inscription about the King of the Confessors? How I longed to see the cross! I cursed Randall violently for not having obtained, just for the record, a set of photographs. That should have been simple enough.

Parsons urged Rorimer to make a date to meet Topic Mimara in Zurich "as *quickly* as possible." He wrote that Topic did not wish to play, through him, "one American Museum against another; and the Cleveland Museum of Art is *profoundly* interested but may have allocated their 1961 funds; but hope with all earnestness that it can be acquired in 1962."

Oh, my God!

Parsons finished his long and breathless letter by saying that it was

> a case of first come first served. I frankly believe he will never cede the cross for less than half a million. He argues that it relates to the present values for paintings. The argument is, I think, unanswerable. The cross, in medieval art, is a world-important masterpiece, which you will realize when you have a chance to study it—not too hastily I hope.

The situation was not hopeless, although it was difficult. The price of the cross, if it did remain at $564,000, would be the highest ever quoted in history for a work of decorative art. A ghastly problem, yet not insurmountable. The irony was that the money was actually in hand. I had learned months ago from the treasurer of the museum that the reserve funds set aside for acquisitions at The Cloisters had built up to the extraordinary sum of $860,000. And even that surplus had been increased on the first of July, the beginning of the new fiscal year, with fresh revenues amounting to $520,000. That meant a grand total of $1,423,000. Commitments had been made for only a fraction of that amount. The money was there, but how to squeeze it out?

Topic Mimara would be a problem, too, I figured, a very difficult opponent. But he could be dealt with. The fact that he had dramatically lowered his price in five years told me I might be able to bargain more with him. I wondered how old he was. I was pleased to learn from Parsons' letter that the man had been deeply disturbed by his operation. Fear of dying plus his recent marriage were promising factors for a deal in our favor. But what if the man died before I could reach him?

Parsons, I thought, would be easy to handle. The only thing he wanted was to see the cross sold. Just where clearly didn't matter. I figured I could whipsaw Parsons by offering him a side commission for putting my rivals off the track. There was a discretionary fund at The Cloisters for such undertakings.

I wondered which museum, or museums, would offer the stiffest competition. Every one of them was a likely enemy, except for Boston. Cleveland would be the toughest. The museum was wealthy, earning through an endowment the incredible sum of two and a half million dollars annually. Cleveland's director, Sherman Lee, was an astute and courageous collector, and so was his curator of Medieval Art, Bill Wixom.

There was no other museum in America I feared. But if the cross really had come from Winchester or some other great center in medieval England, Great Britain would surely pursue it vigorously. Only a couple of dozen English medieval ivory carvings had survived through time. None of the survivors seemed better than the cross, at least according to Hanns Swarzenski. I had no idea what to expect from the Victoria and Albert Museum, since I didn't know who the director was. But I was fully familiar with the brilliance of John Pope-Hennessy. He would clearly have recognized the importance of the cross to the nation, provided it really was authentic.

Pope-Hennessy, one of the most energetic individuals in the museum community, would certainly be rounding up support from his extensive acquaintances in the British government. And with him at the Victoria and Albert Museum was another dangerous collector, John Beckwith. He would fight hard for such a work of art as the ivory cross. The British Museum? I was less concerned about that institution, not knowing Bruce-Mitford. Yet, a year before I had joined the Metropolitan, the British Museum had spent an enormous sum of money for an eleventh-century English bronze sculpture. I also was well acquainted with the purchase power of the National Arts Collection Fund. Six months before, an expensive Rubens had been bought for Great Britain partly from the fund and partly from a donation by an industrialist who had been knighted for his generosity. England could be very, very dangerous.

When I tallied up the problems and listed my opponents, I realized at last that my most serious opponent was likely to be James Rorimer. For reasons still unknown to me, he stood steadfast against the cross. But why? I had no clear idea, but I suspected he was opposed to it simply because I was in favor. He was against it just because I had discovered—or rediscovered—the object. Whatever the case, I knew that the only way to force

Rorimer to a decision would be to play the competition off against him, competition either real or imagined. If a competitor did not exist, I would have to invent one.

I began eagerly. I would obtain photos from Topic to initiate the research and would arrange to see the cross on my forthcoming trip. Because of the letter, I expected Rorimer to allow me to contact Parsons. I also planned to ask Kurt Weitzmann, my old mentor at Princeton, what he knew about the object. The plan seemed simple enough.

But it didn't turn out that way. Rorimer ordered me once again to "stay clear of Parsons. I don't care if he did write me about the damned cross. Stay *away* from him, hear?"

I dispatched an immediate letter to Topic Mimara:

With your permission I should like to ask you for some information about the object—such things as its size, whether or not there is any figurative decoration on it, or if it is inscribed in any way. Naturally I would greatly appreciate any photographic documents on the Cross, if you consider this a possibility. I would keep any information you might impart in utmost confidence.

Topic sent me a discouraging answer: "The ivory cross has a very rich figurative presentation and many, many inscriptions. I hope that it will soon be published, but until then I shall give out *no photos.*"

And Kurt Weitzmann responded ominously to the queries I had sent him. He was deeply concerned that *his* mentor, Adolph Goldschmidt, had never seen the crucifix. "I can only speculate," he wrote, "that if the crucifixus was already in Switzerland shortly before or during the war, the dealer or owner would have tried to get Goldschmidt's opinion, so that the absence of any notes in his papers gives me, indeed, some reason to worry."

CHAPTER SIX

The Cross

I THINK I WAS discouraged. I should have been. But in late September I went off to Europe to close in on the illusory Topic Mimara and his mystery cross. I was to stay abroad for nearly a month and a half. During that time I kept a detailed journal, chronicling my joys, my fears, my premonitions of disasters to come.

Tuesday, September 12, 1961

All is in order and has been for weeks. My tickets are booked, the hotels chosen. I have assembled the names of everything and everybody I want to visit—dealers, collectors, museums, churches and a list of the finest affordable restaurants in each city. As Jim Rorimer told me, "Fine art and fine cuisine must go together."

What will the intriguing Topic Mimara really turn out to be like? And his mysterious cross and collections? My conviction that the object will be superb has been shattered by some disturbing dreams recently. Only last night I imagined the thing set up on a high altar. Before that altar I stood, elevated a little higher than two dark-

*suited colleagues on each side of me. One was Hanns
Swarzenski of Boston; the other, William Wixom of
Cleveland. They nodded politely and respectfully as I
raised my arms to reach for the prize. I had won! Then,
as I was about to take the splendid cross in my arms, I
heard them laugh. The object crumbled away, and turned
into sawdust.*

In my waking moments too, the cross seemed to be
crumbling away. Confident that I could persuade Topic,
I had sent a second letter containing a threat that I might
not bother to examine the cross without first seeing photographs. His reply was icy: "Unfortunately I cannot send
a photo. I have refused to do so up to now although I
have been asked many times."

My optimism was briefly restored when, after weeks
of cajoling, Rorimer finally approved my writing directly
to Harold Parsons. Parsons had written an extremely arrogant letter to Rorimer, the tone of which can be suggested by just one of his sentences: "Topic will make a
definite date to meet Mr. Hoving, although I think it
unimportant for anyone save yourself to see that remarkable object." Rorimer handed me the letter, snorted
contemptuously, and said, "He's all yours."

In my answer to Harold Woodbury Parsons, refined
from seven drafts, I laid down the gauntlet.

Mr. Rorimer has asked me to let you know he has
given me the responsibility of looking into all the facets
of the Winchester ivory and making full arrangements
about it for him and The Cloisters. As you may know,
I have communicated several times with Mr. Topic
Mimara and expect to meet him in October in Zurich.

There is, however, one chronic problem about this
object which I trust you will overcome. This is the
reticence of Topic to send us a photograph of the piece.
I understand that Topic is unwilling to part with photos
until Mersmann has published it. We appreciate this point
of view. Yet at the same time it must be said that the
Metropolitan Museum is hardly likely to leak out any
information on the cross or to show the photographs
indiscriminately. The object and our interest in it is a
matter of obvious strictest confidence. You can assure
Mr. Topic Mimara that the pictures will not leave the
hands of Mr. Rorimer or myself.

I had no deep confidence that Parsons could influence his intransigent client, but I wanted to set the tone for any negotiations we might have. Parsons' response reached me just before I left for Spain on the first leg of my European journey.

I wrote to Mr. Topic Mimara advising him to send you photographs of the Winchester cross for purposes of study. . . . But he replied that he could not accede to my request because it would constitute an "offesa" to the other aspirants for the ownership of the cross, for he has consistently declined to give out photographs. . . .

I know you will be greatly impressed by the cross, as all of those who have seen it have been; but Mr. Topic Mimara's reluctance to give out photographs may be due to the fact that none of the photographs seem to transmit its truly monumental quality. Swarzenski has stated the problem on p. 12 of his "Monuments of Romanesque Art": "The monumental quality of the art of this period is in no sense determined by size. . . . The gilded statuettes on a book-cover from Trèves are the ancestors of the more than life-size statues of Reims Cathedral." This is true of the Winchester cross to the Nth degree.

Do not be disturbed by the number of obviously false objects you will see in Mr. Topic Mimara's small collection of "Medieval" objects. He is, _au fond,_ a rather ignorant student of _objets d'art;_ merely a misguided and untutored, though highly interested and enthusiastic, amateur collector. He really believes that all he has collected is of importance. But having travelled much and seen a great deal, he has actually made a number of "finds," both in the Medieval field and in the field of paintings, of prime importance. I have found him honest and truthful, and now know a good deal about his past life, both from him and from certain others who have known him for many years, such as Fritz Volbach, a good and old friend of mine. You will have an interesting, if rather strange, visit in Zurich.

My first stop on the way to Zurich was Madrid. The bright sun and dappling clouds bathed the city in the pastel tones of Goya's tapestry cartoons. At night I strolled the city for hours. The full moon, veiled by occasional clouds, produced reflections like pewter.

Carmen Gómez-Moreno, a colleague in the Medieval

Department of the Metropolitan, became my guide to Madrid. Her father, Don Manuel, was the most renowned art historian of Spain. Several hundred books and articles had flowed from his pen over the decades. At ninety-two, this crinkled parchment of a human being had, he told me, just embarked upon a twenty-four-volume history of Spanish art!

Don Manuel granted me special permission to enter the sacred halls of the Academia to examine in my two hands a solid silver plate called the Missorium made for and depicting the Emperor Theodosius during his reign in the late fourth century A.D. The massive plate, nearly a yard wide and weighing ten pounds, is one of the most spectacular and beautiful remnants of early Christianity. The custodian of the Academia, a creature even older than Don Manuel, conducted me to a darkened office of the elite institution. He sat me down at a table illuminated by one yellow bulb and disappeared to retrieve the Emperor's great ceremonial dish. When he brought it before me, it was nestled on a red velvet pillow. "Go pick it up," he said, gesturing vigorously. I did. And the thick, heavy plate snapped in two! My God! It had parted down a centuries-old break spanning the object. The custodian cackled with laughter as I tried to catch my breath. When my pulse had slowed to a sedate one hundred and twenty, the custodian gleefully explained that the jest was enacted "only for those whom Don Manuel particularly respects."

Next day I ran into a bizarre proposition from a certain dealer. He resembled an elegant grandee until he opened his mouth and his harsh, grating voice filled the air. "You ought to buy it. The price is good—only two million pesetas. That's thirty-three thousand, five hundred American dollars. Cheap for a twelfth-century painted altar cross. But the owner is an eccentric. He insists that all proper art authorities be informed and the export papers prepared." His aristocratic mouth seemed to twist into an expression of faint disgust. But I wanted the piece. It was imposing—almost six feet high and two and a half feet wide—and its condition was excellent.

"I assume you think the price is just," he rasped.

"I agree," I told him. "I'll buy it—or at least recommend the cross to my director. What I want, I get!"

"Excellent! Excellent!" he responded. "Now, the sum consists of twenty percent for me, seventy-five for the owner, and the customary five percent for you, the buyer."

"I don't want a percentage," I informed him. "I would never do that."

He winced, sat still for a moment or so, cradling his chin in his hand. Then he smiled wanly and said, "Ten percent?"

"I want nothing. It would be illegal," I protested.

There was a long silence, and then the art dealer began to whine. "Fifteen! My God, fifteen is the top. You understand, I will have to cut the amount of my share. Please don't be so harsh."

"Look, how can I tell you? I don't want a cent."

At this lugubrious news, the man moaned, sank into his chair, and virtually wailed, "You are so hard. Never, *never*, have I encountered such a bargainer. Americans are not normally like you. I surrender. It will kill me. Twenty percent! I cannot go higher."

He never got the point, and I never got the piece. I consoled myself with the thought that the painted cross would probably never have received an authorized export permit from Spain anyway.

My visit to Barcelona provided revelations of a different kind. There I immersed myself, day after day, in the works being shown at an exhibition of Romanesque art spanning two centuries and so gigantic that it would be unlikely ever to be assembled again.

It seemed as if a thousand pieces had been jammed into the makeshift galleries in the dilapidated building where the exhibition was held. I trudged through the halls, my mind and eyes reeling, making detailed notes. With typical Spanish efficiency, the exhibition catalogue would not be published until a year after the show had been bundled up and the objects sent home. Unconscionable!

I established a routine. I would arrive at the hall precisely at ten each morning and stay until two o'clock. By that time my eyes were stinging from the effort of scrutinizing several hundred works of art, from heroic stones twenty feet high to lacelike miniatures captured in creamy-white pools of parchment bordering illuminated manuscripts.

I recuperated each day at lunch at one of my favorite

restaurants. Then I slept, falling into a cottony-soft black-out until late afternoon, when I would venture forth from my hotel and stroll to Las Ramblas, the terraced boulevard stretching from the heart of the city down to the docks.

During one of those strolls the most vivid impression of Romanesque art came to my mind. I envisioned a great tree—squat, fibrous, low to the ground—growing out of a hollow, a tree with a tangle of branches extended from its enormous trunk. I saw I could climb into the tree. It would be easy—there were hundreds of branches covered with moss and lichens, crisscrossing the sky like lines in an engraving. At first I lost sight of the sunlight; then a gentle breeze moved the leaves, and glimmers of light and blue sky flashed into my eyes. It was a tree which I soon realized could not be climbed to the top. The upper limbs were too young, too thin. The tree was a curious combination of force and fragility, age and youth, bursting with life.

The next morning I left for Zurich, Topic Mimara and his ivory cross.

At midday I walked into the faded-brown lobby of my Zurich hotel, the Savoy, alive with a sense of adventure. I had invited Carmen Gómez-Moreno to join me when I examined the ivory cross, and she was due to arrive in an hour.

Within minutes, I was speaking on the telephone with Topic Mimara himself. I was incredibly nervous. My hand, sweating, gripped the instrument when he came on the line.

"Mr. Topic Mimara? Thomas Hoving here. I am at the Savoy," I started off in measured, polite tones.

"Hoving. Good. Zurich. Tomorrow. Downstairs. Morning. Bank." The man threw out the words in English like a handful of stones. My small room seemed to resound with his resonant voice.

"Sir, do you mind," I said haltingly, carefully emphasizing "Sir," "if I bring with me a colleague from the museum? Her name is Gómez-Moreno."

"A *what?*" Topic Mimara half shouted.

"I hope you don't mind if I am accompanied by an

associate to examine your cross tomorrow," I repeated, raising my voice.

"Yes."

"Do you understand?" I pleaded.

"Bank. We go . . . to bank to ten."

"I see."

"Bank. Cross at bank. Mr. Hobink, I speak little English," Topic said, bellowing his words.

"Mr. Topic Mimara," I cut in, desperately trying to communicate, "I speak Italian, some French. I understand some German. I suggest—"

"*Va bene,* Signor Hoving. *Italiano. Preferisco italiano.* The language of art and culture," a suddenly jovial voice rang out clearly in Italian. "Now, what did you say before?"

"In order to indicate our serious intentions toward your collection," I began, "I have brought along an associate from the Metropolitan." I was pleased that my Italian seemed up to the task.

"Very good. Two are better. Two curators from the British Museum were just here ten days ago," Topic remarked amiably. My heart sank.

"The Metropolitan comes in pairs, too," I said lamely. "My associate is Carmen Gómez-Moreno, one of the world's most accomplished experts in Romanesque art. She is, by the way, the daughter of Don Manuel Gómez-Moreno, the art historian in Spain." No harm in embellishment, I thought.

"Very good. I met him some years ago. I have just been to Spain, Barcelona, to view the Romanesque exposition. I commend it to you. There are many works of art, but only few were equal to the quality of my treasures."

"I was just in Barcelona myself," I observed genially.

"Too bad we did not have the opportunity to meet. For a time I was with Dr. Hanns Swarzenski of the Boston Museum. He too is deeply interested in my cross. So, Mr. Hoving, let us meet tomorrow in your lobby shortly before ten. I shall telephone your room."

"Fine," I said in a subdued tone of voice. Hesitantly I added, "I trust I'm not too late, Signor Topic?"

There was a pause, a short laugh. "We shall see. Tomorrow at ten," and the line went dead.

I collapsed on my bed. Could the man already have

made a deal? Had he encouraged me to come all the way from the United States just to laugh in my face? I groaned. Had Swarzenski stabbed me in the back? Had Topic concluded an arrangement with the British Museum? It could be. I had to break it up. Perhaps I could offer more money or pledge to buy one or two of the authentic pieces Dick Randall had written on his list. But I had to admit to myself I really didn't know what to do.

The following morning, unable to restrain myself, I descended from the room to the lobby well before ten o'clock. Carmen Gómez-Moreno was already there. Together we waited for our quarry. I had imagined that an historic moment of the magnitude of my first face-to-face encounter with Ante Topic Mimara Matutin might have been accompanied by thunder, flashes of lightning, an earth tremor or at least the parting of the waters of Lake Zurich. Not at all. It came off placidly—at first. He turned out to be a hearty hail-fellow-well-met type with a face like a crowd. He was short and portly, powerful in build, and slightly paunchy. The handshake was firm, warm, lingering.

"I am delighted to make your acquaintance, Mr. Hoving, and particularly, I must add with pleasure, the acquaintance of your attractive colleague, Miss Moreno. Your father, Miss Moreno, is a genius in the field of art history. If I had just a fraction of his knowledge of art, I would consider myself elevated. But I am just a humble painter and art restorer who has collected a few treasures here and there over the years. Come, let us proceed to the bank and my vault to examine its unique treasures."

What I had not expected was a courtier!

The Union Banque de Swisse was on the Bahnhofstrasse a few blocks away from the Savoy. As we ambled toward it, Topic Mimara shuffled along in front of us like a trained bear. Every few yards he would halt unexpectedly, wheeling around toward us to utter a few words.

"Chalices. You will appreciate my chalices. One is gold glass, very early in date, and another is silver and gold."

"I am so much looking forward to them," I said courteously.

We started off again at a leisurely pace. But soon Topic stopped once more.

"Reliquaries. You will appreciate my reliquaries. One is blue glass and comes from Winchester."

"I am certain I shall find them fascinating," I said, trying to sound convincing.

"It is a shame, don't you agree, that one must keep one's valuables in the recesses of a bank. Life can be hazardous in these modern times."

"Well, I am here to try to solve that problem, at least in part," I answered with a leer.

"Yes? Perhaps you will, Mr. Hoving. Now, what do you think you will see in my vault?" He boomed out the words, causing several passersby to look up.

"I think you know. I came to see your remarkable ivory cross," I said as evenly as I could.

"The cross, the unique cross. Yes. And there are many other objects."

We walked into the bank as if Topic Mimara owned the place. He waved a hand casually at one of the guards, who deferentially bowed his head. Just inside the spacious marbled and glistening interior of the building, Topic instructed us to wait until he could approach the *Administration*, so that he could identify us as his guests and make arrangements to obtain the keys for his area.

"I kind of like him, Tom," Carmen confided to me as he departed.

"Be careful," I said. "He isn't exactly what I expected, but I think he's clever as holy hell!"

When Topic returned, we proceeded in single file into the subterranean quarters of the bank as though we were part of a sacred procession. First went the uniformed guard, wearing white gloves, holding a large silver key in one hand. Then came Topic, also bearing a key, moving along like a high priest. The two of us followed like a pair of initiates about to be introduced to the Mysteries. Down and down we went, along carpeted halls and stairs. Warm yellow lights glowed along the serpentine route. A half-dozen portals were opened, then allowed to close with a gentle exhalation of air.

Eventually we reached a spacious room outfitted with small carrels and desks. A few people were already there. One of them was bending over what seemed to be a portfolio of stamps. The vault with Topic Mimara's treasures was isolated from the rows of safe-deposit boxes, which covered three walls of the large chamber. The door of his vault, a dazzling sheet of highly polished steel, was punctuated by two keyholes set some six inches apart. Simultaneously, Topic and the uniformed guard inserted and turned their keys. They removed the keys. The large door didn't move at all at first. Then it sprang open, but only an inch or so.

The guard disappeared. Topic switched on some low lights in his vault. I edged around him to glance at the interior. I caught sight of a series of shelves covered with leather jewel boxes; I saw a dozen or so small sculptures in wood, bronze and ivory, a stack of old books and, in a corner of one partition, what looked like a foot-high stack of fresh currency. Topic Mimara smoothly shepherded me away from the enticing doorway. With a quick smile, he directed Carmen and me to a conference room. The light was superb. Thank God. There was a bright incandescent lamp in the center of the ceiling, and two frosted windows furnished considerable daylight from outside.

Topic turned to us. "Please sit, accommodate yourselves. This is where you will see great treasures."

"The cross," I urged.

"In time," he said.

I sat down and blanked out my mind for objectivity. I wanted to drive out all preconceptions. Be calm, be neutral, I instructed myself over and over again. I became quiescent, even dreamy. Detached. A perfect state of mind for examining the cross.

With a subdued grunt, Topic Mimara placed an object on the table before me. It was covered by some cheap yellow fabric. I lifted my eyes to look at it as he removed the covering. Damn! It was not a cross delicately fashioned in ivory. It was a disgusting caricature of a work of art. I saw a two-foot-long chalk-white puckered and pockmarked wooden replica of the world-famous bronze the *Lupa Romana*, the she-wolf, symbol of Rome, made in Etruscan times, with two ugly figures, Romulus and Remus, reaching up, awkwardly trying to suckle the beast. It was a horrid travesty!

I sat there dumbfounded while Topic chatted on brightly, and apparently with utter conviction, about the wretched thing. It had been found in an excavation undertaken in the 1920s on the edge of the Palatine Hill in Rome. "Unique in the world!" he proclaimed. "It is the only *sculptor's* model yet unearthed from the Etruscan civilization." It was, he claimed, far finer than the original bronze—and smaller, too, which was always better. He shrugged massively, turning down the corners of his thick gray lips. Certain archaeologists who had inspected the great *Lupa*, "my wolf," had been incredulous, he admitted. "They did not believe it." But *he* knew it was an original. He had faith. He saw it and believed it. It was a matter of the heart, the inner consciousness which a true connoisseur brings to a work of art. Didn't I agree? I just nodded, a stupid smile on my face.

What had I gotten into? I became anxious, then petrified, then furious, then bored as an hour passed. An almost unending stream of ugly objects appeared before me. They were worse than fakes. No respectable forger would have touched them! I saw milk-white bleached "Gothic" ivories that seemed to have been squeezed out of some kind of toothpaste tube and frozen. There was a chalice in a metal I could not readily identify, ineptly gilded, a rotten facsimile of a well-known example in a famous monastery on the Rhine. The gold glass chalice, which he characterized as early Christian, and which I had already condemned from the photography so many months before, seemed in physical presence to be diseased. Topic showed off dozens of items—figurines, caskets, goblets, enamels, pieces of jewelry, parts of ancient weapons, fragments of stained glass, drawings, small oil paintings— all unappealing or wrong. I became desperate to find *something* authentic.

"Here is a treasure you will greatly admire," Topic told me. "It is a glass reliquary vase. See if you know what it is. I shall give you a hint. These enamel floral decorations on the rim are the same as the flowered patterns in the Benedictional of Saint Aethelwold in the British Museum, and they date to the early tenth century."

Although my immediate reaction was that the vase was doubtful, I forced myself to retain an open mind. The vase did seem to exude age; the painted ornament was fluid, natural, what an illuminator of the tenth century might well have done. But in a few seconds I realized

I was kidding myself. The glass was too thick and, from what I could see, uniform in thickness throughout. At the bottom of the vase I found, not to my surprise, a mark which clearly indicated the piece had been made by a glassblower. Could that have happened in the tenth century? I decided the glass jar had to be a product of the nineteenth century coming from Venice, painted by someone in modern times. I suspected it had been Topic Mimara himself.

"What you have before you is the rarest reliquary on earth," Topic Mimara announced proudly. "It is, I have been able to determine, a vase of Saint Aethelwold. It was made for Winchester Cathedral."

"How do you know it comes from Winchester?" I asked.

"The style. It is clear the glass was painted by the same artist who painted the benedictional. I found it with four other works of art in a small church on the Continent which had historical connections with Winchester before the invasion of William the Conqueror. A priest at the church told me the works of art were always thought to have come from Winchester Cathedral."

Fatigued by the onslaught of fakes and his ridiculous claims, I had become almost giddy. Would I never find something genuine? At length I was able to compile a list of only five—just five—medieval works which were authentic and might conceivably fit into the collections of the Medieval Department and The Cloisters. A boxwood Virgin and Child of the thirteenth century; two carved wooden heads, presumably of Saint John the Evangelist and a warrior saint; a four-inch-long ivory casket, decorated with floral bindings of gilded bronze; and an ivory soldier on horseback of the fourteenth century which may have been a chess piece. This discouraging lot would be my bargaining chips.

"You see, a museum of treasures," Topic bragged. "I can imagine my pieces are greater in number and, perhaps, even better in quality than most of the Metropolitan's medieval objects. Wouldn't you like to have them all?"

How in God's name would I deal with the eccentric? I needed time; I had to slow him down.

"Signor Topic, I am staggered by your collection. It

is truly amazing!" I spoke out with all the enthusiasm I could manufacture.

"And to think," he crowed, "that these are merely a few of the whole. I have many more elsewhere, some here in Switzerland and others in Tangier. The finest in the world. I might allow you to make a choice. But I cannot part with all, you know."

"Yes, and I believe I know why," I told him warmly. "To part with *everything* would be an offense to your personal code of collecting."

"You have a keen sense, Signor Hoving. Tell me what, of all you have seen, what would you want *most?*"

"It would, sir, be discourteous of me to say at this moment. If you understand me, it is just . . ." I paused as if to collect myself. "I have formed such a . . . strong . . . impression of your objects that it would be ungracious to *them* for me to comment right now."

"Excellent, I delight in seeing you are a man of sensitivity," Topic Mimara said. "And now it has become the time for another one of my unique treasures. It is on a level with the English blue-glass reliquary."

"I do not want to see it, Signor Topic," I told him, softly and a shade piously. The man shot me a quick look which was perplexed and ice cold. There was an intensity of black evil in that gaze. A beast within him had almost come to the surface. I was fascinated and amazed.

I let him smolder a bit and then added in just the right tone, "The objects I have looked at have moved me so deeply, sir, that I beg of you to allow me some minutes alone to regain my composure."

Topic Mimara became subdued. He smiled, reached over and awkwardly touched my arm. I restrained myself from flinching. He got up and left the room, removing all the objects.

"Jesus," I whispered to Carmen Gómez-Moreno, "have you ever gone through anything like that?"

"So many pieces," she said. "Where do you suppose he got them all?"

"From a bordello, I think," I muttered.

"How many real things did you see?" she asked.

"From all that mess, I counted just five. I have the awful feeling that Dick Randall was right."

"Can you imagine what the cross may look like?" she said in discouragement.

Looking like an aging acolyte, Topic Mimara entered the room holding something in the air as if he were displaying the Holy Grail. It was shrouded in black velveteen. Would it be the cross? If so or if not, would it be Act Two of this comic opera? He set the thing on the table before us with exaggerated care.

With a flourish he drew the shroud up and away. It *was* the cross. My instant feeling was that it was soft, yet powerful, supple yet strong. It seemed to curve delicately as if it were bending in the winds of time.

How many works of art have been created since the dawn of history? Hundreds of millions? Who knows? Whatever the cipher, only an infinitesimal few are imbued with pure magic. The cross was magical. Magic? A work of art with magic will survive forever through warfare, rape, pillage, fires, earthquakes, storms and seizure. It can be broken into fragments, strewn throughout the corners of the world; the pieces can be hidden for hundreds of years; still, it will surface somehow. Ignore it; mock it; spit upon it; revile it; the magic will never disappear. A work of art with pure magic has the power to change the lives of those who come into its proximity. Such a thing will resist forever those who try to alter it, ideologically or physically, or attempt to force it to conform to their ambitions, desires or greeds.

Golden buttery in color, every surface and facet of the cross shone and glistened with tiny, delicately formed figures silently conversing with each other by means of artfully held scrolls. I touched the cross gently. It was worn smooth and oily with age, yet it was rock hard and unyielding at the same time.

I became enclosed in a pocket of silence. All light in the room seemed to fade except for a tunnel of yellow-white refulgence at the exact point where I stared—the circular center of the cross. Converging toward the center, vertically and horizontally, as if drawn to it, were two budding branches of a great tree. My mind seemed to fill with music, a rhapsodic, deep, tonal series of chords forming into words and eventually a visual image. And that image became a stalwart, deep-rooted tree with feathery young branches, striving to reach the sky. As

I gazed at the ivory cross, its golden surfaces seemed to move and shift. The more I examined it in that first moment, the more I felt myself transported in some mysterious fashion into the shaded interior of my imaginary tree. I saw myself climbing easily, steadily—grasping branches which were firm, yielding but tensile strong. And I ascended swiftly. Soon I could clearly see the sun bursting through the clouds in a brightening sky.

It was, I thought, a *holy* object and a holy presence. As soon as the words came to my mind, I felt a slight shock. I had never in my life called any work of art *holy*. Now, confronted with the cross, the word "holy" did not stick in my throat. The cross exuded strength, confidence, an all-encompassing serenity. It was authentic beyond question. And surely twelfth century. Of that I had no doubt at all.

I attempted to conjure up some specific stylistic comparisons, but my mind seemed to resist the effort. I just didn't *care* about analyzing art-historical evidence. I abandoned the effort of running down my examination checklist. I simply consumed the beauty, the complexity, the twisting, tangled yet ordered concatenation of the figures. Who could have made such a thing? None but a genius! *Who* could have sculpted and arranged the host of figures in so harmonious a manner? Would I ever learn the identity of the master?

My initial attention was drawn to the central circular medallion on the front of the cross, just above a bronze figure of Christ about six inches high which had obviously been added later. The medallion was bursting with figures. A powerful individual with a daggerlike beard stood right in the center, poised with the same tense energy as a ballet dancer about to spring into the air. The powerful figure was garbed in a sumptuous robe which appeared to flow about his limbs like water around a partly submerged stone. With his right hand he vehemently thrust a carved ivory scroll out and into the air. His left hand was clenched unmistakably into a fist. The scroll, carved in high relief in the golden walrus ivory, was inscribed in two neat rows with tiny writing in superbly formed capital letters. The figure, whoever it was, was only about as big as my thumbnail. Unable to take my eyes off the stunning figure, I grabbed notepaper and pen and, concentrating hard, copied the Latin inscription:

SIC ERIT VITA TVA PENDEN
S ANE T Ø N CREDE VIE TVE

I couldn't make any sense out of it. But I didn't care. I knew I could decipher the text later.

This dominating figure was peering at a snake curled and wriggling on the fork of a minute stick. Around that clustered a dense crowd of heads, some wearing distinctive conical hats. The scene was that of the Brazen Serpent, and the main figure was obviously Moses. The raising of the Serpent was, as Hanns Swarzenski had told me, the beginning of the drama, the prefiguration in the Old Testament of the Crucifixion of Christ.

In a flash of time my eyes went from one scene to the next, figure by figure. I must have counted sixty figures in less than half a minute. My senses had become that acute. As I studied the object and took notes, I carried on a dialogue with myself:

"My God! Absolutely splendid piece! How crisp, how finely carved, how strong in composition! I can hardly believe the figures are so deeply undercut. They almost look carved separately and *pegged* in afterward. I'll test that later. A master artist of world history was *here!*

"Now, calm down, slow down. Go over the thing, scene by scene. Find the correct and logical order. There must be a chronological order. The Serpent medallion starts it. Okay. A central figure which must be Moses, with three others, each one with a carved and inscribed scroll. Quickly, let me see, how many inscriptions *are* there on this cross? My God. About *fifty*, even more. All of them are small, barely readable. *Ah.* There on the front side of the long, curving, thin walrus ivory tusk of the upright are the two large inscriptions Hanns talked about: TERRA TREMIT . . . I'll get them later.

"How exciting! How beautiful! The style is confident, a bit youthful. No, *not* young; *fresh* is the better word. Okay. *Fresh.* And very realistic. I'm amazed at how some of the little figures bend and twist their bodies back and around. Unusual for the twelfth century.

"My God, I must find out who the genius was who

made this triumph! He's incredible in his skill. I hardly believe it, but on the face of one of the four—I guess they are prophets—in the central medallion on the front, a face only about a quarter of an inch wide, I can make out *with no trouble at all* the eyes, the eye-lids, the lips, the delicate nostrils. And how pliant and beautiful are the hair and the sharp daggerbeards.

"General style is knifelike, elongated. Could the figures in the Psalter of Saint Albans be at all comparable? What is the date of that illuminated Psalter of Albans? It is, let's see, 1110, 1120. Yes. But these figures here are later, more mature, better formed. I'd say, offhand, roughly 1150! Sure! Good. Calm down, Hoving. You're racing. Slow down your eyes.

"Have I seen anything like it? No, never. It *is* unique. Who would have thought that this idiot, Topic, would have found such a piece!

"Now go through the scenes. At the center of the front is the Brazen Serpent with Moses. The block on the right, which flows from the horizontal branch of the growing Tree of Life—*that's* a sweet touch—depicts the Deposition and the Lamentation. The block on the bottom? Gone. The blank block carved out of elephant ivory isn't old. Who put that there? Topic? Probably.

"Next? Up to the block on the left. The Three Marys at the Tomb. An angel sits on the rim of the tomb. Its wings and draperies look like sheaves of wheat falling to the ground. Stunning! The angel holds a scroll. Let me see with my glass. I can write it down: QUERITIS NAZ IHM: RENUM CRUCIFI. Heavy abbreviation! Is it in code? I'll figure it out later.

"Aha! There, behind the angel, is Christ resurrected. Head up, arm in the air, imploring, reaching out—about to be lifted. To *what?* The little Christ is magnificent. I can even see His ribs. And the wounds—*so* small—in His hands and side. Incredible!

"And look! Beneath the tomb, a group of sleeping soldiers, lying horizontally. Five of them. In armor. Armor can sometimes date a piece. Elongated, almond-shaped shields cover the soldiers' bodies like insect wings. They look just like a nest of crickets! Incomparable! Nothing nearly like this cross exists anywhere! To think that Topic Mimara found it! God!

"What's next? Yes. There's a hand, carved right on the placard, blessing, reaching out and down to the resurrecting Christ, the hand of God helping Christ to complete His journey from death. Poignant and sensitive. The hand is on the placard. A series of writings surrounds the hand. . . . That is where Randall's 'King of the Confessors' must be. I'll return to it.

"Three figures are standing on the top of the placard. Again the conical hats appear. Who *are* these people? Two wear pointed caps; one has a sort of crown. His scroll reads: Q. SCRIPSI. *Scripsi*—what's that? I'll find out later. At the very top, the block at the summit of His holy mountain depicts the Ascension of Christ. Classical English iconography with the figure of Christ rocketing into the clouds surrounding heaven, His body half swallowed up by the clouds.

"Now to the back. The little bust-length figures in windows along the vertical bar of the cross are so magnificent. There are . . . *nine* of them, and six on the horiontal bar. Each one different, each face so alive. Who *are* they? Wait! They are identified by names inscribed above their heads. The first is DD; he wears a crown. Double D? David! Must be David. Next, SALMN. Of *course*. Solomon.

"Just look at him! Solomon's quiet, composed face seems big as life. All the features are there—perfectly rendered eyelids, lips, nostrils, strands of hair and matted beard. What's written on his scroll? These words are not heavily abbreviated: ASCENDAM: IPALMAM: APPREHENDA: FRUCTUS: EIVS:

"Let's see. 'I shall ascend . . .'; IPALMAM—that must be *In palmam;* APPREHENDA—that means to take hold; FRUCTUS is 'fruit.' I know. I *do* know the phrase from that seminar with Weitzmann on typology. It means 'I shall ascend into the palm tree and take hold of the fruits thereof.' Classic, clear, obviously typology from Old to New Testament signifying the Crucifixion.

"It's my *tree*. It is written there. My tree! Uncanny. Incomparable! The cross is *incomparable*. I have to have this thing. I must get it! I have to possess this magnificent cross. My God, I have to make this thing mine! How? But how?"

CHAPTER SEVEN

Sleight of Hand

I KEPT LOOKING, staring for at least half an hour. Probably more. My mind was exploding with the excitement of confronting the incomparable work of art set before me. I knew all about it, yet knew nothing. I realized it would take years, perhaps a lifetime, to root out its subtle meanings. Of course, now it was time for restraint, the moment for analysis, *not* euphoria. But I could not hold myself in check. I just kept staring at the ravishing work, turning it on its base one way and then another. The complexity of the sculpture and its simple harmony were awesome. Finally I managed to shake myself out of my trance.

I saw that Topic Mimara had been observing me quietly. When I looked up into his impassive moon face, he curled up the corner of his mouth slightly as if to say he had seen similar reactions before and was only moderately impressed.

"The cross is the most magnificent and moving work I have seen from the entire Middle Ages," I said without hesitation. It was no time to be coy. "And its quality goes well beyond that. It is universal. The piece compares to masterworks like Duccio's *Maestà*, or the Ghent Altarpiece. It conveys a similar sense of order, equanimity, quiet power. Peace. Although I had conjured up something grand, I have to admit that, experiencing it, your cross is far greater and more transcendent than I ever would have dreamt. I am captivated by it. I intend to inform James Rorimer of my feelings."

Carmen Gómez-Moreno, who had been schooled in the classic mode of negotiations, looked at me askance. Topic Mimara moved over beside us.

"I believe you, Signor Hoving. I am a man seldom fooled. I see your reactions are from the heart—genuine, impressive, highly gratifying to me as a humble collector. If you had acted too casually, too quickly, or if you had reacted to my world masterpiece in such a way as to assume the pose of a bargainer, I would have urged you and your colleague to leave my presence. I have no time for anybody but those who are genuinely fascinated. If Mr. Rorimer listens to you the way he should, he will be impressed. If he is a man of action, he will move. He will come over to Zurich now. And I advise you to tell him to do so."

"Signor Topic Mimara," I said, injecting a deferential note into my voice, "Mr. Rorimer wanted very much to meet you and examine your works of art. He instructed me almost a year ago to communicate with you. I sent almost a dozen letters. But you never responded. After a while I began to suspect that you didn't exist. There was not much more I could have done. Rorimer is the director of the largest art museum in the world. You must understand that he cannot just drop all his other activities and come instantly, however much he would like to. His schedule is set for months in advance. But *I* have been granted full authority by Mr. Rorimer to negotiate for your cross. Yet I can't do it alone. You must help me. Your help will be simple. Indeed, I ask of you almost nothing. All I ask is a superb set of photographs of your cross. Nothing will excite Rorimer more than photos. With them, within weeks, I am convinced, we will be able to conclude our negotiations."

Topic Mimara studied my face for several moments, rubbing the gray stubble on his chin.

"I shall think about it," he said. "While I do so, you

may examine my masterpiece a little longer. I will leave you alone for a time and I shall ponder your request. But, Signor Hoving, I must tell you right now that I am doubtful. I am not sure I should give you photographs, much as I would desire to do so. You see, I have given my word to others, your rivals, *never* to give out pictures. I like you; I have come to respect you. I shall leave you now. We shall discuss the issue further when I return. I will not be long. But I am doubtful."

"Let me offer a suggestion, Signor Topic," I added smoothly. "*You* don't have to give me photos. Let *me* take the pictures. I have a camera here in my case, a Rolleiflex. It is perfect for the job. The light is adequate. If I have to use a tripod, that's fine, too. I brought one with me. Such photographs are all I need. And they will not be so fine that I or anyone else would be able to publish them. I will swear by all I consider sacred never, *never* to publish so much as a detail without your written permission. If you will allow me to take my own snapshots, technically you will not have violated your word with my rivals."

Topic Mimara roared with laughter. Then he came over and plucked the camera right out of my fingers and slipped out the door, closing it behind him. I could hear echoes of his laughter as he walked down the corridor.

As his footsteps faded, I reached inside my pocket and withdrew a second camera, a miniature Minox I had brought with me just in case.

"I have no choice. I hope he doesn't come back too soon," I muttered, holding up the Minox for Carmen to see.

"Is that little thing really a camera?" Carmen burst out, looking stunned.

I nodded.

"Do you really think you should use it?" She was bewildered, anxious. "What if he finds out? We might lose everything. I say you should not."

"I've made up my mind. Don't confuse me," I barked rudely. "Go to the door. Listen for him. Lean against it. Do anything. I *must* have photos. For some damned reason, Jim is against the cross. Only a photographic record will change his mind. If I don't get that, then we are really lost."

Nervously, Carmen Gómez-Moreno did what I had demanded. She clung to the door like a frightened bird. I took the Minox and measured off the appropriate distance with the focusing chain. I tried to take close-ups of the large inscriptions on the front and the sides, so that later I could decipher the writings at leisure. And I attempted to shoot as many details as I could—each side of the central medallion, the square terminals, and as many of the bust-length figures on the back of the cross and their scrolls as possible.

"I think he's coming back," Carmen suddenly cried out. It had been no more than three or four minutes. "Hurry!"

"Just a shot or two more," I whispered hurriedly, clicking away, poking the miniature camera over the entire surface of the cross, approximating the correct distance with the focusing chain. I had no idea if the pictures would come out.

The door opened as I cocked the camera for a final shot. Just in time, I stuffed it back into my pocket.

"Are you discovering interesting things, Signor Hoving?" Topic asked.

"I was just registering my impressions," I remarked casually.

"Fine. Did I inconvenience you by taking this?" Topic said, laughing as he handed back my Rolleiflex.

"I didn't miss it at all," I told him as I took the large camera in hand. "Have you decided to give me a set of photographs?"

"I cannot. I would like to, but I cannot."

"Without them, I may never be able to interest Mr. Rorimer in the cross," I observed sadly.

"Too bad. The rules are the same for everyone. Mr. Rorimer can come here as often as he likes and for as long. Just like everyone."

"Signor Topic, come, now! Just how many museum directors have really come here?" I asked.

"Many. Dr. Sherman Lee of the Cleveland Museum has come. And Mr. William Milliken before him. They came. There have been many others whom I do not wish to name. And others will also come. I have received expressions of profound interest from every great museum, except for the Metropolitan."

"What about me? *I* have expressed interest," I protested.

"That is true. Now, however, it is time for Mr. Rorimer to do the same," he replied.

I gazed at the shining cross before me and listened to the man's words, wondering whether what he said about everyone's interest was a lie. But when he had finished, I was totally convinced he was telling the truth. A wave of depression suddenly swept over me. I conjured up images of my opponents vigorously coming to decisions, drafting agreements, dispatching telegrams to Topic Mimara. I half expected to see a messenger rush into the room with a fistful of cables and hand them over to Topic, and to hear him proclaim, his voice rising in triumph, that not one, but *three* museums had agreed to his "most reasonable" terms.

I tried to remain calm. "I will ponder your words very carefully, Signor Topic. Do you mind if we examine your cross in detail? If you do not grant permission to obtain photographs, at least I must have careful notes."

How I hoped the man would leave just once more. Then, for insurance, I would take a second set of photographs with my miniature camera. But Topic waved a hand toward his work of art, sat down at the far end of the table and started reading a newspaper. I could see he was not about to leave.

I settled in for a closer scrutiny of the cross, and a deeper sense of wonderment came over me as I conversed with my colleague in tense, excited whispers.

"What do you think of this bronze Christ?" I asked as I tapped the chest of the unprepossessing figure attached awkwardly to the ivory. "Can it possibly be an original? I can't believe it is. It's ugly as hell. Undoubtedly a fake. Listen, Carmen, do you have any doubts about the cross? Could it possibly be a fake? Could Dick Randall have been right?"

"Absolutely not! That's ridiculous," she remarked testily. "Something *this* ambitious, this mysterious, cannot be wrong! The cross is a triumph!"

"Still, we have to prove it's authentic. I think I'll ask our friend a couple of questions," I said.

"Perhaps you should let sleeping dogs lie," she remarked.

"Signor Topic," I called out. "A couple of questions. This bronze crucifix, where did it come from? Do you believe it's the original? And what about the bottom square block? Is that a replacement? Did you put it there?"

"Your eye is perceptive, Signor Hoving," Topic said. "The bronze Christ is rare, beautiful. Truly exceptional. It is English and dates to the early eleventh century, just like the ivory cross. Because of that, I placed it on the cross to keep my two English pieces together. Who knows, it may have been the original Christ. The bottom block of ivory? I carved it and put it there. And I repaired the bottom of the upright, which was shattered. Interesting. At some point in its history, the cross must have been snapped violently off its base."

"I wonder what might have been carved on the bottom block," I mused. "I suppose we shall never know."

Topic Mimara half rose from his chair. He seemed about to tell me something. Then he shrugged with a curious heavy gesture and settled back once again into his chair.

I dismissed this peculiar man from my mind and began a detailed examination of the cross. I felt like a detective starting off on the most difficult and challenging case of a career. I decided to begin with what had brought me to the underground vault in the first place—the inscription "King of the Confessors."

I studied the minute writing carved on the placard. The inscription had six different lines, crowded around the

hand of God. A few letters were missing; the upper corners of the rectangular ivory placard had apparently been slightly whittled away. I adjusted my magnifying glass and looked closely, losing all awareness of the room around me. I transcribed the letters and the punctuation marks at first without thinking about what they meant. My only objective was to be accurate. Deciphering the marks, breaking the code, would come later.

I sat back to study what I had sketched and the notes I had written down. Carmen and I carried on a whispered and animated discussion about what we had discovered. We also shared a sense of frustration about what we were not able to fathom.

We agreed that the placard had given us our first important clue to the mystery cross. The inscriptions were definitely composed in three languages: Greek, Latin and, at the bottom, what seemed to us both to be an attempt at Hebrew.

We were able to decipher little of the Greek lines and none of the Hebrew. But the Latin was crystal clear. We found the name "Jesus" followed by the Latin for "Nazarene"! Then "King." And then to our intense pleasure the word CONFESSORUM. "King of the Confessors." Dick Randall had been right. And so had Topic. Amazing!

We pursued the translation of the large inscriptions on the front and the sides of the upright. We both felt that the capital letters were so beautiful they must have been carved into the ivory by a master calligrapher. And we both were convinced that within these inscriptions the key to the meaning of the ivory would be found.

We copied down the inscription on the front. It said: TERRA TREMIT MORS VICTA GEMIT SURGENTE SEPULTO VITA CLUIT SYNAGOGA RUIT MOLIMINE STULT . . . The last letter of the final word was gone, snapped off. Much as we tried, we could not translate the Latin. We recognized certain words and eventually pieced together only "Earth trembles. Death conquered." We knew that SYNAGOGA meant the Synagogue or possibly the Jews, but the context was obscure. We had no idea of the meaning of the words RUIT, MOLIMINE and STULT.

It suddenly occured to me to ask Topic Mimara if he had a list of the two prominent inscriptions plus all the tiny ones carved on the scrolls. I suspected he or, more likely, his scholar wife had identified and translated them all.

I turned to the quiet man at the end of the table. "Signor Topic, I am having difficulty reading some of these inscriptions. Can you supply me with a list?" I injected the warmest possible tone into my voice.

"No," he responded in more of a grunt than a word. "If you can read them, fine. Until the publication appears, I shall keep the list to myself." Without a further word, he turned back to his newspaper.

I took the greater part of two hours to copy every one of the minute inscriptions and names. It was agony. We could barely see some of the letters engraved into the scrolls. The words were heavily abbreviated. Yet we both realized that obtaining these writings would be crucial and would probably tell us virtually everything about the ivory cross. As we counted up the writings, Carmen and I began to look upon the cross as a book, a literary object, in which the writings were equal in importance to—or even more significant than—the carved scenes.

We were astounded to find no fewer than sixty-three inscriptions. At the completion of the meticulous and taxing work, I recognized even more deeply how complex and arduous a process it would be to crack the code. I hated to admit that my once adequate Latin was so rusty that I could readily translate only one inscription. For the rest I needed a Latin dictionary or a Latin Bible. The only feature that made me at all optimistic was that each one of the prophets holding scrolls on the back of the cross was identified by name. Those writings, I figured, I could easily track down in a Latin Bible.

After we had copied the inscriptions we tried valiantly to translate the large ones, running along the sides of the upright. What at first seemed easy remained, in the end, almost a total enigma. The pair of verses read: CHAM RIDET DUM NUDA VIDET PUDEBUNDA PARENTIS; IUDEI RISERE DEI PENAM MOR . . . The last word was probably MORTIS, or "death." The word CHAM was a puzzle; RIDET was the verb "to laugh"; NUDA—that was "nude"; PARENTIS was, obviously, "parent." Yet the whole phrase was maddeningly obtuse, something about "He laughs at a parent who is naked." Was it some sort of jest? The second

phrase was even more of a mystery: IUDEI signified the
Jews; RISERE was, again, "laugh." Curious, but the second
part of the inscription seemed to be saying something
about the Jews laughing. But at what? What a puzzle!

We gave up on the writings, confident that they could
be—had to be—solved in time. We concentrated instead
on the rich visual drama packed in a breathtaking manner
with dozens of lacy figures and beautifully carved vi-
gnettes. As I stared at them I was reminded of what the
philosopher Bernard of Clairvaux had taught in the
twelfth century about how to look at a religious work of
art. He urged the observer to cast his eyes over every
inch and fraction of an inch of an object, crawling over
it more slowly than a snail would, in order to comprehend
the full meaning and the ultimate beauty. It struck me
in sharp wonderment that Bernard might have seen this
very cross. It was the perfect example of what he was
talking about—a work of such profuseness, depth and
subtlety that each figure, each gesture, seemed to carry
a profound meaning.

After another hour of scrutiny Carmen and I believed
we could identify most of the scenes on our cross and
had come to grips with the basic program of the masterpiece.

We knew it was no mistake that the artist had chosen
for his cross the flowering tree, the budding palm, instead
of unadorned pieces of wood. He wanted to emphasize
life, the living nature of the true cross which was a palm,
and the eternal life of Christ. The palm tree was invariably used in connection with a typology, or the
practice of using Old Testament scenes and events to
predict and explain the New Testament. This cross provided uniquely rich typology in its carved scenes. We
were convinced that the typology would be reflected in
the inscriptions as well. The one scroll I had deciphered,
held by the second prophet down from the top on the
back, was from Solomon: "I shall ascend into the Palm
Tree and take hold of the fruit thereof:" To a theologian
of the twelfth century those lines constituted an obvious
reference to the palm tree of the cross upon which Christ
was crucified. And the lines also signified to that theologian that Jesus had willingly climbed into the tree,

voluntarily given himself up to the cross on behalf of mankind.

The palm tree as life and the inevitability of the Crucifixion were strongly emphasized throughout the cross. At the bottom two figures, one male, the other a female, were vividly depicted as if they were climbing out of the depths of the earth. And they were. We saw from their inscribed names that they were Adam and Eve emerging from their grave at the moment Christ died on the cross. Adam embraced the cross so powerfully that his body became almost a part of it. Eve, an ancient crone, hugged Adam. Both looked up the cross in exultation.

What they were gazing at, we could not be certain. There could originally have been a figure of Christ. But just as properly there could have been no Christ at all. The palm tree itself could have symbolized the Savior. Whatever the case, it was clear that Adam and Eve were also looking up to the medallion at the crossing, which, we figured, symbolized the wheel of life carried along by four vigorous angels. This central medallion was jammed with figures. There seemed to be a couple of dozen of them. We were unable to identify them all, but we recognized the one at the center, the hub of the wheel, the dancer who threw out his scroll as if it were a proud outcry of triumph. He was, I believed, Moses. Just above his magnificent head appeared a little snake curled around a forked stick. The creature was the Brazen Serpent sent by God to cure the stricken Israelites, and was the typology for Christ and the Crucifixion.

After a while Carmen pushed her chair back from the table and exclaimed, "I've never seen anything more powerful in all of medieval art."

"I was thinking the very same thing," I remarked and then asked, "Can I borrow a strand of your hair?"

"What?"

"A hair. I want to try to thread it behind Moses. He's carved in such high relief, I wonder if the artist carved him separately and then pegged him in place."

She laughed and did what I had asked. I tried to push the hair behind Moses and several of the other figures. I whistled in amazement. None of the tiny figures had been carved separately and then pegged into the cross.

The undercutting was incredibly deep and daring, a stunning tour de force, particularly for walrus ivory, a material far more fragile and prone to flaking than the denser elephant ivory. The artist was also a genius in technique!

My colleague observed that the sequence of the scenes on the cross had the same circular motion as the central wheel. The story which began at the medallion followed in the square terminal on the right side of the cross. There, carved in a spectacularly vivid style, were the two episodes in the New Testament that come immediately after the Crucifixion, the Deposition and the Lamentation.

The dominating figure of the Deposition was the dead Christ on the cross. The carving of the tiny figure was matchless. One could see His miniature ribs and collarbones. To the left of Christ stood the Virgin Mary, who tenderly held one of Christ's arms in her veiled hands. John the Evangelist stood opposite her, grieving deeply. Nicodemus was depicted behind John, pulling a nail from Christ's right hand with a pair of pincers. And behind John were a number of heads gazing intently at Christ. There were, including Nicodemus, exactly eight of them. It was just the same number as in the central medallion. We didn't know what the number eight meant, but we knew it was not coincidental.

On the left side of the crucified Christ, just behind the Virgin Mary, was the centurion, holding shield and spear and wearing a helmet. Behind him were a few more soldiers, represented just by helmeted heads. Finally, above Christ's head were minute roundels with bust-length figures weeping. *They* had to be the symbols of the sun and the moon.

Below the Deposition was a representation of the Lamentation over the body of Christ moments before He was entombed. On the left sat a majestic bearded individual, shown crying. He was the only figure in the scene with a scroll. Carmen was able to translate the abbreviated words. They were from the Book of Zechariah and said: "They weep for him as for an only begotten son." The artist had not missed anything! Under Zechariah's scroll he had carved tiny skulls representing Golgotha, the hill where Christ was crucified.

"We've simply got to convince Topic Mimara to sell it to us. What do you suppose his price will really be?" Carmen said in a hushed voice.

"I hate to even ask him the price," I told her. "But forget prices. We'll get it somehow."

The next block, the one which would have appeared on the bottom, was gone. Whatever it was, we knew it had to be a chapter in the drama of Christ immediately after the Deposition and the Entombment and just before the subject on the left terminal, which was clearly the Three Marys coming to the empty tomb where the Angel of God was sitting.

The scene was one of the loveliest on the object. The three Marys, hooded and veiled, approaching the empty tomb were splendid, with elegant, tall bodies. The artist had depicted them as surprised but not fearful. They seemed calm, motionless, waiting trustfully for the next thing to happen. Only the right hand of the first holy woman was raised in slight alarm.

"It's *all* marvelous, isn't it?" I whispered to Carmen. "My God, we have got to get this thing! That angel of God beckoning to the Marys is so fine. The draperies caress his body like flowing water. But, Carmen, look here, at those hard, precise, chevron-shaped drapery folds falling between the angel's legs, and at this face shaped rather like a lima bean. See it? And the slender knife-blade bodies of the women! Does that style remind you of a specific English manuscript illumination? To me it could be close, you know, to the figures in the Saint Albans Psalter. There, I recall, you find similar chevron folds, knife-blade bodies and dramatic gestures. I wouldn't be surprised if it turned out this cross has a definite link with Saint Albans and England."

Together we confirmed what I myself had suspected was the next act in the drama. It was almost hidden behind the splendid seated angel. There, emerging from the tomb, was the resurrecting Christ, holding the cross, raising His arm to a pointing or blessing hand of God carved just under the placard which bore the words "King of the Confessors." There were two dramatic people standing on top of the placard who had at first confused me. They seemed to be arguing. The figure on the left leaned forward aggressively and, quite literally, jabbed

his finger into the face of the rather dignified individual
on the right, who drew back in disdain and pointed his
finger decisively down, seemingly to the placard itself.

Carmen supplied the clues to their identification. The
high priest of the Jews was complaining to Pontius Pilate
about the precise wording of the placard to be placed over
the head of Christ—a very rare scene in art. My colleague
explained that when Christ's trial was over, Pilate, according to the texts, wrote a placard saying, "Christ, the
King of the Jews." And the priest objected violently,
saying, "Don't write 'King'!" But Pilate answered back
that he would leave the inscription the way it was. But
where the unique variant of the strange word "Confessors" had come from neither Carmen nor I had an idea.

The final episode on the front of the cross was carved
on the top square block. It was the Ascension. It too
was highly dramatic. Christ was shown soaring—rocketing
—into the clouds surrounding heaven, with His Apostles
looking on.

The back of the cross was more complicated than the
front. And even more beautiful. There were three Evangelist symbols: Mark, Luke and John, one on each block.
They grew out of a series of prophets. Those on the upright bar peered out of little windows; the prophets on
the crossbar were full length, and were conversing with
one another.

From top to bottom, there were eleven prophets:
David, Solomon, Obadiah, Hosea, Isaiah, Micah, Habak-
kuk, Zephaniah, Joel, Daniel, Ezekiel. Then suddenly,
below Ezekiel, we encountered an evangelist, Matthew.
We had no idea why. And originally there had been one
more, a thirteenth figure which had been broken off.
His identity was easy to ascertain, for his name was still
inscribed—Jonah.

On the horizontal bar of the cross were six prophets:
Nahum, Haggai and Balaam on the left side of the central
medallion, and three more on the left, Malachi, Amos
and Job. All carried scrolls. But we could decipher none
of them.

The central medallion of the back was unimaginably
beautiful—and enigmatic. It portrayed the Lamb of God.
We knew that the Lamb had to be the final chapter of
the cross. But the full significance of the scene escaped

us. We did know that with the magnificent Lamb the
genius artist of the unique cross had surpassed himself.
The animal threw back His head toward a splendid angel,
garbed in a flowing gown. The Lamb had to be Christ,
triumphant for eternity. What a crescendo of joy! The
frustrating thing to both of us was that the rest of this
complex scene remained a puzzle. Behind the Lamb, to
the left, was a hooded man weeping. Who? We didn't
know. Underneath the Lamb there was a bust-length individual. Again, we didn't know who he was. Above the
Lamb was another hooded man. He looked like a monk
flying along horizontally with his fist raised in the air—
most singular. He was a total mystery, particularly since
he looked as though he had been carved separately and
slipped into the medallion.

But even more mysterious was the female figure on the
far left of the Lamb. She was hooded, partly veiled and
blind. Her head was downcast. She turned sharply away
from the Lamb. In her upraised arm she held a long
spear, which she was literally ramming into the breast of
the Lamb. She held a scroll which fell downward as if
in sorrow. The inscription—the whole thing is on one line
—stated: MALEDICTUS. OIS. QVI. P. I. L. What the individual letters meant, we couldn't guess. But we did
know what *maledictus* was. It was a malediction! A curse!
That troubled me. Why would the cross of Christ, the
symbol of love, eternal life and righteousness, have the
word "curse" on it? Who was cursed, and why? Who was
the blinded female piercing the Lamb?

Again I didn't know. All I did realize was that we had
to have the cross.

I pushed my chair from the table and gazed at the
cross from a distance. I was mentally drained, but not
tired at all. I knew I was in the presence of one of the
most powerful and splendid monuments of art I had ever
contemplated, something rich, compelling and profound.
All the mystery of life seemed to lie within it. As I gazed
at it, I recognized again its power. And I recognized the
power it would have over me. I knew, at that moment,
I would do anything to possess it.

CHAPTER EIGHT

Harsh Conditions

I LOOKED TOWARD the end of the table where Topic was hunched over his newspaper. I wished I could walk into the recesses of the man's mind and determine just what he would take for the cross. Would he be reasonable? What the devil would the price come to be? I had concluded that three hundred thousand dollars would be fair for Topic Mimara and The Cloisters. It was also an amount I felt I could persuade Rorimer to go along with, after some agony.

"Your cross is truly fabulous," I assured him. "But, frankly, I see there will be some problems in our purchasing it. I hope to persuade Mr. Rorimer that it will be done, but the outcome depends on your price."

"Not entirely." Topic snapped.

"What do you mean?" He had surprised me.

"The outcome, Signor Hoving," he said coolly, "depends upon your rivals—Boston, Cleveland, the Louvre, the British Museum, and the Victoria and Albert Museum. I have not ruled out an auction at Sotheby's. Mr. Peter Wilson, the director of Sotheby, wants the cross very badly."

"You mean to tell me seriously all these institutions are going after your cross? Even Boston?"

"Yes. Of course. Only Swarzenski tells me they probably do not have the money. Interest, yes."

Suddenly I plunged into another pit of despair.

"Is there anything I can do to ensure that the Metropolitan gets it?" I asked eagerly.

"I can only say, the suitor first with the money gets the girl," Topic said, smiling broadly.

"And what kind of a dowry does a suitor have to bring?"

"For you, the Metropolitan Museum, the price will be six hundred thousand dollars."

"Is that the same price as for the others?" I asked in a subdued voice. The price seemed astronomical. James Rorimer would never think of that.

"No, the price is *not* the same for all others," Topic stated flatly.

"Is that fair?"

"Yes. Being fair is the precise issue when one is holding in trust for the world such a masterpiece as my great Winchester Cross. I have decided for various reasons, principally because the cross is English and dates to the period before the Norman Conquest, to offer it to the British for one hundred and fifty thousand pounds. That is approximately fifty thousand dollars less than to you."

"Mr. Topic, what about Cleveland? And the Louvre?"

"For them, for you and everyone but the British Museum, it will be six hundred thousand dollars."

"That is an exceedingly high price, sir," I observed quietly. "Some people might even call it absurd."

"This cross is exceptionally great. Those people who quarrel with such a fair price, it is they who are absurd. Do you feel, Signor Hoving, that this price is absurd?"

"Is there any chance at all the price can be lowered?" I said.

"Absolutely no chance, Signor Hoving. You must try to understand. Many great and wealthy institutions understand my price. They came to me. I did not travel throughout the world, begging from them. If you must know the true facts, I am not so deeply interested in selling the cross. I have no need for money. My price is small. My cross is the finest cross surviving in the two thousand years of Christianity. Truly, have you ever seen anything like it, Signor Hoving? Tell me, how many crosses are equal to it? And where are they to be found? You have undoubtedly encountered hundreds of medieval crosses. Name me—quickly, now—one that exists any-place on the entire surface of the globe which compares to the cross belonging to Topic Mimara. There is only one ivory cross which is almost equal to mine. You are familiar with it. It is the processional ivory cross in the Museo de Arqueologia, Madrid, made for King Ferdinand and his Queen Sancha. But *that* cross, no matter how royal, majestic, large and impressive, lacks any carvings other than decorative motifs and a few animals. If you have seen it, as a scholar and a connoisseur you have to admit it is far less impressive than mine."

"Please, please," I protested vigorously, breaking into the man's litany, "at least the Madrid cross has its original Christ, a spectacular ivory figure."

"My cross has a Christ," Topic countered.

"It doesn't belong. That's clear," I snapped.

"Well, perhaps when my ivory cross was made it had no Christ. At any rate, it doesn't matter. My cross is here on the table. For sale. Now. Or soon! You know, there's a chance I might remove it from sale. Please be under-standing. I want to be very friendly. The fact is, Signor Hoving, you cannot buy the ivory cross in Madrid. You have a chance at mine, but only a small chance, I am beginning to believe."

I shrugged. I knew I had an obligation to negotiate strenuously on behalf of my institution. Yet I resented the petty bargaining. The object was awesome, and I had begun to find Topic's arguments compelling. As I gazed again at the ivory cross, I felt myself surrendering com-pletely to my desire to obtain it. The Cloisters, after all, was rich. Plenty of money was in hand. More would pour in year after year. The funds could not be used for pur-poses other than collecting the rarest treasures. Perhaps the best course was to go all the way, give the man what he demanded. There might even be peripheral benefits. Medieval art might be accorded a certain cachet by the expenditure of a stratospheric sum. Surely, I concluded, money was insignificant in a circumstance of this sort. Art, beauty, the unraveling of the mysteries of the cross—

these were what seemed significant. How could you put a monetary figure on that?

But I couldn't tell that to my committee, or to Rorimer. I needed specific terms. "Could you, sir, spell out your wishes so that I can communicate your proposed arrangement on the sale to the museum?"

"Willingly, Signor Hoving. The price is six hundred thousand dollars. *You*, the Metropolitan, will have to pay for the insurance premiums and the shipping expenses plus the costs of packing the object. Signor Hoving, you realize, of course, what has happened in recent years to the prices of paintings. A Rembrandt just sold for half a million dollars. A Rubens went in England for three quarters of a million dollars. And how many crosses are there? Available? Well, now I think I have persuaded you, no?"

Dutifully, I nodded at him.

"So," Topic continued in his rapid-fire Italian, "now you know my price. And my price will never dimnish, even by one dollar. In fact, after a certan date I will increase it to one million dollars if no one agrees to my current price."

"What about Harold Parsons?" I inquired. "Is he getting a commission? And, if so, from whom? Me? You?"

"Harold Parsons has done only a small amount of work. *I* have done it all. His commission will be a flat fee, and I will pay for that. But there are other conditions. *No* photographs will be available, and under no conditions will the cross, or any part of it, leave this vault for examination."

"But, Signor Topic," I protested, "you certainly must know it is common practice, at least at the Metropolitan, for a vendor to send photographs and the object—I repeat, the object itself—to the museum for study. We will pay for all costs."

"That practice, Signor Hoving," Topic said acidly, "is no doubt the reason why the Metropolitan has lost already once before the unique chance to acquire my great cross. Any scholar, specialist, museum director, curator—anybody interested must come here. And I must be present always."

"But surely you recognize," I pleaded, "that for a work of art of this magnitude we have to utilize certain scientific tests. Ultraviolet light, for example, which, as you must know, can establish the general age of an ivory and determine the nature of whatever restoration there may be. Mr. Rorimer was personally responsible for having developed the ultraviolet-light technique."

"Mr. Rorimer may flash his black light upon the cross all he wants. Here! But I made what minor restorations there are and I will point them all out to you. Mr. Rorimer has no need for ultraviolet light. But if he insists, he must bring his machine here to the vault."

"I want you to know that I shall have an insurmountable problem if the cross cannot be sent to New York for physical examination. You see, it is not simply the decision of a curator or even the director which commits the Metropolitan to purchase something. We have a board of trustees and a special committee of the board which must by our internal laws study a proposed acquisition and vote on it. It is mandatory, especially with such an expensive thing."

"Excellent!" Topic shot out. "These trustees can come here to the vault."

"But, good God, they won't do that. These are important and busy people."

"The cross is more important than they. The cross, after all, will live forever. Of course they will come, Signor Hoving. You can easily persuade them. Surely the trustees of the great Metropolitan Museum of Art in New York City can afford a trip to Zurich. I shall be pleased to greet all of them here. On the steps of the bank."

"It simply won't work," I muttered gloomily. "Why can't you make it simple, Signor Topic? You could easily bring the cross to New York and show it in person to James Rorimer and key members of our board. Three, four days is all it would take."

"Signor Hoving, as I told you, I do not intend to go begging throughout the world. The suitor who wants the girl must woo her, and to do that successfully he must come here."

"Your conditions are harsh. Are there any more?"

"There are certain conditions which will make the proceedings very easy for you. If you find the money hard to raise at once, I would be pleased to allow you to buy the cross over a period of years—say three years—without interest payments. And I will guarantee the authenticity of my masterpiece. I will sign a document stating that if at any time solid proof is forthcoming from the appropriate experts indicating the great cross is not genuine, I wll take the treasure back and will make full compensation, as well as interest payments. The final condition will also be beneficial to you. I will not sell my cross to anyone prior to the first of January, 1962. The reason for this is that I plan to publish an extensive article on it in a distinguished art publication before the beginning of the new year. That allows you almost three full months to persuade Mr. Rorimer and the trustees."

I fell silent while I pondered the truly impossible situation. Was there hope at all? Probably not! If it was acquired at the price Topic named, the cross would be the most expensive example of decorative art in history. And nothing of such value had ever been bought by the Metropolitan Museum without weeks of minute examination in our laboratories and a number of presentations to the board.

"Signor Topic," I spoke up at length, "I am going to tell you things which I should not. What I shall say is against our regulations. You must promise never to repeat my words—to anyone!"

The man nodded eagerly and looked at me gravely. "Speak," he said in a half-whisper. "I pledge silence forever."

"The Cloisters is a great and wealthy museum on its own. Richly endowed. Twice, and more, the amount you seek for the cross is already in the bank. Each year, funds equal to what you ask accrue from our endowment. I personally have no objection to our paying six hundred thousand dollars. I will struggle to achieve that goal. But despite my powers of persuasion, I cannot, alone, make the deal. James Rorimer *must* be fully in favor. He is a brilliant man—and a vain one. If he does not have a significant role in examining your ivory, 'discovering' it, negotiating for it, making the final decision, the purchase will never occur. Only he will be able to persuade the trustees. My job is to entice him to see the cross. I must persuade him to come here before it is too late. To do that quickly, I absolutely *must* have a set of professional photographs. So you must think over your refusal. Please, don't tell me now. Let us meet briefly tomorrow. Think it over tonight and tell me tomorrow. Mr. Rorimer is not someone who takes kindly to competition. He would prefer having an exclusive option on the cross."

"Who would not?"

"But I have a way of eliminating my rivals to your advantage."

"And that is?" Topic demanded gruffly.

"I propose, and I believe Mr. Rorimer will agree, that The Cloisters purchase one or two other works of art in your collection in addition to the cross. Perhaps that beautiful chess piece, the ivory knight, or the precious boxwood Madonna and Child. And after we have bought the cross and these additional objects we will also exhibit, under your name, a selection of your other English pieces in the grand gallery at The Cloisters for a certain period of time. This way, you will find, the value of all your objects will rise substantially. I can assure you, no other institution will offer what I have suggested."

Topic Mimara shrugged heavily. "Interesting. I shall think about it. But now we must depart," he said abruptly. "It is three-thirty. The bank wishes all guests to leave by four."

I couldn't believe we had been there more than five hours. I should have felt exhausted, but I was not tired at all. I could have remained until midnight.

Just as we were about to walk out, something stopped me. I realized I had overlooked something vital to the examination of the cross. "Please, Signor Topic Mimara, grant me a favor. Would you kindly remove the bronze figure of Christ?"

He did not offer the slightest objection. He merely shrugged and grasped the bronze Christ in his large, stubby hand. The figure came off so easily, it almost seemed it had never been attached. Relieved of the incongruous decoration, the cross became even lighter, more sinuous. I could immediately perceive subtleties I had not noticed before. The bottom shaft bent almost imperceptibly to the right. And the top shaft curved delicately to the left. Optically, the cross seemed straighter than it actually was. The artist had overcome, ingeniously, a problem inherent in the curved material he had used.

And soon I noticed something else, which had been partly obscured by the bronze figure. The two branches of the Tree of Life were directly linked to the content of the carved scenes. The vertical shaft sprang from the figures of Adam and Eve and grew directly to the Ascension of Christ. From death to eternal life. The horizontal shaft of the tree stretched in one unbroken span from the dead Christ, entombed, to the figure of Christ resurrected. Again, from death to life. And where the two shafts crossed stood Moses, who, pointing to the Brazen Serpent, proclaimed Christ and eternal life. So a part of the complex message of the ivory cross was that death would become life through Christ.

It was almost four o'clock, and now I saw still something else that had been obscured before. Along the center of the two branches of the Tree of Life ran a series of circles with a dot in every center. Each dot was painted red. The motif continued along both shafts except in one key area. About halfway from the bottom of the vertical the dotted circles vanished. The rest of the tree was smooth. I knew instantly what that meant: a figure of the Christ *must* have originally adorned the cross. Where the body of the Savior would have covered the circle, the sculptor had not bothered to carve them. Within seconds, I discovered other undeniable signs of a missing Christ. Just under the central medallion I found a single ivory peg cut down flush to the surface of the shaft, which obviously was where the head of Christ must originally have been attached. And what about the hands? Now that I knew what I was looking for, I found their fittings easily. Along the horizontal shaft of the tree, on each side of the medallion, were two holes filled in and concealed no doubt by Topic Mimara.

By some chance had the Christ survived? If so, could I, by some incredible stroke of luck, track it down? I concentrated hard and was able to bring to mind Adolph Goldschmidt's omnibus catalogue of medieval ivory carvings. For my doctoral thesis I had studied each page of the Goldschmidt *Corpus*, several hundred of them, a dozen times. My visual retention had always been keen. In the volume devoted to ivories of the twelfth century made in England or France, I recalled two ivory figures of Christ. Both were large enough to have been the

original Christ on Topic's cross. One I captured in my eye
as being closest in style; it was thin, with drapery folds
cut into sharp chevron patterns, very much like some
figures on the cross. I would explore that further.

Topic was becoming extremely impatient, but I couldn't
bring myself to leave. I wanted just a few more minutes
to determine what was missing from the cross. For sure,
the bottom block. One side would have been carved with
the angel of Saint Matthew. The other? I was confident
that in time I could identify what had been carved there.
What if that missing piece existed and could be found!
It could provide the strongest clue, even proof, of where
the cross had been created and by whom. It was logical
to assume that the bottom block would carry the name
of the artist or the patron for whom it was made.

"Now, it is *absolutely* time to depart," Topic said
crisply, taking hold of the cross. "But first I shall show
you how the first Crusaders took my ivory cross to the
Holy Land. It was made to be taken apart so it could be
placed in saddlebags. There are no pegs or nails to fasten
it together. The three principal pieces are held in place
by a clever system of tongues and grooves, which press
together to form a bond."

Topic Mimara gently took hold of the horizontal and
vertical shafts at the medallion. With his right hand, he
grasped the vertical shaft at the top. With a slight tug
it came away from the rest. "Like the head of Christ,
falling forward on the cross," he whispered.

Then he removed the horizontal shaft and inclined it
to one side. "The arms of Christ free from the nails which
pierced his hands," he said.

Finally Topic pulled the bottom shaft from its fitting
and slowly laid it before us. "The body descends from
the cross."

What a curious mixture of a man, I thought, as I left
the underground vaults.

CHAPTER NINE

A Certain Vision

I THANKED TOPIC PROFUSELY for allowing us to examine his "magnificent, unique treasure," and arranged to meet with him the next morning. Then I headed for a religious bookstore at the Schifflände, overlooking the charming river Limmat, which wends its way through the center of the city. There I purchased two Bibles, one in Latin and the other a standard King James version. I was annoyed that I could not obtain a Latin version with an index of key words from most-quoted passages. Without such an index, my task of identifying the sixty or so inscriptions would be more difficult.

I returned to my hotel and, in a feverish state of mind, began to race through the Latin Bible, seeking the phrases that appeared on the cross. No sooner had I begun to scan book after book, chapter after chapter, verse after verse, than I sat back horrified. God, where to begin? I was riffling through the thousand pages of the Latin version with a deepening sense of discouragement, when I happened to stop at Solomon's Song of Songs. I'd start there, searching for the phrase from Solomon, *Ascendam*

ipalmam . . ., "I shall ascend into the palm tree . . ."
Why not begin with the magical tree?

There are only eight chapters in the Song of Solomon, but there are few passages more enigmatic. How does one interpret the Song of Songs?

> Behold, you are fair, my love . . . You have doves' eyes within your locks; your hair is as a flock of goats . . .
>
> Your lips are like a thread of scarlet . . .
>
> Your two breasts are like two young roes that are twins . . .
>
> Your lips, O my spouse, drop as the honeycomb: honey and milk are under your tongue . . .
>
> Your naval is like a round goblet . . . your belly is like a heap of wheat set about with lilies . . .
>
> This your stature is like to a palm tree . . .
>
> I will ascend into the palm tree, and will take hold of the fruits thereof . . .

I knew that, during the Middle Ages, theologians did not consider these lines to be a love poem, but a reflection of the adoration of the church for Christ. The phrases about the palm tree were thought to signify the Crucifixion.

I just did not believe it. To me the Song of Solomon was a lusty poem of love. And why not? Why shouldn't a king, even a Biblical king, give way to passion? After all, hadn't King David taken Bathsheba as a lover, and then killed her husband? Despite his transgression, David had not been punished. That, I ruminated, was the very essence of the Old Testament, the Old Law. Under the Old Law, only God could punish; only God could grant forgiveness. That was why, of course, Christ absolutely horrified the Jews, who espoused the law of Moses. Christ advocated that confession of sins *to Him* guaranteed forgiveness. No wonder the Jews had looked upon Christ as a heretic. Imagine the mere confession of sins producing full absolution. When that thought came to me I sat straight up on my bed. *King of the Confessors!* I suddenly understood the implications of the text on the cross. With that one phrase, the cross embodied the root of Christianity!

My mind raced. I was at last getting somewhere. Christ was *not* the King of the Jews. Never wanted to be.

Never said it, really. Never cared. Being king would be merely secular, temporal. Christ was God. Only God could take confession and forgive those who confessed to Him. Confession was the cornerstone of the New Law. The cross was the symbol of the most fundamental revolution in religious history.

I left the hotel, feeling elated, and strolled the city. It was late and the streets were virtually deserted. I contemplated the cross and considered carefully how I might convince Rorimer of its incomparable importance. Eventually I returned to the hotel and slept fitfully through the night.

I had visions of crosses, dozens of them, swirling on the ceiling above me. All kinds, all shapes. The rich "tapestry" crosses of early Christian Ireland; the elongated crosses of Byzantium; crosses as weapons, swords, hammers of war; the expressionistic crosses of the tenth and eleventh centuries; the ivory cross owned by Topic. What was it? Where had it been for centuries? What message did it impart? The last thing I remember from my dream was a shadow passing over the cross, blackening it as if ink had been spilled over its glistening branches.

The new day was bright, lucid. Topic Mimara came to my hotel promptly at ten, and for the first few minutes I had the disquieting impression he had forgotten our long meeting the day before. He looked different, older, haggard. His face was grayish-brown, well worn, like a used rucksack. When I asked if I could go to the bank to examine the cross one more time, he asked, rather desultorily, "Why?"

Eventually he consented. This time there was no ceremony. He pulled out the cross and set it on a small table near the door to his vault.

Had it been a mirage? Was the cross as magnificent as I had thought? I gazed at it intently. The chain of figures seemed even more exquisite than before, and the symbolism more audacious. As I gazed at them, my nerves became taut. What if I were unable to obtain the cross?

Topic allowed me no more than fifteen minutes, and then draped the black cloth over his treasure and placed it back in the vault. This time he did permit me a glance inside. There, on one of the shelves, was a foot-high stack

of new bank notes. Topic laughed. He plucked the top
bill off the pile, gave it a snap, and held it out.

"This is a one-thousand-Swiss-franc note, Signor Hoving. You are wondering how many there are. I shall not
say exactly, beyond suggesting that the sum approaches
one million of your dollars." Topic smiled wanly. "Now
what do you want to talk to me about?"

"Surely you recall," I muttered in some confusion.
"Your final decision on photographs? The purchase of
certain other works of art? The exhibition of some of
your things at The Cloisters?"

"The rules shall be the same for everyone who wants
my cross. I shall give out no pictures before my publication of the cross is complete. The price is six hundred
thousand dollars until the publication. Afterward, it will
go up. Or I shall not sell it at all. At this moment, I do
not know which. The Cloisters may purchase a small
number of other English works of art, modest pieces, but
those purchases will have no bearing on the cross. The
rules must be the same."

A hard anger began to burn within me. "Signor Topic,
why don't you come out and say it? You do not wish to
sell your cross to the Metropolitan under any circumstances. Right? I'll bet last night after our meeting you
telephoned the officials in England at the Victoria and
Albert or the British Museum or both and told them I had
seen the cross and would do anything to obtain it. Didn't
you let them know of my interest? Didn't you urge them
to move swiftly before I could advise Rorimer? Isn't that
true?"

"You might be right," he said evenly.

I was furious.

"I want the rules to be the same for everyone."

"You damn well know the rules are *not* the same.
You've arranged it so I don't have a chance."

"The rules to the English are a bit more favorable,
you are correct. The reasons are simple. The cross is
from Winchester Cathedral. By all rights, it should be
returned to the country of its origin. The British are not
as wealthy as you. After all, as you told me, the Metropolitan does have more than enough money in hand."

"Did you tell the British that?" I demanded.

"I simply observed that the Metropolitan and The

Cloisters together were rich. No. I would never have violated my pledge."

"Why continue this charade, Signor Topic?" My voice rasped. "Why not just tell me to forget it? I have other works of art to pursue. Your blessed cross isn't the only object in the world, you know."

"Signor Hoving, sit down. Calm down. Listen to my words," he said in a soothing voice. "If you work hard and if you are tenacious, you may win the prize. You are further ahead in the race than you suspect. The English know they must raise the money, and quickly, or they may lose to you. They informed me that they will use some of their museum funds and then will apply to Parliament for the rest. They are confident they will succeed. But I personally am not so sure. Work hard and you may win. It requires only a certain vision."

"Who are you, anyway?" I said, my voice rising.

"I . . . am . . . I am nothing more than a humble painter and restorer who has no secrets. I have searched for the greatest art treasures and have, by luck, and by my eyes, discovered a few. That is all."

"I mean who are you *really*, Mr. Topic Mimara?" I repeated coldly.

"A friend. Let us be friendly."

Later that day I sat listlessly in my lonely room, gazing dully at the wall. Before packing for my evening trip to Florence, I decided I would write as eloquent a letter as I could to Ante Topic Mimara.

Dear Mr. Topic Mimara,

It is difficult to describe my feelings of profound pleasure after seeing your masterpieces and the chief of all masterworks of English Romanesque art, your great cross. I was and continue to be profoundly impressed and moved by the experience. The opportunity to meet you has been one of the most important experiences in my career so far. The chance to encounter a collector of such brilliance, of such commanding forthrightness and of such modesty will seldom occur again. I am convinced of that.

Although I am as yet young *and* inexperienced as you so correctly pointed out, I have learned one key thing regarding collecting which I feel constrained to point out

to you. *That is:* the love of an institution toward a work
of art transcends all other considerations—money, scholarship, anything else. A real collector should always place
his most cherished objects where they will be loved. I
must impress upon you that no institution other than
The Cloisters, no curator other than me, will ever convey
an equal appreciation for your cross. To my way of
looking at it, your transcendentally fine cross belongs in
New York for this reason beyond all else. And, as I
told you and wish to repeat (my Italian can be somewhat primitive when I get excited), The Cloisters does
have money to support my zeal for the breathtaking
object. Please, think hard, and give me the chance to
make it possible for my Director to come speedily to
Zurich and examine and then acquire your majestic work.

It was definitely not the kind of letter I wanted to read
more than once. I sealed it immediately and carried it
by hand to Topic Mimara's hotel and saw to it the thing
was placed in his mailbox. Then, after returning to my
hotel, I wrote in a different vein to Jim Rorimer.

About Zurich and Topic Mimara I will say for the
moment nothing. There is nothing to do at this time
anyway. Two things only: this cross—all morse ivory,
60 cm. high, with literally *dozens* of beautiful figures and
inscriptions—is one of the most exciting ivories I have
ever seen, and those words are not to be taken lightly.
Topic still cannot give photos. He promised the British
Museum that he would not until publication in January.
But I pulled a bit of a sneaky. When he left the room
of the bank vault for a minute I took five quick pictures
with a concealed Minox camera. I hope they came out. . . .

I told the story to Peg Freeman straight.

The Zurich operation was exciting but bizarre. Topic
is big, hail-fellow-well-met, and, thank God, he spoke
Italian, so communication was easy. The cross—something like this, 60 centimeters in height—is one of the
most thrilling objects I have ever seen.

It has five full scenes, some nineteen large Apostles
and Prophets and, I swear, no less than 50-55 inscriptions. The style, it seemed to me, is around or near St.
Albans and circa 1120 A.D. The price for this *beauty* is
also a "beaut"—for him, not us. It rests at a comfort-

able $600,000. To me it is worth it—but as it was with the Hugo cross, I know Jim will not be at all interested. I did manage to take a few pictures with my "apparechio d'espionnaggio," so we have something to tempt him with.

By the time I reached Florence my energies had been renewed. Within a few days I swept through eight dealers and visited some of my favorite galleries and museums. During my whirlwind tour I managed to pick up some fascinating, and disturbing, information about Topic Mimara.

One of the dealers, Salvatore Romano, a totally honest individual, and immensely charming, had met Topic five years before, in 1955, and had been shown several black-and-white photographs of an "ivory processional cross." According to Romano, Topic had wanted to sell the piece quickly for a fairly modest price. Nothing had come of the encounter; when Romano tried to reach him for further discussion, the man had mysteriously disappeared.

"Salvatore, do you know anyone else who is acquainted with Topic Mimara or might have had dealings with him?"

"I did not trust the man. If you are going to have dealings with him, be cautious. Yes, I do know of someone who is said to have had dealings with this Topic. The *avocato* Albrighi knows him."

I had no desire to meet with the *avocato,* or lawyer, Albrighi. He had a poisonous reputation, having been jailed and disbarred several years before for being part of an art-smuggling ring. But I thought it necessary to see him.

"I was framed, of course," Albrighi breezily explained to me when we met over espresso in a hole-in-the-wall café I had chosen in a back street off the Piazza della Repubblica.

"Of *course*," I said.

"Some of the insidious dealers—I shall not name them —had established an efficient and brazen method of illegal exportation. Deplorable! Think of it! Certain art treasures, the very artistic heritage of my cherished country, were leaving Italy openly like rich tourists. Then the Carabinieri infiltrated this scandalous ring. There was panic. Some very renowned and influential gentlemen of Florence were involved and feared for their careers and fortunes. The police became fearful, too, when they *saw* how many *commendatori, professori* and men of exalted position in Florence were a part of such disgraceful proceedings. And so you see, it was arranged that *I* would be framed—I along with a restorer of paintings who, by chance, was one of my clients and may actually have been marginally involved in the operation. I was arrested, tried and convicted. I appealed. I was convicted again— falsely. With a clear heart and conscience I went to jail. But not for long. The affair is over. I have not really been damaged. I still work in the law, though not officially. But that does not matter. This, after all, my friend, is Italy. Say, are you here seeking works of art? Is there something I can do to help? I have been quietly a part of some important arrangements over the years, particularly for America. One of my favorites—ah, what a story I could tell!—was a rare marble panel, coming from a renowned sanctuary right here in—"

"Albrighi, Albrighi," I cut in frantically, not wanting to hear more about what I was positive was going to be the Annunciation relief. "I care nothing about works of art right now. Only about a man, a collector whom you know."

Albrighi leaned back comfortably and gave me a thin smile.

"The fellow's name is Ante Topic Mimara," I said. "He is Yugoslavian, but apparently holds an Austrian passport. At one time he lived in Italy. His collection is large, containing all kinds of materials—objets d'art, antiquities, sculptures, paintings, drawings, stained glass. Do you know him?"

"I know him well," Albrighi answered in a whisper.

"He was once a close friend and partner, of a sort. Topic Mimara is dangerous. He can at times be foolish. Always a bothersome mixture. He is an art dealer, a painting restorer, a forger, a thief, a genius at survival. He has been involved in some highly questionable affairs outside the field of art, too."

"My God, tell me," I croaked.

"Topic Mimara was the chief of the Yugoslavian mission at the Allied Art Collecting Point in Munich in 1948 or 1949. As such, he was a powerful man. He worked ceaselessly for his country, Communist Yugoslavia. You will hear from time to time that Topic Mimara hates Tito and Communism. That is a sham. He is part of the regime. But Topic Mimara Matutin also works ceaselessly for himself. From time to time the two masters, state and self, become blurred. As an example, when Topic was at the Collecting Point in Munich, he tracked down an amazing hoard of gold and silver ingots which the Nazis had deposited at the bottom of a small lake. Topic Matutin sent most of the ingots to Belgrade, but retained a certain portion for himself. He placed his share in some bank in Zurich. Overnight he became rich, and began to collect massively—sometimes well, sometimes foolishly. As far as I know, the Tito government never raised any objections to his taking the precious metals, which can mean only one thing."

I sat there, stunned by the information. In one part of my mind, I yearned to hear more. In another, I wanted silence. Every piece of news, real or imagined, fact or rumor, which tended to tarnish the man's reputation was an impediment to my gaining the cross.

"From the look of astonishment on your face, young man, I am not sure it would be prudent for me to say more about Topic. Anyway, I'm not conversant with all the facts. Which pieces in his collection are you after? No, don't tell me. But I'll tell you who really knows this character. Volbach. Fritz Wolfgang Volbach. In Rome. *He* knows. Perhaps you should talk to him. Then again, perhaps not. In art, sometimes it's better to listen to a *portion* of a tale. Art is the only thing that matters, not the people surrounding art. Art is pure. Human beings are not."

I remained a few more days in Florence simply to savor

the artistic treasures of the city. My first stop was the
Bargello, the sculpture museum containing works by such
giants of Renaissance and Baroque sculpture as Ghiberti,
Donatello, Michelangelo and Giambologna. The place is
a veritable pantheon of Florentine sculpture, but it also
has some medieval artifacts in an upper gallery. Visitors
seldom bother to go there, climbing the steep and narrow
flights of stairs. I did, partly because I wanted to pass
some time before dinner and partly because I remembered a collection of decorative arts, primarily medieval,
gathered together in the late nineteenth century by an
obscure French collector named Carrand.

Carrand had acquired some good medieval reliquaries
and a number of fine French ivory caskets and diptychs
of the fourteenth century. He had also managed to get
his hands on one of the rarest objects in the medieval
world—a fan carved in ivory, used to keep flies away during the Mass. The carvings on the handle depicted
dozens of saints, prophets and church fathers, all crammed
together along with scenes from the life of Saint Nicholas.
The fan was described as French, possibly English, dating
to the twelfth or early thirteenth century. Fascinated by
the piece, I made a slow circle around the glass case,
identifying the scenes, making notes.

Suddenly I froze. In a nearby case, a small ivory
plaque caught my eye. From a few feet away my eyes
recorded all: the sharp undercut beard of the individual,
his beady eye, the slender index finger pointing expres-
sively, the chevron folds of the drapery, the profusion of
circles with dots painted red, and the creamy surface of
walrus ivory.

I didn't rush over to it at once. I had the incongruous
feeling that if I did, a guard would jump out from nowhere and apprehend me. I walked over casually, never
letting it out of my sight. The ivory was about three
inches by three, with a peaked roof decorated with a
sunburst identical to the one on the cross. The figure was
bust length and carved in profile. Its right hand pointed
to a budding tree, whose trunk was decorated with the
same circles and dots as those on the cross. *Everything*—
the facial features, hair, beard, costume, drapery—was the
same as on Topic's crucifix. There was even a scroll
inscribed VIRGA: AARON—the rod of Aaron. The bold

capital letters were identical to the writings on the cross;
even the punctuation was the same.

I had to get the ivory in my hands! The back might be
marked or inscribed in some way which would help me
unlock the secrets of the cross. I turned toward the stairs
to seek out the director of the museum, or the curator
in charge of the Carrand collection, to request the re-
moval of the piece from the glass case. Abruptly I
stopped. Permission might take days; I would have to
suffer through interminable meetings with the museum
bureaucracy. After all, I was in Italy. And when in
Rome . . .

I scouted the gallery on tiptoe, listening at the entrance
and the stairs. The place was deserted. The guards probably glanced into the upper galleries no more than twice
a day, at opening and closing. I looked at my watch.
There was plenty of time.

I examined the case containing the walrus ivory plaque
with the eyes of a professional curator. I could see no
wires or electrical fittings for an alarm. I kneeled down
and placed a fifty-lire coin under the case. In the event a
guard suddenly appeared I could pretend I had dropped
the small change and was retrieving it. Dropping to my
knees, I studied the wooden floor at the base of each of
four legs on the glass case. There was no change of
color in the wood indicating passage for wires. Good! I
looked carefully up at the bottom of the case. No signs
of a drawer for dry-cell batteries. Then I rose and studied
the interior of the case, to see if there were signs of a
pressure alarm mechanism. Nothing. I put my ear to the
case and gave it a gentle kick. No muffled reverberations
of bells which would have told me there was an alarm
system activated by a spring.

The case had no locks or keyholes. There were only
four screws, one on each side, holding the glass top in
place. I got out my Swiss Army knife. I hesitated for
several seconds, listening like an animal. I chuckled to
myself and started in. Within a few minutes, I had un-
screwed them all.

Carefully touching the glass with my knuckles—I had
heard somewhere that this technique would yield no
fingerprints—I lifted the vitrine. It came off smoothly. I
set it back on its base like a cocked hat, reached in and

with a slightly trembling hand picked up the walrus ivory. Breathlessly, I turned it over. There were no inscriptions: just the smooth surfaces of walrus ivory, crosshatched randomly by thin lines.

I studied the diminutive work with fierce determination, assimilating its details into my memory. As I cradled the piece in my hands I became even more convinced that the representation of Aaron and his budding rod or tree had to have been carved by the artist of Topic Mimara's cross. The tiny plaque was definitely a part of it. But what part? Where did it belong? I had no idea. I swore to myself I would find out.

For an instant I even thought the unthinkable. Then I smiled to myself and replaced the piece, the glass top, and the screws. When the task was done, ten thousand needles of excitement and pleasure pricked me. I remained in the gallery studying the ivory until closing time. No guard ever appeared.

The next morning I introduced myself to a totally uninterested member of the curatorial staff of the Bargello and asked to study what might be written about the Aaron plaque in the catalogue cards of the museum. Two days later I received permission for this routine scholarly request. Ah, Italy! The catalogue entry noted only that the collector, Carrand, had purchased the ivory in Paris in 1867. No specific art gallery, dealer or collector was mentioned. That was all.

I politely asked the official if the vitrine containing the Aaron ivory could be opened, to allow me to inspect the ivory more closely. I explained that physical examination would be critical for my researches. The facial expression of the curator—part disdain, part mock exhaustion—put an end to that fantasy. It took me another half day to obtain permission just to enter the sacrosanct room of the city library to peruse the four volumes of Adolph Goldschmidt.

The Aaron plaque was described in the fourth volume. Unfortunately, even Goldschmidt had dug up little factual information about the piece. He seemed to vacillate between a French and an English provenance and could not decide on a specific date other than the decades from 1170 to 1200. The distinguished scholar had made a quality judgment which matched mine. He called the ivory "excellent in workmanship." Goldschmidt also explained who Aaron was and what the tree signified. The story was to be found in the Book of Numbers.

Jehovah had commanded Moses to gather all heads of Israelite families and tribes to place their wooden rods, the symbols of authority, in the temple. The tribe or family whose rod flowered into a tree would be made perpetual priests of Israel. Aaron's rod had flourished, so he and his progeny became the holy men. In medieval times, the episode must have been taken as a clear reference to the living wood of the cross upon which the Messiah would die for the salvation of mankind.

I sat in the cool, dim recesses of the library, luxuriating in the smell of ancient books and the feel of the great leatherbound elephant folios of the Goldschmidt *Corpus,* which I leafed through, page after page. On each appeared several superbly printed black-and-white reproductions of medieval ivories from collections throughout the world. I marveled at the grandiose quality of the books. And then, as I turned the page, I almost yelled out loud in the quiet hall. I was looking at a photo reproduction of what seemed undeniably to be the original figure of Christ from my cross.

Eagerly, I scanned Goldschmidt's description. The figure was in the Decorative Arts Museum in Copenhagen, and I wondered how quickly I could go there to see it. The Christ was definitely walrus ivory. According to Adolph Goldschmidt, it was either Norwegian or English in origin.

I translated Goldschmidt's convoluted German with my heart beating loudly, hoping for some sort of proof. Then, as quickly as my hopes had been raised, they were dashed. For, according to Goldschmidt, on the back of the figure of Christ was carved a portion of the Tree of Life. "Damn," I exclaimed softly as I slumped into my chair. Since the Tree of Life on Topic's cross was intact, the Christ in Copenhagen could not possibly be the original. I studied the photograph intently. It had seemed so plausible! But I knew, of course, that the punctilious Adolph Goldschmidt could not possibly have been wrong. I finally decided that the superb Christ must be another masterpiece by the gifted artist of my cross, no doubt a vital part of yet another cross.

I quit Florence feeling elated by my discovery of the Aaron plaque and the Christ. I was not at all discouraged that the Copenhagen Christ did not belong to the cross. I had convinced myself that, in time, I would find the real one. I was hopeful that Volbach or Harold Parsons would provide some positive information. When I reached Rome I settled into a modest *pensione* situated halfway up the Quirinal Hill. I chose it for sentimental reasons: I had lived in the same building with my wife for close to a year in 1956 and 1957, studying art and archaeology.

I telephoned Parsons and arranged to meet him late the next evening. I politely declined his offer to escort me around Rome with his car and chauffeur. I wanted nothing to compete with my own personal embrace of my beloved city, which I prided myself on being more passionate about than anyone else in the world.

Fritz Volbach's name was not to be found in the phone book. But in time I obtained his address and telephone number by appealing to an assistant librarian at the German Institute, where I had spent hundreds of hours in my studies. I finally got his wife on the phone, but not him.

"But why do you want my husband?" she asked me.

"Oh, just to pay my respects, because I'm a student of early Christian art, a pupil of Kurt Weitzmann and an admirer of your husband's works." I paused, and then plunged ahead. "I also want to ask Dr. Volbach about a man he is said to know, Mr. Topic Mimara, and a very special work of art he owns, a large ivory cross."

There was such a lengthy silence on the phone, I thought the woman had put down the receiver.

"I'm not so sure," Mrs. Volbach replied hesitantly. "Yes, he is acquainted with Mr. Topic Mimara and the cross. I am afraid I cannot say anything. You will have to ask him."

"Is your husband at home?"

"No. Right now he is in New York."

Damn!

"Would you kindly let me know where your husband

can be reached in New York? Perhaps one of my col-leagues at the Metropolitan Museum can contact him."

There was another long pause from Mrs. Volbach. "He moves around a great deal," she finally told me. "You might try Dr. Alfred Rosin on East Seventy-fifth Street. Goodbye."

I dispatched an express letter to Peg Freeman urging her "to meet Volbach while he's in town, because he knows more about the cross than anyone. It is important!"

I rented a motor scooter and next morning, at dawn, started off on an all-day tour of Rome. I followed no pre-ordained route; I simply launched off at top speed and roared from one section of the sprawling city to another —from its outskirts on the Via Appia to its heart at the Capitoline, stopping to render homage to my favorite remnants of art and time.

I visited dozens of monuments. One which particularly intrigued me was the red brick early Christian church of Santa Sabina. What I had come to see was one of the marvels of the early Christian epoch, a massive wooden door dating to the fifth century, carved with panels showing episodes from the Old and New Testaments. Though primitive in style, they seemed to burst with the kind of artistic vitality that can only issue forth from true religious faith. Here I gazed at the earliest representation of the Crucifixion. Three stark crosses. Three tortured men. No ceremony. No pomp. The pain of poverty.

I could not resist touching the figure of Christ, over one thousand five hundred years old. Suddenly I recog-nized a powerful similarity between the style of the doors and Topic's cross. Could the artist who created the ivory actually have seen the wooden doors of Santa Sabina and have been inspired by them? The sculptor could easily have been trained in Rome, and then traveled to England. During the twelfth century the ties between English and Roman monasteries were strong indeed.

As I wended my way toward the heart of the city, I paid a visit to the church of San Pietro in Vincoli and Michelangelo's *Moses*. What an image of strength and anxiety! The awesome, shaggy head of the prophet loomed like a mountain above the tangled thick beard falling in twisted thrums through his massive fingers. I had forgotten how highly polished the Moses was. The skin of the sculpture was almost a glaze, like ancient Greek pottery.

On an impulse I made up my mind to look again at another of Michelangelo's sculptures, one which I had always disliked. It stood in the church called Santa Maria Sopra Minerva, and was an eight-foot-high marble image of Christ striding along briskly, holding an immense cross as if it were weightless. I had always found this Christ too vibrant, too robust. I imagined Christ to be an ascetic, someone with burning eyes, *not* an athlete vigorously striding along.

Without warning, something came over me. I seemed to be transported into a world of uncompromising distress and pain. I had what can only be described as a vision, a vivid sense of what it was like to hang upon the cross. There was no physical pain. But I could imagine an agony of unspeakable intensity, stretching every sinew. I could imagine a thirst so dry that it cracked the mouth, the lips and even the body. I could feel the heat of a dozen suns, and then a gradual dulling of the agony. The words "My God, my God, why have you forsaken me?" came into my mind.

I shook my head violently. The vision faded as suddenly as it had come. I remained perfectly still for some minutes, and then I slowly left the church.

The sun was lowering, the shadows were lengthening. The city was beginning to turn into gold as I made my way up the Capitoline Hill. I gazed for a few minutes at the bronze, gold-flecked sculpture of Emperor Marcus Aurelius astride his horse. Then I walked the short distance to the terrace where I could watch the Forum turn from a pale golden to the slate blue and silver shadows of dusk.

CHAPTER TEN

The Singer and the Song

IT WAS LIKE MEETING in the flesh a gentleman of leisure who had stepped right out of an elegant portrait of the turn of the century, perhaps by John Singer Sargent. Harold Woodbury Parsons turned out to be courtly, soft-spoken, witty—and charmingly dishonest. His first words summed him up. He had picked me up in a chauffeur-driven Lancia and started off toward the Piazza Navona and a fashionable restaurant there, I Tre Scalini. He turned toward me, smiled like the proverbial silver-haired uncle, and with a bland expression that added a dash of deviltry to his words he told me, "I am, my boy, a *marchand amateur* who dabbles from time to time in the amusing avocation of making the perfect marriage between a collector, a sublime work of art and a rich American art museum, for their mutual benefit—and for the benefit of yours truly."

Cool, gossamer streams of fresh air caressed my face as I sat at the table on the terrace of the Tre Scalini. October imbued the timeless Piazza Navona with hues of azure, silver and red. I was alive with anticipation to learn what Parsons would say about the cross, Topic Mimara and the many mysteries which surrounded them. But I had decided not to make the first move. I would be casual, detached, and an exemplar of savoir-faire.

Parsons seemed perfectly willing to carry the burden of the conversation. But he too had chosen to be oblique. He started off by lecturing me like a concerned maiden aunt.

"*Never* sit in a draft in Italy, and *always* wear a belly-band."

I stared at him with my face contorted into what I hoped passed for a sincere smile. What the *hell* was a bellyband?

"Note, young man, that Italians never, never sit in drafts," Parsons churned on. "The sun intrigues and tempts; but the wind, which is very slight in Rome—it is the most windless city I know—comes down from snow-capped mountains and is the stealthy stiletto which gives the unnoticed stab in the chest or guts. In fact, cold in the guts is the common complaint, particularly of foreign travelers who exhaust themselves when sightseeing. When one feels cold or shivery in Rome, one has, usually, already got cold. Wear much thicker underwear than at home; clothes which may seem unduly warm in the sun are on the light side when visiting galleries or churches. Never walk to your destination and then—in a state of perspiration, or 'all of the glow,' as the ladies of Boston used to say—plunge into some Frigidaire of a church. It is best to carry a lightweight coat along, to slip on going *in* and peel *off* coming out; just the reverse of our American custom. A very light flannel *panciera*, or bellyband, put on next to the skin and worn for several days, together with instant and complete repose and a light purge, then clear soup, light tea, et cetera, comprises the sovereign remedy for 'cold in the guts,' or *colpo d'aria*, as the Italians call it. Many people wear a light *panciera* all through the winter. The military are obliged to keep their guts and kidneys warm; the rest doesn't matter."

"Well, sir," I told him respectfully, "I sure could have used one of those *panciera* today when I toured this heavenly city starting at dawn. You see, I lived here once years ago for almost a year, and fell in love with the place."

"Oh, *do* tell me about your little tour. I have lived here on and off for, well, sixty years, but I'm always eager to hear how someone else, another expert, would see the city."

I rattled on about where I'd been, what I'd seen, not leaving out a thing, except of course that vision in Santa Maria Sopra Minerva. Parsons took it all in delightedly, breaking his avid silence occasionally by a sharp laugh or a gleeful hand clap. A couple of times he broke in to interrupt when I happened to mention a work of art which he too obviously adored.

"Ah, *ah*," he cried out as I told him of my fondness for Caravaggio's Saint Matthew paintings in the nearby church of San Luigi dei Francesi. "Ah, the figure of the executioner. What a wonderful anatomical drawing! And such a contrast to the equally wonderful but very different draftsmanship of that soft and provocative young Bacchus of his in the Uffizi. Here the hand is cruel, *hard* right down to the glinting highlights on the nails and the formaton of the sinews and underlying *ossatura*. And the blood from the neck of Matthew! It spurts like a gush of Chinese red lacquer. That is the Rome I love."

"The Rome I know and love," I countered, "is Rome the time machine. If you scratch around not very far below the surface or examine the architecture with care, or scramble through museums or stroll the archaeological sites, you are sure to find something from virtually each moment of that unbroken history stretching back from today twenty-seven hundred years to the founding of the city. You can dig into your cellar to replace a hot-water heater and, only inches down, hit upon a perfectly preserved piece of ancient wall built by Oscan masons who were here long before the Romans arrived. It's pure magic. In Rome I have always lived as though I were sitting in a time machine."

Caught up with the pleasing reminiscence of my whirlwind tour and wanting to impress, I filled Parsons' ears. I told him I must have passed through a dozen eras—Paleolithic, Etruscan, Imperial, early Christian, into the full Baroque of the late seventeenth century. I said that on my route, and in my imagination, I trod the

narrow, slippery clay streets of Rome which were there
before the Forum was ever conceived or built. I had
looked through my mind's eye into the abyss where the
legendary Castor and Pollux had plunged. I stood where
the Emperor Augustus planted his feet and uttered his
famous words "I came to this city built of brick, and
left her in marble." I passed along the triumphal route
and rested where Belisarius may have sat in A.D. 536
when he contemplated Rome, once the greatest city of
the ancient world, degenerated by his time into a decrepit village of broken walls, weeds and dust, inhabited
by fewer than five hundred wretched citizens.

I regaled Parsons with how I felt the awesome sense
of human and artistic continuity in the ancient city.
Despite all the upheavals, the sieges, the battles, the
plagues and the pestilences, the violent shifts in religion
and the vicissitudes of human behavior, the city of Rome
seems to remain unchanged. To me the city is the very
symbol of how mankind has survived and will survive in
a delicate balance between soul and matter. Rome, to me,
is proof that both spirituality and materialism exist in a
continuum.

I told him how intrigued I was that, by looking carefully at the stones of a building in Rome, whether it be
temple, church or palace, you can decipher its entire
history, year by year, over centuries. You can tell when
it was built, what it once looked like, when it was
changed, added to, subtracted from—whatever. Each
fragment of Roman architecture is tattooed with its own
history, whether by the shape of the bricks, or the cutting
and style of the marble decoration, or the writings to be
seen covering every structure, writings from ancient
Roman times to the Papacy of the twentieth century—a
palimpsest of history. The depth of the city fascinated
me, too. Exactly fourteen feet down from the level of the
modern city was the level of ancient Rome. I had been
taught by a great professor of architectural history that
the fourteen-foot difference in levels is constant. So one
could go anywhere and dig down fourteen feet and be
two thousand years and more back in time.

"My dear young fellow, you astonish me," Parsons
spoke up when I had at last finished. "I had conjured
up a different image of Thomas Hoving, assistant curator

of The Cloisters, than what I have found. I imagined you as a dour and humorless art historian—a short, fairly fat young fellow—powerfully steeped in some obscure soup of the Middle Ages. A junior James Rorimer. Now, I hope that doesn't offend you. How utterly at odds with my image is reality! Here I find myself conversing with a thin, angular individual with an aristocratic face, refreshingly articulate, seasoning his conversation with wit and sensitivity. I find it all enormously pleasing. Tell me about yourself."

I described my undergraduate years at Princeton and my service in the Marine Corps during the Korean War. I told Parsons I had been planning to become a career officer, but they stopped the war. I was furious. So I quit. I had loved the Corps!

"When I left the Corps," I said, "I went back to Princeton and got my Ph.D. in art history and archaeology. Then to the Met. I'm a professional art collector now. No other activity surpasses the excitement of hunting down a great work of art, probing and searching to reveal its secrets. It's an unbeatable combination of thrills. It's a love affair, a hunt for a mysterious and dangerous beast, a detective story full of perils."

"I'm afraid my life has not been as exciting as yours," Parsons reflected. "I have been a gentleman of leisure ever since I graduated from Harvard in 1904."

He told me he had been blessed with a modest independent income. While he was confident he could have done many things—law, teaching, Wall Street—early on Parsons recognized that he was supremely lazy. So he decided at an early age to become an art advisor.

"The hub of my wheel of life is Italy," he said with enthusiasm. "Its spokes are the glories of Italian art, from pre-Etruscan to modern, although I am *hardly* a modernist. I was brought to Rome by my mother, in 1895, when I was twelve. I remember being taken to the top of the Janiculum Hill within a day or two of my arrival, and that first glorious impression of the auburn-and-gold city stretching forth beneath me never left my mind or my heart. I devoted my life to art, studied art history at Harvard and everywhere else in the world where great art is to be found."

Despite his excellent education, Parsons' first formal

job had come somewhat late in his life. At thirty-seven,
in 1920, he became the official art advisor in Europe for
the Cleveland Museum, which paid him a modest annual
retainer. He explained forthrightly how he received a fee
from the art dealer or collector whose work he placed
with the museum. He had, he assured me, placed some
splendid pieces.

"In the old days it was easy," he sighed. "The market
abounded with masterpieces. Not so today. Ah, well, but
there are still a few hidden here and there, don't you
agree? But we shall discuss that in due time. William
Milliken became the director of the Cleveland Museum
and, being a friend of mine from the beginning of time,
called upon me to alert him to whatever treasures might
be available in Europe, primarily Italy. You know William, don't you? A most extraordinary man, vibrant,
athletic, gifted, opinionated, a true *enfant terrible*. You
know, he's in his early seventies and still skis each year
at Aspen or Vail or at some Alpine haunt. Remarkable!"

"I certainly do know Milliken," I interrupted. "He's
high on my 'envy list.' He has seized, for Cleveland,
some of the most breathtaking medieval works of art ever
gathered together. Thank God, he's retired. I would hate
to have an active William Milliken scouting the world
for medieval pieces, especially with all the cash Cleveland
has to spend."

"He would adore hearing that. I must tell William, if
you permit me."

"Of course," I said.

Together, William Milliken and Harold Parsons had
acquired some "world-class pieces." There had been a
canvas by Claude Monet "so colorful that looking at it
was like living inside a highly tinted vase." He had once
chanced upon a painting by Titian which, Parsons said,
"possessed such an impression of life that the portrait's
eyes glimmered with wisdom and humor, and the man's
chest could almost be seen to rise and fall gently in
anticipation of speech." Cleveland had occupied most of
Harold Parsons' activities up until the war. Not that
Cleveland had an exclusive right to his services. His
agreement allowed him to place certain works of art
elsewhere, even with the Metropolitan.

"You know, of course, the sleeping child in bronze,

most certainly Hellenistic, which is the pride of your Greek and Roman Department? I found that! I love it. The sculpture has about it a resounding ring, like a finely cast bell. That child is as pure as mountain stream water."

"Mr. Parsons, I think it's one of the top three pieces in the collection. My congratulations!" I said with genuine admiration.

"Please, my boy, it has to be Harold. And, I assume, Tom—or, better, Thomas. Well, I thank you. I am complimented."

Parsons explained that his work with Cleveland had come to an end after the war. He still worked on an informal basis, placing various works of art. Why the official arrangement had lapsed was somewhat of an enigma.

"My dear friend William Milliken was becoming a little crusty. Perhaps he wanted to make all the discoveries on his own. Perhaps he thought I was getting too old. At any rate, I was promptly retained by the William Rockhill Nelson Gallery in Kansas City and also by the Joslyn Memorial Museum in Omaha, Nebraska."

"But why not the Metropolitan?" I asked. "Didn't that possibility ever come up?"

"Never," Parson snapped. "The director then, Francis Henry Taylor, disliked me fervently. He said I was a snob, which is amusing—so was he. He called me superficial, which is deplorable, for he was the most superficial of men. He used to tell people—who then informed me—that I was, to quote, 'probably devious, possibly not crooked, but shifty, weak, intellectually and morally flabby,' which is exactly what *he* was. I still have an aversion to him these many years after his passing. Oh, but not really. I have never loathed anyone. And anyway, how could one deeply dislike a museum director who once defined trustees as 'sacred cows intended to be milked'? And then came James Rorimer. I am, Thomas, nothing if not frank. At my age I have fallen into utter honesty. I find your boss, Rorimer—who may be a man you respect, or even your friend—a pompous and stiff fool, and a liar. But in the same breath I must assure you I consider him the best man in his profession, an absolutely superb eye. Jimsie suspects me of something untoward, and I cannot for the life of me figure out why. Unless, of course, he is unhappy that I know that the famous Etruscan warriors at his museum are forgeries. But that is between him and me."

I just looked at him openmouthed.

Parsons rushed on with his story without noticing my surprise. When he returned to Italy, as soon as expatriates were allowed in the spring of 1946, he found Rome to be a sad place. The city was struggling for survival, and so was the art market. Parsons claimed he was among the first to recognize a profound change in the art scene. He had been appalled by the great scarcity of works of art, as well as by the enormous number of forgeries, some of which were frighteningly skillful. The scarcity of art Parsons blamed on rich manufacturers and producers in northern Italy who had made incredible fortunes out of Italy's misery. They had plunged into art collecting, partly as a hedge against inflation, partly from a desire to possess what the aristocracy used to own. To Parsons, the sinister side of the situation was that many of the painting restorers, excellent ones too, had become forgers. It had become for them far more profitable to create old masters than to restore them. Their work was often spectacular.

"To make matters worse," Parson added grimly, "university professors, caught between the anvil and the hammer of high living costs and stationary salaries, had turned to writing expertises validating these spurious works of art. Those supporting and laudatory documents, to quote Dante, had 'fallen thick as the leaves which strew the brooks of Valambrosa.'"

Old-master paintings had not been the only excellent counterfeits manufactured in a shattered postwar Italy. There was a run of Romanesque bronzes, formed from casts taken from small museums and a private collection or two, and hundreds of masterful Greek and Roman marbles. Parsons vowed to tell me, someday, how he discovered the works of the great faker Alcide Dossena and how the Fine Arts Museum in Boston spurned his news that their vaunted Greek sarcophagus and their Ludovisi throne had been carved by him. To this day the "stuffed-shirt curators in Boston" did not believe the truth.

Parsons may have discovered many sad things in Italy when he returned, but he also made the find of his life—not a work of art but a human being, Professor Giuseppe "Pico" Cellini.

"I had known for years the boy's father, a truly distinguished illuminator of books who, though modest in his upbringing and financially limited, was what we used to call a man of 'high New England principles.' He was rather spartan, and was a *lion*, disguised in double sheep's-wool wraps, when he came up against fraud or pretense. Pico is the same, but he is tempered by the fine breeding of his mother, an Orsini, who is a modest and devout Catholic, and so is he. Thus you have a man of humility and geniality with the smoothness of the Vatican good manners—he has the run of the place from the Pope on down—on the one hand; on the other, Pico has an incredible artistic temperament, and an implacable hatred of the forgers, most of whom he knows personally."

Pico Cellini had been brought up by his father to draw and to study the artworks of Italy. He had accumulated a vast cultural and iconographical knowledge. In addition Cellini was to Parsons one of the most accomplished painting restorers in the world. He had worked for years at the Vatican, the Villa Borghese, Siena, Perugia, and for honest dealers like Salvatore Romano in Florence. Pico knew the work of forgers on sight—people like Ioni, Vangelli, Catani, Latini, Dossena.

"My God, I went on a trip with him throughout distinguished American museums and collections in 1948. The fakes he found! And most of them are still on display, their curators and directors being too stupid to see the true light. Someday Pico will write a book about the massive, truly monumental industry of the forgers. It will sear most museums and the pompous directors in their *derrières*."

To Harold Parsons there was not the faintest doubt that all pieces Pico had listed on his visit to America were the cleverest of forgeries. There were at least twenty, even more. At Boston, the Metropolitan, the National Gallery in Washington, Detroit, Chicago. The "harvest" of fake medieval pieces at Detroit was great; of Renaissance at the Metropolitan, even greater. Parsons had been amazed to hear him say of the big Verrocchio in the Robert Lehman collection, "Look here! A master-piece by Ioni." According to Parsons, Pico had even doubted Michelangelo's spectacular drawing of a figure from the Sistine Chapel, one of the Metropolitan's finest treasures.

"The great forgeries lurk everywhere, dressed up to kill the fancy dude of pride, greed and ignorance, and protected by the armor of fear. Jimsie hates me because I am trying to tell him and his curator of Greek and Roman Art that the Etruscan warriors, all bought by Gisela Richter through my dear friend and colleague Johnny Marshall here in Rome back in the 1920s, are the masterworks of a sublime faker, Fioravanti. I gave Rorimer many opportunities to listen, and then I informed the New York *Times*, which published the sordid story."

I had more than a few reservations about the validity of Harold Parsons' claims, and those of his colleague, Pico, but there was nothing to gain in getting into a fracas with him. I was also seething with impatience to get to the subject of the cross and was about to break my self-imposed silence on it when Parsons abruptly asked, "If you were director of the Metropolitan, or, let me say, when you do become director—I have a sixth sense about these things, Thomas—what will you do about the fake Michelangelo?"

"Oh, on that one, Harold, I'd say nothing. Too political. Too explosive an issue. I might call in two or three specialists, very quietly, and obtain their opinions. But I don't believe I would have the courage to explode a powder keg. The drawing *is*, after all, regarded by others as one of the ten most important works of art among the entire holdings of the Met."

"Excellent answer! Just what I am beginning to expect from you. Prudence, not cowardice. Now I must ask you —I simply cannot bear it any longer—what did you think about Topic Mimara's cross and what are you planning to do about it?"

I smiled inwardly. I had beaten him. I knew what James Rorimer would have done. He would have shrugged, muttered, "It's of certain interest, all right, but there are so many fine works of art in the world . . . I have no plans really." And I knew Rorimer would be outraged if I tipped off my real feelings to a dealer, particularly to a dealer the likes of Harold Parsons.

"Harold, I found the cross of certain interest," I began. "But, as you know, although the resources of The Cloisters are vast, there are many works of art I have seen on this trip to Europe. Honestly, I have no plans regarding the cross at this time."

Parsons looked into my eyes with a steady, bland expression.

I returned his gaze, studying his cherublike pink face. "That's what I am supposed to say," I went on. "In the first set in the game of art collecting, I know I should be reserved, cool. But that would be a sham. I shall tell you instead what I really think and feel! To me the ivory cross is beautiful, mysterious, magnetic, awesome. I'm obsessed by it. It is the finest medieval piece I have ever seen, so redolent with power. It is also deeply disturbing, I can't say why. I have no clear idea what its meaning it. But I know, I sense, that it will reveal, within itself, marvelous and frightening things. I recognize the beauty and harmony of the object, but the inscriptions are the key. They are so enigmatic, so complicated, I don't know if I shall ever crack their message. You know, the placard actually says 'King of the Confessors'! That alone is mysterious. Sometimes I have the curious and awful feeling I'm chasing something menacing in the case of the cross, something which exudes an evil force."

Parsons seemed about to speak, but sat back with a look of intense concentration.

"I am being devoured by this cross," I whispered to him. "I want it, I *need* it. And I need your help. I want the truth. What do you know? What do you really have to do with it? Do you have any influence over this man Topic? Will you help me? Will you go *my* way and help force aside my competition? You know, Harold, I had thought of offering you a payment to drive out my competition—Cleveland, Boston, the British. And if you wish, I'll still make that possible. You deserve remuneration, if you do the work."

"I am touched by your frankness and your generosity, my boy," he said. "Not necessary. I will be well taken care of."

"I am going to get that cross," I told him. "Somehow

I shall outbid the others. But my worst problem seems to be Jim Rorimer. He loathes the cross, although he has never seen it."

"Young man, I had virtually given up on your museum. Jimsie had played his typical standoffish game too long and too well. Before I heard about you, I was prepared to deny the Met another chance. In the past months I have been very close to making a deal with Sherman Lee at Cleveland. At the same time I have been encouraging the British Museum to plunge forward, while simultaneously shepherding Boston on its way through Hanns Swarzenski and Perry Rathbone, that erratic director of his. What I will do about these forces I have set in motion I do not know right now. We can discuss that. In the meantime, however, I shall do something no dealer should ever do. What *is* happening to me? Perhaps this mystery cross has begun to obsess me too. Perhaps it is because in my late years I have converted to Catholicism. What a thing for a proper Bostonian to do! At any rate, let me tell you everything I know. I shall truly sing about the man and his arms."

In the winter of 1956 Parsons had suffered a light heart attack and had begun to be fearful that he was going to lose his health forever. And, although Pico and he had found some splendid works of art in the early 1950s which he had placed in Kansas City or Omaha, he began to suspect that all his resources had finally begun to dry up. However, all his discouraging thoughts dissipated abruptly in April 1956. That month, Rome had the most pellucid spring Parsons had ever enjoyed.

"I shall never forget it. From my apartment high up on the Trinità dei Monti where all Rome lay spread out before me, the great blue bubble of St. Peter's dome seemed to be sinking into a golden haze as the sun slipped behind Monte Mario. Distant bells were ringing for vespers, and thousands of swallows screamed through the sky playing tag. The scent of orange blossoms from the Pincian Gardens—anciently, the gardens of Sallust— was breathtaking. As I gazed out over that incomparable vista, I felt the years, the weight of my illness and gathering depression lift away from me. Suddenly I was far more alert than I had been in years. Do you believe in psychic phenomena, young man?"

Sure, I nodded. I felt it would be useless to argue with the man.

At that precise moment, Parsons told me, the telephone rang. It was Pico Cellini saying he had stumbled on a sizable private collection containing paintings, ancient and Renaissance glass, medieval antiquities. The collector was a man of mystery. No one, or at least few people, had ever heard of him before. And, best of all, according to Pico, the chap kept his material in Zurich and Tangier, Morocco, which Parsons emphasized was a free port. If anyone else in the world had uttered such words *other* than Pico Cellini, Parsons would have laughed. But the news had been like a bolt of electricity. Who was the collector? When could he meet him? What was his story? Where had Pico heard about him?

Pico told Parsons he knew little but was going to meet the man that evening. All he knew was that the chap was Yugoslavian. He had come to Rome with his female "collaborator," who had been his secretary when he was chief of the Yugoslav mission at the Allied Art Collecting Point at the end of the war. Hearing *that*, Parsons became even more alert.

"Thomas, you must know about the Collecting Point. Jimsie was in it, very highly placed, even wrote a book about it."

"Sure," I answered. "The Collecting Point was in Munich and a few other cities in Germany, I remember. It was the name for the commission set up by the Allies to gather together those hundreds of thousands of works of art the Nazis had stolen and return them to their rightful owners. So Topic Mimara had a role in that?" I asked very casually.

"Yes. Fascinating, isn't it? When I heard the news it immediately struck me that anyone who had maintained a position of high stature at the Collecting Point must know where a great many art treasures were hidden throughout Europe."

"Aha!" I exclaimed, wondering if I should probe Parsons on what Albrighi had told me. I decided to hold off for the moment.

Parsons took up his story once again. When Pico had told him the name of the collector, he had laughed. Ante Topic Mimara! He had never heard of a name as bizarre as that. Parsons asked Pico how he had learned about the individual. Pico said that Fritz Wolfgang Volbach, the medievalist, had informed him. Volbach had been acquainted with the man for twenty-five years. He described Topic Mimara as a painting restorer, art collector and dealer in Berlin before the war. Parsons asked me if I knew Volbach. I told him I had read his studies on early Christian ivories, but had never met him. I recounted that I had tried to reach Volbach two days before and informed Parsons that the scholar was in New York.

"Volbach is an extraordinary character—garrulous, drinks a bit, has a memory which, ah, *varies* from moment to moment. But he is honest. Definitely *not* one of those academics who supplied the postwar forgers with expertises. Fritz was director of the Early Medieval Department of the Vatican during the war years and for some years thereafter, which is unusual, he being non-Italian and Jewish."

Parsons explained that Fritz Volbach had told him that in the spring of 1956 he had received a call, out of the blue, from Topic Mimara, who said he was just in from Tangier and wanted to see him right away. Over the years Topic Mimara had asked Volbach to examine and identify various pieces. Around 1948, when Volbach was living in Koblenz, Topic Mimara had brought a small square ivory carving which he insisted was fifth century A.D. Volbach hadn't believe the early date and had told Topic that the piece, which he described as exceptional in quality, seemed to be eleventh century and Anglo-Saxon.

When Topic Mimara telephoned Volbach in Rome he said he wanted to show him a work of art which belonged, he claimed, to the little ivory. Volbach agreed to see Topic Mimara and his associate, Dr. Wiltrud Mersmann, whom Volbach remembered vaguely as the daughter of a professor at the university in Bonn or Cologne. When they met, Topic Mimara completely dominated the conversation. The woman retired into a shell of silence. Topic explained how, over the years, he had assembled a vast collection of works of art from all civilizations and in all media—paintings, furniture, ivory, glass, stone, gold and silver, wood, amber, precious and semiprecious stones, drawings, manuscripts. And each piece was, according to Topic, a "masterwork." The impression he gave Volbach was that the majority of his pieces had been commissioned by renowned members of royalty, had been forgotten by scholars and were treasures only *he* could recognize. Topic had brought dozens of photographs. Volbach saw some fairly promising objects. Many others appeared suspicious, although Topic Mimara seldom gave him the chance to examine anything closely.

At length, Topic had pulled out a series of large photographs from an envelope and held them up for Volbach. He described the object they depicted as the preeminent work of art in all his holdings. He called it an early English ivory altar cross, made for Winchester Cathedral. Fritz Volbach had confessed to Harold Parsons that he fully expected to see something ludicrous. But when he saw the photographs he could scarcely believe his eyes. It was the cross. Volbach had been astounded at its large size and the vivacity of its dozens of figures, who seemed to be conducting spirited conversations with one another. There began a lively discussion about the date of the surprising object. Topic Mimara somewhat plaintively had again suggested an early Christian date. Volbach had disabused him of the idea. "Suddenly, Mersmann spoke," Parsons recounted, "displaying surprising erudition and an unexpectedly advanced knowledge of art history. Her theory was that the ivory was English, made possibly at Winchester in the first half of the eleventh century, perhaps in honor of England's most illustrious royal saint, Edward the Confessor. She could point to hard evidence for her idea. One of the inscriptions—that one on the placard—was inscribed 'Jesus of Nazareth, King of the Confessors.' "

Volbach had told both Topic Mimara and his companion, Dr. Mersmann, that from photographs alone he could assure them the cross was one of the finest works of medieval art in the world, was definitely Anglo-Saxon, and dated to the first half of the eleventh century.

"Then," Parsons said in a voice filled with pride, "when Topic Mimara asked his advice on how to go about selling the cross, Volbach very graciously mentioned Pico Cellini and me. He knew, of course, that no other dealer had sufficient caliber to handle an object of such magni-

tude or had contacts on such high levels both in America
and in Europe."

"How fortunate for the world of art," I said sancti-
moniously. Through Volbach, Topic Mimara had gotten
in touch with Pico first, which was when he had called
Parsons. The American had decided to stay out of the
affair at the beginning. Pico had met the man twice, once
at his conservation studio in Trastevere, the second time
in Topic Mimara's hotel. The circumstances had been
strange, and fascinating.

"Pico had disliked, and feared, Topic Mimara the
instant he met him," Parsons said ominously. "Yet Pico
found himself mesmerized by the man and unable to
remove his gaze from Topic Mimara's moon face."

According to Parsons, Topic had entered Pico's studio
lumbering like a bear. He had identified himself curtly,
blurting out his name and that of Fritz Volbach. Then,
without another word, he had sat down in Cellini's sofa
couch and had rummaged through his jacket pocket until
he had extracted a small black velvet bag. He pulled the
tight drawstring loose with two fingers and his teeth,
drew open the little sack and casually dropped onto the
marble table a square chunk of yellowed ivory—the same
piece, as it turned out, he had shown Volbach years
before.

Pico had been impressed with the superior quality of
the block. Topic Mimara then showed off a number of
photographs of Italian paintings, some of which Cellini
considered to be very good indeed. While all this was
going on, Pico wondered how it could be that such a
coarse-looking and dangerous man could have acquired
such rare treasures.

A day or two after their first enigmatic encounter, Pico
had gone to Topic Mimara's rooms at the Hotel Inghil-
terra. Pico was somewhat at a loss to describe the meeting
to Parsons. He was still frightened by the man and had
to force himself to proceed. But when he met Topic
Mimara at the hotel, he had the sharp feeling he was
meeting someone he had never before seen. Whereas
earlier Topic Mimara had been abrupt, now he was
charming, almost courtly. Except that he treated the
woman, Mersmann, like a slave. She uttered barely a
word and seemed thoroughly cowed by her consort.

Topic Mimara extracted from under one of the beds in the room a valise of beautifully tooled leather and unlocked it. The interior was fitted out, in velvet, specially for pieces of the cross. There were six of them. Parsons described how amazed Cellini had been by the way Topic Mimara handled the object. In his studio he had almost thrown the ivory block down on the table. But at the second meeting the man fondled the pieces as if he were an archbishop performing High Mass. Pico had been struck by the complexities of humanity and had remarked to Parsons, "So many men exist within each one of us." Topic had assembled the cross, placed it before a window and stepped aside rather humbly.

"Pico told me," Parsons said softly, "that the evening light, muted by the thin curtains, surrounded the object with an aureola. It fairly shone! How beautiful it was! Topic's fingers caressed the cross as he described a number of the scenes carved upon it. He pointed out with particular emphasis something which Pico found puzzling and troubling—a scroll held up by a prophet. Topic Mimara told Cellini that the Latin words referred to the Jews who spurned Jesus and crucified Him. Topic Mimara looked right into Pico's eyes and remarked that his cross did not hide the truth about the Jews who conspired against Christ and killed Him. Pico was concerned by the fire in the man's eyes."

At these words I recoiled. My mind captured the phrase in the large inscription on the cross, the one which seemed to imply something about the Jews laughing. But Parsons continued rapidly, and I had to concentrate on his story.

Topic Mimara had explained to Pico that he wanted to sell most of his extensive collection because he was planning to marry Mersmann and wanted to establish a trust fund. He hinted several times that he was an intimate friend of the royal family of Yugoslavia, particularly the ex-King. It had been Pico's impression that Topic was trying to suggest that he had obtained the cross from the royal treasury. But Pico didn't believe the story at all. It had been Pico's firm impression that Topic Mimara had pillaged the cross from somewhere. When Pico had given a detailed account of the meeting he advised

Parsons not to have anything to do with the peculiar individual.

"Incredible tale!" I blurted out. "Then what?"

"It gets even better, Thomas. Here, waiter, another bottle of the Frascati. Fine art and fine wine do get along, don't they?"

I nodded enthusiastically.

"As you might imagine, Thomas, nothing could have kept me away from this fascinating gentleman, so crude and yet so beguiling. I reckoned that Signor Ante Topic Mimara would be a welcome relief from the mixed bag of the nobility, the wealthy and the exalted museum types I customarily deal with. I did wonder, though, how even the most adroit art collector could have amassed anything of note from such an unlikely source as Yugoslavia. But, art collecting being the fantasy occupation it is, and collectors the obsessed creatures they usually are, *anything* is feasible—even in that tortured land of Serbs and Croats dominated so cruelly by Tito and his band of Communists."

After Pico's description, Parsons had been pleasantly surprised. Ante Topic Mimara was a small, rather delicate man, and not at all forbidding. He impressed Parsons by being "frank, direct, charming to me *and* to his companion, Dr. Mersmann, who I am sure disliked me." Parsons found her intelligent, attentive, but stubborn. He had taken the couple to one of the best restaurants in Rome, the Osteria dell' Orso, where Topic at once recommended himself to Parsons' heart by unerringly selecting the pick of the menu, including a little-known but radiant Frascati.

"Modestly, Topic Mimara told me the story of his life. I have no reason to disbelieve it. You see, I am uncanny when it comes to judging people and their autobiographical stories."

Topic related to Parsons that his family were rich Yugoslavian shipowners who were also in pharmaceuticals, a business which Topic still dabbled in. When he was a young man Ante Topic Mimara chose not to go into commerce. He studied to be a painter. He fought in the First World War and was taken prisoner by the Italians. Afterward he lived in Italy for some years, then in Germany on and off for twenty-five years. He supported himself by collecting and by putting pieces into auctions. Yet he was never actually a dealer, only a collector who sold those items he did not desire to retain. And he made a fortune. His life to Parsons had been very like that of one of his friends, a legendary American art dealer, Joseph Brummer, who collected fabulous treasures by prowling little shops and out-of-the-way churches and monasteries.

Topic collected, discarded, and improved his collection constantly. He informed Parsons he intended to leave the bulk of his "incredible holdings, covering all fields of European art and the Near East from ancient Egypt on," to the state of Yugoslavia—specifically, to the city of Zagreb—where he had already given scores of paintings. Topic told Parsons that when Yugoslavia went Communist in 1945 he had broken with the new regime and become an Austrian citizen, although he still kept strong ties to his homeland. During the Second World War Topic had lived in Berlin, and he had saved his collection from the Russians after the fall of Germany. With the help of American Military Intelligence, to whom he had been useful, Topic said, he got part of his treasures transferred to his bank in Zurich and the bulk, including some two hundred paintings, to Tangier, where he established residence. Topic hoped to move eventually to a house near Salzburg. He planned to give another part of his vast collection to that city.

"He's most unusual," Parsons ruminated. "Even now, Tito is making every effort to have him return to his native country and would appoint him Minister of Fine Arts, with an absolutely free hand."

Parsons had expected to be able to examine the cross while it was still in Rome. But Topic put him off coldly, informing him he would have to see the piece in Zurich. His reason was that he had to leave very early in the morning. Thereupon he handed over a series of black-and-white photographs of the cross.

"At first sight I was, I have to admit, deeply worried. The cross, from the photo, mind you, appeared to me thin, wispy, curiously insubstantial. But I couldn't tell *him* that. To Topic, I'm afraid I dissimulated a little. I told him I thought it was impressive. He seemed to be fully taken in by my words. He eagerly placed photographs of other objects before me and started chattering away in a staccato Italian. It was unforgettable. I can recall the sense of his words clearly. He said, 'The cross is from Winchester. It was taken away from the cathedral some-time around the invasion of William the Conqueror. There are five other English pieces, some even earlier than the eleventh century, which I found with the cross. These too I want to sell. The first is a unique glass reliquary. It is about a foot high. The glass is deep blue. You will notice the enamel decoration at the rim. Acanthus. Clearly of the same type as the borders on the most famous manuscript in the British Museum, the Bene-dictional of Saint Aethelwold, which dates to A.D. 950. Unique in the world. The second and third are a pair of heads, life-sized, carved in wood, showing the Virgin and Saint John. They were once on statues of the tenth century beneath a crucifix in Winchester Cathedral. And here, the fourth, is a Virgin and Child sculpture in box-wood. About eight inches high. The Virgin's eyes are made out of sapphires. Also Winchester. Tenth century. And the fifth is this ivory casket with golden fittings. It is about four inches long. Very beautiful. English. Eleventh century. I want to sell these pieces as a group with the cross.'

Parsons found himself at a loss for words. He was intrigued, but was not sure he wanted to proceed.

"Now, Thomas, I shall reveal certain things which I suppose I should never tell you. But why not? I have grown, even in this short acquaintance, to admire you greatly. My only wish is to help you gain the magnificent cross for The Cloisters. Listen carefully, I am going to reveal to you *everything* I told Topic Mimara and Frau Doktor Mersmann. All my secrets. You will be able to use the information to win out over your many com-petitors."

Parsons told Topic he was the only man in the art field who could help him. But he urged Topic to judge for himself. He explained that he was anything but an art dealer. He took pains to describe himself as a retired advisor on works of art to some American museums, who from time to time gained pleasure from placing choice works of art in their proper sanctuaries. Parsons firmly told Topic he was a specialist in *positioning*. He was not an avid searcher, one of those restless, peripatetic hunters digging around private collections, rooting through auction houses long before the objects in a forthcoming sale were announced to the public. Nor was he associated in any way with an art gallery. And, of course, he was not a scholar, signing expertises for a fat fee when something good came along. Works of art came to Harold Parsons and to his associate Pico Cellini. Together they would sift through them, cast away the routine or mediocre, and place what little there was left of excellence with the right collector or the appropriate museum.

It took time, Parsons explained. A great deal of time. But time was money. Over the years, he had developed one unswerving manner of bringing about a sale: utter, almost bewildering relaxation. Collectors and museum professionals, Parsons pointed out, had profound suspicion of making a quick decision or a hasty deal. If one allowed them to think they were being pushed, they would disappear. So the pushing had to be delicate, gentle. Parsons' preferred technique was to prod easily and, in a soft way, remind his client that the object was available, was *very* worthy, but that it might not *always* be there. Sometimes what he did involved nothing more precipitous than seeing to it that his carefully worded letter reached the right eyes. Sometimes Parsons proceeded so slowly with a prospective purchaser that it seemed he was hesitant about completing a sale. He never became associated with a work of art an owner was eager to sell quickly. Time, he said again, was money.

"To show my mettle, I then gave Topic a totally unexpected piece of advice," Parsons said and chuckled. "I did not know how much he would ask for the Winchester cross, or the other objects. But I advised him, whatever price he had in mind, go higher. I have learned through the years that the most important museum directors and the wealthiest collectors tend to consider a work of art beneath them if the price seems too reasonable. And my buyers positively insist upon bargaining. So I told Topic to establish a high price. I wanted that price to drive away those who are not capable of reaching for a true masterpiece. I wanted to focus in on the two or three most likely purchasers and, over time, let them bargain the price down. You see, even if you have to drop your price eventually, it doesn't matter, since the price was so high at the start. There are always hosts of plausible excuses why one is willing to accept a lower price—illness, the wish to purchase a choice piece of real estate, a marriage in the family."

Of utmost importance in Parsons' technique, he explained to Topic, was to select at once the institution, or the private collector, that he was convinced would be the likely eventual purchaser. He would let that institution know about the cross, and give it a clear option to buy. But the option would last no longer than three months. Most of the time, Parsons had discovered, the likely choice did not act right away. He would fail at the beginning, particularly with something as unknown and mysterious as the cross. With the cross Parsons was convinced he would receive a firm turndown. But wait.

He told Topic Mimara and Wiltrud Mersmann that if he agreed to take on the cross he would offer it, and the rest of Topic's objects, to two or three other institutions. It was vital that no single institution know that others had been informed. Parsons counted on natural competitive drive and simple human greed to forestall any communication or cooperation among them. At this moment, Parsons expected to receive some offers. But he believed none would be truly tempting. At this point in the game interest in the cross would lag. So, in order to close the deal and obtain the highest bid, his practice was to let the word out gently to each institution, including the primary one which had rejected the object, that he had been forced by the owner to inform several institutions that the object was available at a price lower than the initial asking price—but not too much lower.

Parsons went on to explain that it was crucial to keep two or possible three prospective clients in competition up to the very end. And if two collectors or great museums vigorously set after the cross to the bitter end, "Well, that is Paradise!"

"So you see, Thomas, Topic Mimara appeared to be delighted with my little discourse. He asked me directly what my terms would be. I answered that five percent of the selling price would be customary and honorable. I assured him I would not seek a penny from the institution or individual with whom I eventually placed the treasure. And, Thomas, I assure *you*, I won't. Topic Mimara agreed to my modest fee.

"I casually asked him what price he was thinking about for his cross and the accompanying English medieval works of art. And without any hesitation or embarrassment, the man spoke the most utterly astonishing words I have ever heard in my life! He wanted two million five hundred thousand dollars for the group—one million dollars for the cross!

"I totally lost that reserve for which I am known. Preposterous, I told him. No medieval object in history has ever fetched that! Not even a quarter of the amount. Why, when the Cleveland Museum purchased the best pieces from the Guelph Treasure in 1930, the price for the whole lot—eight pieces—had been a tenth of that. I told the man I considered him to be a dreamer. Although I *had* urged him to think high, I told him that one million dollars for the cross was astronomical. Impossible."

Topic Mimara had bluntly told Parsons that he was no longer living in the 1930s. He pointed out that the value of money had changed. He argued that decent works of art were difficult to find and that there was nothing like the great cross. He was insistent that "this unique survival of the entire Middle Ages in England, a cross made at Winchester Cathedral for King Edward the Confessor," would obtain that price. He was adamant that the object was equal to the value of a painting. He argued that if one of the many paintings by Rembrandt or Rubens could fetch seven hundred and fifty thousand, his cross was worth an equal sum. Then he said something which enchanted Harold Parsons: "We have a saying in my country—'The more a man dreams, the more solidly his feet are planted on earth.'" Topic emphasized he was a wealthy man. He told the American he was only toying with the idea of selling his cross. He was not compelled to sell it.

"And I believe he is not compelled to sell, my boy. Well, I was utterly confused. Nothing had prepared me for this astounding turn of events. The man, I thought, was not merely an eccentric with a ridiculous fantasy, he was worse, perhaps he was a bit touched. I was convinced then the sale of the cross could never be consummated at such a figure. But then I began to ruminate on the

vast changes that had occurred over the past three decades
in the prices of works of art. Prices had tripled, quin-
tupled, since the war. Nonsensical as the deluded Yugoslav's arguments sounded coming from him, actually they
were not all that unreasonable. So I decided to go along
with his evaluation. And, of course, I yearned to plumb
the rest of his collection. If the cross could not be sold
at first, or even ever, perhaps other of his holdings would.
I had been through it all before with other collectors.
Invariably, the rich ones who had not truly made up their
minds to sell a particularly favorite work of art started
with the same attitude. Then later, under the pressure
of rejection and my own relentless persuasion, they had
all come to terms with reality. At seventy-one years of
age I decided I had nothing to lose in playing along with
this quixotic individual."

Parsons informed Topic he would take up the chal-
lenge. But he warned him that from the photographs he
had been unconvinced of the grandeur of his object.
Without the strong recommendations from Volbach and
Pico he would have avoided it entirely. Therefore he
cautioned Topic to use his photographs sparingly. He
instructed him to ask prospective purchasers to come and
inspect the treasure in person at the bank. Parsons pointed
out that the clients would strenuously object to such
rigid requirements, knowing that museum curators and
directors normally insisted upon seeing photographs before
they would even consider making a purchase. But no
work of art, particularly sculpture, and most especially
this cross with its network of tiny figures and inscriptions, could ever be photographed effectively. Parsons
remarked to Topic that if he were absolutely strict in
insisting that clients come in person, a vital sense of
mystery would begin to surround the object.

"I informed the man bluntly that the work of art, at
its extraordinary price, was an institutional object. I
could not think of a private collector who might be
attracted by it. No. This brilliant object had to go to a
great and extremely well-endowed museum. There was
at that moment, and perhaps is still, only one logical
choice. But I told the Yugoslav that to convince *that*
museum would be hard work and would take a very long
time.

"Mersmann broke in unexpectedly and questioned me rather sharply as to which museum it might be. I named The Cloisters, of course. Neither of them had any idea what I was talking about, so I quickly described the nature of your museum. I told them that the appeal of The Cloisters was threefold. First, it was rich; Rockefeller money was behind it. Second, it devoted itself exclusively to the art of the Middle Ages. Third, the driving force behind it was James Rorimer, who had just become the director of the Metropolitan. Rorimer, I said, was a pompous fellow, always strutting and parading himself. Vain as a peacock. But I told them Jimsie was the most ambitious collector at any museum in America. I thought Rorimer eventually might be attracted to the cross. I explained how, in 1949, Rorimer had purchased the majority of the Joseph Brummer collection—incomparable medieval material—for just under a million dollars. But I cautioned Topic Mimara that the Brummer material had constituted a hoard of objects, several hundreds, not just one piece or even six. I also explained that Rorimer could be indecisive. The only way to get him to strike would be to supply him with a highly enthusiastic competitor, real or concocted, but absolutely convincing nevertheless.

"Now I named the one genuine threat to Rorimer, the Cleveland Museum of Art. I explained that Rorimer's family came from Cleveland; he had always wanted to outshine the place. I told Topic of my friendship with William Milliken and my acquaintance with Sherman Lee, who was then their curator of medieval works of art and was a promising professional collector. He still is, as you must well know. We all agreed to use Cleveland as bait to attract Rorimer.

"Dr. Mersmann became vexed at this point. She exclaimed that the cross should not go to America, but to England, where it had been created. According to her, it belonged either in the Victoria and Albert Museum or, better, in the British Museum. I tried patiently to persuade her that the cross would only go where the money was. England did have funds, but they were principally government moneys, and governments tend to move slowly with works of art. At the same time I did realize that, although Great Britain offered no tax advantages similar to the United States, Britannia did possess some-

thing potentially as effective—the promise of a peerage
for a wealthy donor. I described my impeccable contacts
in Great Britain, primarily with Lord Crawford, who was
at the time highly placed in the National Arts Collection
Fund, and with Sir Kenneth Clark.

"As an important ingredient in my carefully structured
strategy of placing the cross, I urged Topic Mimara to
seek out the most eminent medieval historian in the world
to publish a study of the object. With that, his companion
broke in to assert that she was working on such a major
study herself. She had almost completed, she said, a
lengthy treatise which she expected to be published in
the journal of the Warburg and Courtauld Institute in
London or in an equally prestigious scholarly bulletin.

"Well, Thomas, I thought that was a bit ridiculous.
One needed a world-famous name. I was thinking of
Fritz Volbach, of course, to entice the likes of Jim Rorimer.
But what could I do? So I told her she would be the
perfect choice. Topic Mimara agreed. Immediately, I
put the game into play, alerting New York and then
Boston, Cleveland, the Victoria and Albert and a few
other places. I did give the Metropolitan the edge."

Harold Parsons leaned contentedly back in his chair
and sipped the last of his wine. I almost jumped across
the table and grabbed him.

"What happened?" I cried out. "Who's got the edge
for the cross now?"

"Ah," Parsons sighed. "That, my young friend, is the
second canto of my song. It is late, even for Rome.
Tomorrow I shall tell the rest."

The unique inscription of the Bury St. Edmunds cross: "Jesus of Nazareth, King of the Confessors."

The front medallion with the Israelites gazing upon the Brazen Serpent slung over the forked tree. The figures holding scrolls are: God the Father in the center; Isaiah, lower right; Saint Peter, lower left. Upper left, John the Evangelist. The figure with a scroll lying on top of the medallion is Jeremiah.

The ivory panel, measuring 2¼ by 2¼ inches, the photo of which was found by Professor Kurt Weitzmann in the files of the scholar Adolph Goldschmidt. The scene depicts Christ being dragged before the High Priest. On the upper left, two Jewish priests wearing conical hats crane their heads upward. The scroll refers to the words of John, "They shall look upon Him whom they have pierced."

Opposite: *The front of the "incomparable" Bury St. Edmunds cross. About two feet in height. In the center, the Brazen Serpent. On the right, the scenes of the Lamentation and the Deposition. On the left, the Three Marys at the Tomb and the Resurrection. Standing on the placard jutting out from the upright bar with the hand of God inside the sunburst are the figures of the High Priest and Pontius Pilate. Above is the Ascension of Christ into the clouds of heaven.*

The Ascension of Christ into heaven. Below, the High Priest points vigorously at Pontius Pilate and orders, "Write not, King of the Jews, but that he said, I am King of the Jews." Pilate pulls back disdainfully and answers, "What I wrote, I wrote."

The right side of the cross showing the large Latin inscription: "Cham laughed to see the shameful nakedness of his parent."

The Three Marys make their way to the sepulcher where they meet an angel who tells them, "Ye seek Jesus of Nazareth which was crucified." Behind the angel is Christ resurrected, holding the double-hafted cross with banner. The soldiers, stacked like cordwood, sleep, unaware of the miraculous events.

The Deposition and Lamentation. The Virgin Mary stands on the left and holds Christ's arm tenderly in her cloaked hands. John the Evangelist, grieving, flanks Christ. Behind the Virgin is the centurion and his soldiers. Behind John, Nicodemus pulls the nail from Christ's hand. A dense crowd of soldiers and Jews looks on. The personifications of the Sun and Moon, in roundels, flank the cross. Below, the body of Christ, wrapped in shrouds. The prophet Zechariah sits on the left.

The eagle of Saint John. The scroll carries phrases from his book: "They shall look upon Him whom they have pierced" and "Not a bone of Him shall be broken."

The central medallion with the Lamb of God. The figure on the left, directing the spear against the Lamb, is the personification of Synagogue. The hooded figure in the center of the inner rim is a monk, possibly the abbot of Bury St. Edmunds, Samson de Tottington. This figure appears to have been carved later than the rest of the cross and carefully inserted.

The lion, symbol of Saint Mark.

The bull, symbol of Saint Luke.

The back of the splendid cross. In the center, the Lamb of God. On the right, the bull, symbol of Saint Luke. On the left, the lion of Saint Mark and above, the eagle of Saint John. The upright and crossbars are decorated with a spectacular series of prophets proclaiming by their scrolls the glory of the church triumphant.

A detail showing the Ascension and the High Priest with Pontius Pilate standing on the placard with the lines in Greek, Latin and a pseudo-Hebrew: "Jesus of Nazareth, King of the Confessors."

A reconstruction of the missing bottom block of walrus ivory showing the angel of Matthew and the Harrowing of Hell. This priceless block, last seen in Brussels in 1956, in all likelihood still survives. The question is where.

CHAPTER ELEVEN

Revelations

I AWOKE BEFORE DAWN, my mind stirring with a host of questions I should have put to Harold Parsons the evening before. I was deeply worried that I had been taken in by his considerable and subtle charm. Why had he informed me about his strategy and advice to Topic? Was it because he realized I was already hooked? Oh, why had I impulsively spilled out my true, burning feelings about the cross? If Parsons had spoken so openly with me, what would prevent him from exposing to Jim Rorimer everything I had said? Was Parsons' real aim in being so frank or appearing to be so candid—for I couldn't be certain he was telling the truth—to lull me into believing a network of more important lies? If so, what were they? Who really *was* the competition, and what were they up to? I was dying to know.

We were to meet at noon at Santa Francesca Romana, an obscure church at the corner of the Forum near the Arch of Constantine. I had a leisurely breakfast, walked for several hours through the Borghese Gardens before the traffic clogged its peaceful routes, and sauntered over to the church.

"You had a bad influence on me, my young friend," Parsons said by way of welcome. "I slept not more than two hours last night, reflecting on your thrilling words and your true connoisseur's zeal for the most exceptional work of art to have survived from the Middle Ages. I spent most of the night in my library seeking an essay, very special to me, written on medieval art by my dear late friend Coomaraswamy. Here, allow me to read his poetic words which so poignantly complement your vibrant feelings. He wrote: 'We shall never understand the Middle Ages until we realize how profoundly they strove to find a deeper meaning, a sacred significance in all things. They never forgot that all things would be absurd, if their meaning were exhausted in their function and place in the phenomenal world, if, by their *essence*, they did not reach into a world beyond this.'"

"Those were very special words" was all I could mutter, listening to the banal mumbo jumbo. Such pomposity gave art history a bad reputation.

"Thomas, you may be wondering why I brought you to this particular sanctuary," Parsons whispered as he conducted me to the sacristy of the gloomy, ill-kept church. "You may already know the work of art I am about to show you. But perhaps not. To me, it is among the most striking in the Eternal City, especially since it was created in the so-called dark ages of the early sixth century when few masterpieces were made and even fewer survived."

We entered a low doorway into a chamber furnished with a modest stone altar, above which was—My God, I thought, the crafty old son-of-a-bitch had been right! I stared at an enormous wooden panel, at least four feet square, entirely filled with the face of the young Virgin Mary, so translucent that I imagined a miraculous light had been illuminated behind it. No human face had ever been composed of such unlikely elements—a very long, thin nose; an almost imperceptible mouth; a pair of giant soft black eyes, so large and penetrating they seemed to overwhelm all else. The features, taken separately, were bizarre, but together they bestowed upon the Virgin's face a reality transcending nature. My instant thought as I gazed, dumbfounded, upon the ancient ikon was a sentiment from the writings of the early Christian poet

Tertullian describing why he believed in Christ: "After He died on the cross, was buried, it is impossible that Christ descended into hell, and in three days arose from the dead and ascended into heaven, which, of course, is the absolute proof that He did."

Parsons took hold of my arm, shaking me gently out of my revery. "I *thought* my Madonna would have that effect upon you. I was one of the first people on earth— since the thirteenth century, that is—to see her. It was in the fall of 1950. This divine image was the key reason why I decided to convert and confess to the Catholic faith. Pico Cellini discovered this painting underneath a truly pedestrian painting of the Virgin and Child dating to the thirteenth century. On a particular October morning—as a matter of fact, it was eleven years ago today— Pico took me, Bernard Berenson, his secretary Nickey Mariano, Kay Clark and Lady Clark to see the miracle he had brought to light. He had a studio then in the Palazzo Venezia. With the step of a boy of sixteen, Berenson went up the four enormously long flights of the *grand escalier* of the palazzo on Pico's arm. B.B. was mesmerized. He cried out that nothing since the fading frescos of Santa Maria Antiqua in the Forum can possibly give one a better idea of painting executed by the ancient Romans than this aloof Madonna. The eyes are wonderful, hypnotic, aren't they? And Berenson said he felt the same as a child when he peered into deep water. You know, Thomas, I suppose that proves Bernard Berenson really did have a Narcissus complex after all. Anyway, he made one truly Berensonian remark which I never have forgotten: 'This is one of those instances in art where imperfections add up to a sum total of complete perfection.'"

How could I possibly have harbored suspicions about Parsons after he had revealed such a hidden treasure which not even I had rooted out. I was also moved that he had converted to Catholicism—had he even said "confessed"?

We ensconced ourselves in a modest-looking but superior restaurant near the Forum, and I began gently to interrogate him. "Did Topic Mimara ever indicate to you where he discovered his cross?"

"The man was exceedingly edgy about the provenance;

defensive, I'd say. I asked him at the outset whether it wouldn't be helpful for me to know something about the history of the object. He bristled. I tried to assure him I did not care about the person from whom he had obtained the object. No one, after all, is more sensitive than I about secret sources. But I did wish to know if anyone—any institution, church, monastery, government or, God forbid, museum—might object to the sale of the piece. Would _anyone_ be able to step forward and claim or prove that Topic did not possess full title or ownership?

"The curious man exploded into laughter. He said, 'What do you take me for, Signor Parsons? An idiot? Do you think I would have shown my magnificent cross to Volbach, to Cellini, or to you, were I not totally confident? I have title, do not worry. I will sign any paper, any affidavit, any contract with the American Embassy or Consulate—even with his Holiness, the Pope—to say that _I_ own this cross. Just last month a high American consular official in Tangier examined my collection and signed an official memorandum, clearing it—blessing it.' Well, Thomas, I wondered what in heaven's name _that_ strange statement meant. What could Topic have done, to need such a consular clearance? Well, I decided to steer away from what I thought might be a dangerous issue. No sense in discovering _too_ many things about works of art."

"Exactly what did he tell you about his source—anything at all?" I persevered.

"Only that he discovered it within the innermost recesses of 'a sacristy of a Continental monastery,' together with a number of other medieval objects brought from England—Winchester—at the time of the Norman Conquest and then discarded with changing fashion in the church and relegated to the attic."

"Do you believe that?" I asked.

"Yes. Why not? Volbach could tell of similar finds in provincial Italian churches when, as director of the Vatican medieval collections, he had papal authority to investigate the _sancta sanctorum_ of small, unknown churches and cathedrals."

"Topic Mimara told me," I interjected, "that he would inform James Rorimer where he got the cross after we make final payment, if that ever comes about. Which leads me back to my other question. Who is my competition? Topic mentioned Boston, Cleveland, the Louvre, the British Museum, the Victoria and Albert, and even Sotheby's."

"All of those are, I suppose, effective possibilities against you. I fear I carried out my strategy all too well. But that was before you entered my life. The Metropolitan did have the first chance. But now there are other people and institutions who saw the cross. All of them may be pursuing it."

"Jesus!" I moaned. "Can you tell me?"

"This is what I know," Parsons intoned gravely. "I must admit to you I mentioned the cross to a dear friend at the Cleveland Museum before anyone else in the world, in December 1955. He is Henry Francis, the curator of Paintings and Drawings, a gentle, superbly educated and witty man with whom I have corresponded regularly for years. Henry may have told William Milliken. But at that moment I offered an option to James Rorimer, and I presume you have examined that correspondence. Later I alerted the great Hanns Swarzenski of Boston. I also talked about the cross at length with Kenneth Clark, who then saw it and virtually fell on his knees before it. Clark pledged to inform John Pope-Hennessey of its existence. In addition, Topic Mimara traveled to London several times over the years and showed photographs of the divine work of art to some key experts—Peter Wilson at Sotheby; some functionary at the Victoria and Albert, whose name I have forgotten; and now, in recent weeks, to the keeper of Medieval Antiquities at the British Museum. I think Topic mentioned the piece to a German private collector. Whether or not he approached the Louvre, I am not positive. Probably. Everyone who saw the cross was deeply impressed, and it would seem that everyone is going after it."

"Do you know for certain? Can you tell me more?" I begged him.

"Your predecessor at The Cloisters—Randall, wasn't it? —made a terrible impression upon Topic Mimara. He spent only an hour or so in the vault, barely enough time to examine the one object, much less the series of treasures Topic graciously presented to him. When the cross appeared, Randall glanced rapidly at both sides of the work as if he were performing a distasteful task. He rudely demanded to know the price. Topic was put off and told him it was not for sale. Then, I believe, he said it would be a million."

"Funny," I said. "Randall's notes to Jim mention *two* million."

"Impossible!" Parsons snapped. "I know Topic is a dreamer, but *two* million? Never! Jim Rorimer used a very clever ploy. Randall was instructed to appear to be disinterested for Jim's ultimate bargaining position. Rorimer came to Rome in the winter of 1957, and we talked about the object for hours. He had not seen it—never has, you know—but I am convinced he wanted it badly. And, if you will permit me to say so, your arrival and your attitude prove his continuing interest."

"Harold, let me tell you the facts. Randall wrote a memo to Rorimer just after his visit, saying that the cross was hogwash—a total fake. Rorimer is firmly against it. If I had a set of the highest-quality photographs, I might be able to capture his interest. Can't you get them?"

"Well, I think it might be possible. After all, you have seen the object in the flesh. I shall talk with Topic."

"Great! Now tell me what happened after Randall's visit."

"A few weeks later, William Milliken came to Zurich and studied the cross more than once. He called it 'a triumph.' He described to me how he was bowled over by the exceptional object, so complex, yet so pure, so symbolic of the very essence of the Christian faith. He considered the piece a world-class work of art."

"Then why didn't Milliken buy it for Cleveland?" I asked.

"He wanted to. But he had other obligations. At that moment Milliken was turning over the reins of the Cleveland Museum to Sherman Lee and wanted *him* to deal with the cross."

"Harold, what happened with him?"

"Sherman is a remarkable individual. I remember meeting him for the first time in New York in 1943. Sherman Lee—what a juxtaposition of generals! I took him to see Joe Brummer's magnificent material, and Sherman was humble and devout. I can assure you, had he not been I would have pilloried him with my favorite quotation from old Cardinal Newman: 'No one of us is infallible—not even the youngest.' But before this incomparable combination of William Tecumseh Sherman and Robert E. Lee saw the great ivory cross and fell head over heels in love with it, several other of your staunch rivals came, examined, and went away to plot their various conspiracies.

"Who?"

"I had, as you know, communicated with Hanns Swarzenski. He rose like a trout to a fly. I briefed him fully. My goodness, it was at the very table where we dined last evening. Swarzenski studied the cross in the vault, proclaimed to Topic Mimara his belief that it dated to the tenth century, and was positively English. He wanted to buy it for Boston, but could not raise the funds. This took place only three, possibly four years ago. Swarzenski was immersed in purchasing a spectacular Gothic Madonna and Child which some people claim was part of the clandestine Goering collection. That is yet another art tale. From what I hear, Swarzenski still hopes to pursue the sublime cross."

"After Swarzenski, who saw it next?" I asked.

"Immediately after Hanns must have been Sir Kenneth Clark, who in turn alerted John Pope-Hennessy, who adored it. Topic Mimara informed me Pope-Hennessy made a sizable offer. But it was not enough. Lucky for you. I urge you to be wary of the Victoria and Albert Museum. You are acquainted with Pope-Hennessey, aren't you?"

"I certainly am. And he worries me. He's brilliant and tenacious. Although the Middle Ages is not his field, I figure the 'Pope' would recognize the quality of the cross. His associate, John Beckwith, is pretty capable, too."

"I know for a fact, Thomas, that both of them are in hot pursuit."

Listening to Parsons' story, I became fearful. A strict rule in art collecting is never to chase after a piece that a lot of others have already examined and rejected. Why had this host of perceptive and aggressive professional collectors failed to take any action? Was Randall, after all, not the only person to have branded the cross a forgery? Or was Parsons embellishing the facts?

"It doesn't sound to me as if any of these people is really interested," I observed.

"To make that judgment," Parsons warned, "is to commit a tragic error. The process of negotiation takes time, especially with an object as unusual as the cross, under the control of a man who is essentially a dreamer and an enthusiast but is most unrealistic in the matter of evaluations. I know that now that he has reduced the price from staggering heights to at least a discussable level, all who have seen the cross are, or will be, back in the fray."

"Do you think Topic might be persuaded to come down from the six hundred thousand dollars he quoted to me?"

"Possibly, but it depends upon how many competitors are still in the race. The most serious competitor you have has just left the starting block," Parsons told me with a concerned look on his face. "Only weeks ago the British Museum sent their top medievalists, including Ruppert Bruce-Mitford, the keeper. He studied the cross for four days, longer than we fast-paced Americans seem to manage. He described it to Topic Mimara as the single most important English medieval object in existence. I happen to have a copy of the letter Bruce-Mitford wrote to Topic. I suppose I should not show it to you, so please keep this in confidence."

I winced when I read the key sentiment in Bruce-Mitford's communication: "We want the cross at any price, but the sum you have mentioned will require an act from Parliament. We are proceeding to seek just that. . . ."

That evening I proceeded to write a letter to James Rorimer describing everything I had learned about Topic Mimara. But I left out those points which I thought might cause my director concern. And with that act I embarked upon a path of deception, selecting and screening information, so as not to jeopardize my chance to capture the work of art by which I had become obsessed. I begged Rorimer to find out through his secret sources the true intentions of Boston, Cleveland and the two English museums.

I also revealed my discovery of the Aaron plaque in Florence without mentioning that I had held it in my hand. I cited its existence as "absolute proof the enigmatic cross is authentic beyond question, doubt, hint or suggestion." Finally, I informed my superior that I had made some headway in cracking the messages inscribed upon the cross.

I had been plugging away, a little bit each day, searching through my Latin Bible for the five inscriptions on the scroll in the medallion on the front of the ivory. How difficult it was! To locate three lines had taken me hours. Two I never did find. I had to skim through the entire Bible, Old and New Testaments for each inscription. I would read up one column, down the next, guiding my finger along the Latin text, hardly closing my burning eyes so as not to miss a key word. And then I found it! In the third chapter of John were the words *Sicut Moyses*. What a feeling of pleasure!

I had written down the abbreviated Latin from the cross as SICUT MOYSES EXALTAVIT SERPENTE IDESERTO ITA E. O. F. H. Although I guessed the reference was to the Brazen Serpent, I had no idea what the letters E. O. F. H. meant. The discovery elated me. The full text was: *Sicut Moyses exaltavit serpente in deserto. Ita exàltari oportet Filium hominis.* It was Chapter 3, Verse 14, of John the Evangelist: "And as Moses lifted up the serpent in the wilderness, even so must the Son of man be lifted up." It was obviously a reference to the Crucifixion.

And, after an hour of searching, finding nothing, searching again, I had identified two more scrolls within the medallion. The scroll held by Moses in the center of the medallion, which I had recorded as SIC ERIT VITA TVA PENDEN. S ANE T Ø N CREDE VIE TVE, was actually *Et erit vita tua et non credes vita quasi pendens ante te. Timebis nocte et die et non credes vite tuae*—"And thy life shall hang in doubt before thee. Thou shalt fear night and day and shalt have none assurance of thy life." The phrase, from Deuteronomy 28:66, was intended, I thought, as a direct Old Testament reference to the Passion of Christ. The artist of the cross had not copied the precise text of the Bible, which is why I had such difficulties identifying his wording.

I was worried. Could it be the mark of a forger? It wasn't. The texts of medieval Bibles varied, sometimes a great deal. So a variant would be an excellent argument in favor of authenticity.

The third scroll, held by the prophet looking out and

down from the interior of the medallion, read: QUARE RUBRU IDUMENTU TUU VESTIMENT SIC. C. T. Fortunately the first two words were complete. And it was through them I eventually found the full text in Isaiah: *Quare ergo rubrum est indumentum tuum: et vestimenta tua calcantium in torculari*—"Wherefore art thou red in thine apparel and thy garments like Him that treadeth in the wine vat?"

What this Old Testament passage was supposed to refer to in the New I was not at all sure. At length I concluded it must be either the scourging of Christ or his Passion as a whole.

When I examined the three verses I had deciphered, I saw that Hanns Swarzenski had been right. The inscriptions amounted, so far, to a typology—the use of verses, phrases or even single words plucked from the Old Testament as parallels for the New Testament and proofs that Christ was Messiah, Son of God and Redeemer.

I was pleased that the hardest part of the decoding seemed to be over. All the prophets on the back of the cross were identified by name. Tracing their utterances would not entail poring through the entire Bible. I even hoped that I might be able to match the singular typology of the cross to a known medieval author and thereby possibly learn the place where the cross was carved and when. I believed I was on the threshold of a landmark discovery.

Much as I wanted to press on with my search through my Bible, I couldn't. I had to put it aside and meet Harold Parsons at the studio apartment of Pico Cellini, which was located in one of Rome's oldest quarters, in Trastevere. Pico, a ruggedly handsome silver-haired individual, greeted me with a radiant smile and conducted me through his elegant apartment. I noted a number of drawings by Piazzetta, the Venetian master of the eighteenth century, which were of superior quality.

Cellini's studio, upstairs, was ramshackle in a studied way. The place was crowded with easels positioned like extras in an opera. Each easel had a painting clamped to it, some right side up, some sideways and others tantalizingly upside down. Cellini walked slowly through his forest of art, explaining his conservation work. Few things are more fascinating than an ancient, yellow painting with just part—an inch or two of a face, or a tree deep within a landscape—freshly cleaned. In seconds, I had to admit Pico was an expert.

He discussed the art of conservation in sensitive and persuasive terms. He would scrutinize a painting intently, placing his hand on the side of his face, with his fingers spread like a starfish, while explaining rapidly in a deep gruff voice how he was bringing forth "the truth" and preserving the work for humanity. My respect for him increased by the minute. Then Pico mentioned, almost as if it were an afterthought, an extraordinary little marble sculpture he had encountered in a private collection. It was the head of a man, half life-sized, which Pico claimed was carved in Pentelic marble and which he said was most unusual, since that variety of marble could have come only from Greece.

"This, Dr. Hoving, will most certainly interest you," Cellini said, handing the piece over to me with a sweeping motion. "The owner found it buried in one of the interior walls of his villa in Genoa, built originally in the thirteenth century. The style of the head is, of course, thirteenth century. The marble tells you who it is. What significant individual—what ruler of Italy during the thirteenth century—would have bothered to instruct his official sculptor to obtain marble from Greece?"

I thought I knew whom he meant, but I couldn't believe it.

"This ruler must have been a classicist," Pico continued. "And he could only have been—" here Pico paused dramatically—"Emperor Frederick the Second of Hohenstaufen, who, as we all know, initiated his own Renaissance long before the fifteenth century. Superb, is it not?"

The face of the sculpture was oily smooth, the skin carved so that it seemed to stretch over the high cheekbones under powerful tension. A sort of diadem or crown adorned the man's head. But the head wasn't Pentelic marble; it was alabaster. The style was later than the powerful manner of Frederick's time. Yet, for all of that, it was not uninteresting.

Harold Parsons, who had been circling us like a larger fish at the edge of a school, darted in. "Thomas, this is the only portrait of Frederick in existence, other than the one in the museum in Benevento. It would be perfect for

The Cloisters, a summation of everything that sublime institution stands for and a great personal coup for you. Pico, do you believe you could ever persuade the owner to part with his Frederick?"

Cellini shrugged pleasantly and eased slightly away.

Aha! I finally realized why I had been brought to the studio. Parsons quietly observed that adding the "rare and distinguished portrait" to the collections of The Cloisters might have a beneficial effect upon my career. I got the message. The price was high—twenty-five thousand dollars—but I calmly promised him I'd buy the little head if I won the cross. Parsons touched my arm affectionately. I had taken another step down the road toward mendacity.

"Well done, Thomas, I do like you. And in honor of your most accomplished and executive decision, I shall let you in on a great secret. Within several months I will have procured a fabulous treasure, a sculpture by Giovanni Pisano which once adorned the campanile of the cathedral in Siena and which may—will, I hope—become available in Switzerland or London. When that day happens, you will be the first to know."

"Will this too, Harold, be part of our deal?" I asked.

"Oh, no. And, the head of Frederick isn't really part of any . . . deal," he protested, smiling in a little hurt way.

The ritual of farewell was lengthy, warm, sentimental. There were glasses of excellent Verdicchio, handshakes, inflated promises to stay in touch. After a while I felt a bit cruel for having harbored any unkind thoughts about Harold Woodbury Parsons. The last impression I had of him as he embraced me on the street in front of Cellini's apartment was of a kindly, sincere, elderly aesthetician, perhaps caught up too tightly in the art trade, but a man who genuinely appreciated me and would try everything to help me on my quest. We traded assurances of unflagging friendship, and I parted with yet another impassioned plea for photographs.

"You shall have them, Thomas," he promised as I turned and walked away.

CHAPTER TWELVE

Out of Focus

ALTHOUGH SADDENED TO leave Rome, I did look forward to the last three stages of the trip: Munich, Paris and London, and particularly Munich, for there I would find the proper laboratory where the film from my Minox could be developed. I had waited until Munich, figuring that a German photographic technician would be more able to deal with the film from the German camera. Before checking into my hotel on the Barerstrasse, I found a photographic laboratory and pressed the proprietor to take the utmost pains with my valuable film.

I called Dr. Erich Steingräber, who was then the associate curator of medieval art at the famous Bayerisches National Museum, and arranged for him to join me for dinner. Erich was one of the most brilliant art historians in Germany and had been a key influence in my professional life, despite the fact that he was only a few years older than I. The year I had arrived at the Metropolitan had been the year Steingräber had come for six months to give Rorimer his opinion on the objects at The Cloisters and the Medieval Department. Meeting him, I had at once recognized a superior professional who could teach me more about works of art than even James Rorimer. We had enjoyed many long evenings together in the deserted galleries, examining hundreds of treasures which we removed from their vitrines and spread across the green felt-covered table.

To watch Steingräber approach a work of art was an exciting experience. He seemed to circle around the object at first, like a stalking animal. He would inspect the piece in front of him for several moments without touching it, to satisfy himself nothing was fragile or glued together. His eyes seemed to dart over all surfaces, flickering as though they were on fire.

With a rapid and sure motion, Steingräber would quite suddenly seize the object. He would hold it far from his face, then bring it close, turning it completely around, upending the thing, glancing several times at its bottom and inside. He would stare at it without comment. Eventually, words would slip from his thin line of a mouth in a litany, gathering speed: "Beautiful," "Grand," *"Spezial, nicht wahr?,"* and soon the words *nicht wahr*—"Is it not so?"—would begin to dominate his remarks. Erich would gracefully replace the object on the table, turn to me, eyes glowing with pleasure, and say, "Tom, excellent piece! Condition perfect, better than the examples in Dresden, Berlin, the Louvre and Cleveland. A truly surprising example of brown enamel, *nicht wahr?*" And then he would launch into a learned and intriguing description of how the unusual substance of "brown enamel" had been manufactured during the Middle Ages, complete with statistics on the temperatures required in the oven to fire and produce the enamel.

Steingräber never held back what he thought. Once we were scrutinizing together one of the most valuable reliquaries in the collections, of beaten silver in the shape of an index finger. The reliquary, considered by all the experts who had looked at it to be of the early thirteenth century, perched upon three slim legs. An inscription, which no one had been able to translate, encircled the base of the finger. But the most special feature of the finger reliquary was a large solid silver ring inset with an emerald fully half an inch across.

Steingräber went through the movements of his examination, set the reliquary back on the table and informed me gently, "Tom, this thing is a fake."

"What?" I exploded. "Erich, Jesus, this thing is one of our best pieces! It came from the private collection of one of our most powerful trustees, who collected only the finest—and rarest reliquaries. What makes it a fake?"

"Do you see these three almost invisible stamps on this leg here?"

"Sure. They're the maker's marks."

"Of the thirteenth century?" Steingräber pleasantly queried and then continued, "Impossible. This particular type of mark normally appears only on French goldsmith work of the late eighteenth century."

"Eighteenth century? Well, there's probably a legitimate explanation. They must have been added later," I tried.

"Oh, no. Look through your magnifying glass and you will see that these so-called stamps are cast into the silver. They are clearly not stamped as they should be."

"Ah," I sighed. "Well, Erich, one little deficiency doesn't make—"

But Steingräber interrupted me. "The final proof that this thing is a fake is this emerald ring. One cannot remove it, *nicht wahr?* That is a problem. In every other finger reliquary in existence, the ring can be removed, because these rings were always placed on the reliquary later as homage to the saint."

"I see. What about the emerald?"

"That seems excellent. Perhaps it was put there to make the price of the object really worthwhile for the collector and, of course, for the forger as well."

Steingräber and I reminisced at a small Italian restaurant in Schwabing. Eventually I told him all I had learned about the ivory cross and its quixotic owner.

"I have heard of it, this cross, but only in vague terms. That inscription, 'King of the Confessors,' is highly convincing to me, even if it's not absolute evidence of authenticity. You must discuss this piece with my director, Theodore Müller. He was at the Collecting Point and may have become acquainted with this Topic Mimara. You must also talk to Ludwig Heidenreich and Florentine Mütherich at the Central Institute for Art History. They too were at the Collecting Point."

I had no inkling that the dinner with Steingräber would

be the prelude to disaster. But it was. When I returned to my hotel the concierge informed me, with a smile, that in my absence he had moved my luggage to another, more spacious room with a better view. I was delighted, for the chamber was superior. It was not until I had unpacked and slipped into bed that my mind registered that something was amiss. Everything I had brought from Rome was there—except for one item. It was the folder I had removed from my suitcase when I had gone to my first room, the folder with the Latin and English Bibles and my lists of all the inscriptions on the cross. Missing. The concierge and the porter who had moved my possessions did the best they could, but the folder never turned up again.

I sank into one of the deepest depressions of my life. I desperately tried to phone Topic Mimara in Tangier, and then in the hotel where he had stayed in Zurich, to attempt to see the cross again before I returned to New York. It was as though he had vanished.

But all was not lost. At least I remembered the three inscriptions I had deciphered. And I was confident the Minox photographs might reveal the others. In the morning I called the photographic laboratory and was told the prints would be processed in two days. My spirits improved.

Theodore Müller, the genial director of the Bayerisches National Museum, listened to my story about the cross and burst out, "Topic Mimara? Oh, I remember him! But I'm not sure that was the name he used during our days at the Collecting Point."

"What about just Mimara, or perhaps Matutin?" I volunteered. "That's what Dick Randall and Hanns Swarzenski remember him as."

"Mimara. Most of the time it was simply Mimara," Müller replied and laughed heartily. "The man was quite . . . comical. He showed up at Munich very late in the history of the Collecting Point. It must have been 1948. He wore a uniform, a uniform of the Yugoslav Army. He was a full colonel, I believe. Very flamboyant. I could be mistaken, but I recall he carried with him some sort of swagger stick or marshal's baton. Gave parties. Was exceedingly polite and charming. Had a distinctive, perfectly

groomed little black Vandyke beard. Everyone liked him
—and wondered who he really was."

"What do you mean?" I asked.

"This Mimara was rich. Threw his money around la-
vishly. In 1948 one wondered where that money could
possibly have come from. There were rumors, of course."

"Do you remember their substance?"

"It has been so very many years. The period just after
the war was strained. Some people acted in ways that
today would be considered contemptible, but then—well,
few cared. Some of us assumed Mr. Mimara was involved
in the black market."

I asked Theodore Müller if he had ever seen Mimara's
ivory cross.

"I have heard about it, but I never saw the piece
either physically or through photographs."

"Could Topic have found the cross at the Collecting
Point and simply walked off with the thing?" I probed.

"Highly unlikely," Müller replied. "Once something of
that unusual nature had been brought to the Collecting
Point, it would never have disappeared. No! Now that I
think about it, I was told of the existence of the cross
by Hermann Schnitzler at the Schnütgen Museum in
Cologne. He saw it and may know a good deal more
about it."

"What about Fritz Volbach? Did he ever discuss the
cross with you?"

"Never."

"Anything else you can tell me, sir?"

"Only that this Topic Mimara Matutin was a peculiar,
mysterious character, and you should be prudent in your
dealings with him."

Within minutes I was conversing with Hermann
Schnitzler on the phone at the Schnütgen Museum in
Cologne.

"It is very strange, Dr. Hoving, that you have telephoned, since I was thinking of the curious Topic Matutin
just last week, wondering what had happened to him. I
remember the individual vividly. He came to see me after
the war—I believe it was 1951 or possibly a year earlier.
He arrived at my offices unannounced. What an apparition! The man looked like a Turk! He was wearing a red
fez and had a luxurious mustache. How can one forget

such an individual? He carried with him a leather satchel from which he drew out an old chamois bag. Out of that Mr. Matutin extracted an ivory carving, telling me it was the top of a large processional cross made for Emperor Constantine. His theory was outrageous. I attempted to inform the man that whatever he had chanced upon was certainly not early Christian. Would that it were! Anyway, the ivory looked as if it had never been cleaned—it was the color of creamed coffee—and was carved with a variety of impressive images. I recall the Ascension, a most unusual depiction of the High Priest and Pontius Pilate standing upon a special platform, probably the stairs of the Temple . . ."

"Dr. Schnitzler, how do you know the scene was the High Priest and Pilate?"

"Simple. In Latin I could see Pilate's famous phrase 'What I have written I have written.' You know it, of course."

"Of course, of course," I said quickly.

"The Book of John." Schnitzler seemed to bark the words.

"Do you recall," I asked, "what the priest's scroll said?"

"Yes, of course. It was from the well-known passage in John where the High Priest, Annas, came to Pontius Pilate and said, 'Write not King of the Jews, but that he said, I am King of the Jews.'"

"Curious," I remarked half to myself.

"Yes. The iconography is exceedingly rare," Schnitzler said.

I described to Schnitzler what I now knew about the cross, giving particular attention to the "Confessors" inscription.

"'Confessors,'" he intoned. "That is most extraordinary. Offhand, I do not know what it could possibly signify. But do look into certain very early Irish exegeses on the nature of the cross. I seem to remember dimly that a certain sect in eighth-century Ireland used the word 'confession' in an unusual manner."

"What is your opinion of this piece?"

"I have to say that I never give an opinion without examining a work of art in its entirety. So I am very sorry. You will understand that I can say no more than that the piece seemed to be, I suppose, early to mid-twelfth century."

"Authentic?" I tried to pin Schnitzler down.

Whereupon the scholar drew sharply away from the conversation, saying he could not be certain. I would surely understand. I asked him who else might know about the piece. He advised me to try Erich Meyer in Berlin. The last words he uttered lifted my spirits: "From your description of the cross and what I remember, the object sounds authentic beyond question. It sounds very ambitious."

The voice of Erich Meyer, curator of Decorative Arts at the National Museum in Berlin, practically pierced my ear when I reached him on the phone. "Topic Mimara? Oh, yes, I do remember him. He is still living? You want information about him? I recall our last meeting clearly. It was just before the war, in 1938. The man *and* his object were unforgettable." As I listened, I feverishly made copious notes on what he told me, and as soon as I could I reconstructed his remarks.

Erich Meyer's first reaction when his secretary informed him that the "sinister Yugoslav art dealer" had shown up again in his outer office without warning was that anyone who could enter and leave Germany in 1938 to collect works of art had to be an agent for the Third Reich. Then, instantly, Meyer was furious with himself. National Socialism, he reflected bitterly, seemed to reduce everyone to suspicion.

Meyer had no desire to see the fellow. It was late and he had just packed and locked his briefcase, an act emphatically symbolizing the end of his working day. Damnation! It would be fruitless, as it had been several years before when this same mysterious man had shown up with a "golden treasure trove." Every piece in the "trove" had turned out to be worthless. "Balkan things," Meyer had characterized them disdainfully at the time. The man obviously had no knowledge of art. How could he survive as an art dealer? Who would buy such ludicrous pieces?

Nonetheless, he consented to see him. His decision was made partly out of guilt for having labeled the visitor a Nazi without the slightest actual knowledge, and partly because Meyer, one of the most gifted connoisseurs in

Europe, could never resist examing any work of art, no matter how unpromising the circumstances.

"I deeply appreciate the honor, Herr Doktor Professor, of having the opportunity to see you," Topic Mimara said deferentially. "I always value your observations. I have always hoped that someday I might discover a work of art measuring up to your standards. And I have. It is this plaque of walrus ivory which I humbly believe is Italian and dates to the early Christian period, probably the beginning of the fifth century." With these words, Erich Meyer recalled, Topic Mimara laid a square block of ivory on a small velvet cushion. The ivory seemed to shine against the deep-blue fabric.

Meyer's trained eyes reacted instantly to the object before him. A torrent of words, phrases, associations, dates, titles of books and articles surged through his mind. As he studied the piece, Meyer carried on within his mind a high-pitched conversation with himself. "Now, *this is* something, not so? Splendid piece. Crisp, finely carved and strong in composition. The work of a master. The claim that it is early Christian is nonsense! The figures are far too thin, elongated, but they could have been inspired by something early Christian. Yes. Remarkable. Have I seen anything like it? No. Never. It is unique. Who would have thought this Slavic bumpkin would have found such a piece!"

Erich Meyer readily identified the scene as the three Marys coming to the empty sepulcher where the majestic angel of the Lord sat. Aided by a magnifying glass, he gazed raptly at the minute letters carved into the scroll held by the angel. Taking up a pencil, he copied the inscription: QUERITIS NAZ. IHM: RENUM CRUCIFI. He mumbled to himself, "Ye seek Jesus of Nazareth, which is crucified."

Meyer interrupted his study of the piece to make a few notes describing the scene. He jotted down the titles of several reference books on the iconography of the scene. When he returned to the object, his eyes took in the virtuosity of the carvings. "Aren't the little figures beautiful? I can even see the delicate bones of Christ's naked chest. Incredible! And the wounds in His hands—so tiny, yet easily visible. Such an accomplished chain of little people. So alive! One would like to pluck them out of their diminutive world and set them out here on the desk and hear their eager and excited words as they might describe their awe and rapture at the empty sarcophagus, the angel and the risen Christ. Ah!" Meyer's eyes took in the tightly bunched group of sleeping soldiers lying beneath the open sarcophagus. There were five of them. He examined the differing shapes of helmets and noted with interest the apronlike tunics, slit on each side, worn by the warriors. Late eleventh—early twelfth century, he thought. Distinctly early twelfth century, he concluded.

Meyer set the carving back on the pillow and looked into the face of his visitor. "The piece is fascinating," he said with a smile. "It is of extremely high quality. But it is definitely *not* early Christian. What is key to the date of the ivory are the draperies which cling to the figures as if they were slightly wet, so that the limbs are subtly revealed. This is an element which can be dated with assurance: I would say somewhere within the first half of the twelfth century.

"Now, as to the place of origin, I cannot be sure. A lengthy comparision with other pieces would be needed. But, offhand, my impression is that this ivory—and it has been carved by a master, I can assure you—is probably a product of what we art historians term the Channel School. Not that the piece was made on an island in the middle of the English Channel. 'Channel School' is simply a convenient way to describe those works of art which could have been made either in England or in France during a time when there were frequent associations between monasteries and artistic workshops both in England and on the Continent."

"Is the piece valuable?" Topic queried.

"I should say so. Yes. Do you intend to offer it for sale?"

"No, no, I cannot," Topic insisted. "You see, it is not really mine. It belongs to a certain private collector. I simply cleaned the piece."

"Would you mind telling me who the owner is?" Meyer asked.

"I am sorry, but I am not allowed to do that. You must understand."

Perfectly understandable, Meyer reflected. In times like these, who in his right mind would reveal ownership of any work of art, particularly one like this, one of excellence and portability? "Well, you can tell the owner that if he ever thinks of selling the piece, I would be most interested in having it for Berlin."

"Unfortunately, Dr. Meyer, I know the owner will never sell. Never."

"I see," Meyer responded. He saw he would get no further with the man. "I have some advice for you—and the owner. Take the ivory to Dr. Adolph Goldschmidt, professor of art history at the University of Berlin. He is the world authority on medieval ivories. He has completed several volumes of a comprehensive catalogue of the known pieces throughout the world. Adolph Goldschmidt would be able to tell you a great deal more about this fine object than I. And there is another scholar who might be illuminating—one of Goldschmidt's pupils, a certain Kurt Weitzmann. And, yes, a third individual. His name is Fritz Wolfgang Volbach, an expert in early Christian and medieval ivories. But he no longer lives in Germany; he is in Rome. They might be helpful. Your piece is of the highest quality and I will tell you again, I would be interested in acquiring it for Berlin under the proper circumstances.

Meyer's story thrilled me, and his observations gave me confidence in the stature of the cross. After I had spoken to Meyer, I went over to the Central Institute, where I met the director, Ludwig Heidenreich, and one of the professors, Dr. Florentine Mütherich.

Ludwig Heidenreich turned out to be a heavyset, square-headed man who looked like the archetypal Hun out of a World War I poster. But his personality belied his physical appearance. He was a gentle humanist and responded graciously to my inquiry about Ante Topic Mimara.

"I was not concerned directly with the work of the Collecting Point, but I helped out in any way I could. The task of bringing together, cataloguing, researching and eventually returning the hundreds of thousands of works of art was simply incredible," he explained. "Mr. Mimara does stand out in my memory. I met him two, possibly three times. He intrigued me because he seemed to be German, yet was demonstrably working for Yugoslavia. The man was charming, gregarious and active.

Munich was, as you probably know, the major center. Subsidiary centers were in such places as Weisbaden, Stuttgart and Berlin. Most representatives of the various missions were assigned to one city. Topic Mimara was unusual in that he traveled frequently to each place. Perhaps this is of no significance. It is possible that Yugoslavia, being a poor country, could provide only a few people and had to move them around. Oh, yes, there's something else I remember. The Yugoslavs in the mission seemed to me an unlikely group of men to have been assigned to the field of art. They all looked tough. Their knowledge, including that of Mr. Mimara, seemed sparse.

"Here's something which may interest you," he went on. "There was an American, the chief of intelligence for the United States mission, who had grave suspicions about what Mimara was doing. I seem to remember that the American felt Mimara had done something wrong and that he was determined to investigate his affairs.

"Who was the American?" I asked.

"Edgar Breitenbach is his name. A charming man, born in Germany. He is an art historian, studied with Erwin Panofsky. He is now at the Library of Congress in Washington. Here, let me write his name down for you."

Dr. Florentine Mütherich, a beautiful woman in her mid-fifties, laughed gaily when I brought up the name Topic Mimara. At my mention of the cross, she drew back in mock horror. "Him!" she smiled. "Watch out for him; he is a bad man. Anything he has to sell may be . . . strange."

"How? Why? Tell me," I pleaded.

"There are some famous stories about Topic Mimara. No proof, just stories. That is the kind of man he is. Topic Mimara was, and still is—you say he still lives? —an art dealer. His works of art are said to be of poor quality. No one knows how he really makes his living. I have heard that at the Collecting Point Topic Mimara seduced a young art historian assigned to his mission— each one had a German representative—and that she, I cannot recall her name now—"

"Would it be Wiltrud Mersmann?" I cut in.

"Mersmann? Yes. That's it. Topic Mimara is said to have seduced this girl. Together, they were supposed to have expropriated some works of art from the storerooms at the Collecting Point."

"They stole works of art?" I asked.

"Of *that* I am not certain. Perhaps the material was not technically stolen."

"But how could that have been?"

"Certain things happened. Perhaps the authorities had given permission—of a sort. And I recall hearing somewhere that in the early 1950s Topic Mimara got into some difficulties with the German police. A woman from Czechoslovakia complained to the authorities that this Topic Mimara had taken a number of old-master paintings from her to sell on her behalf and then disappeared to Tangier. My advice," Florentine Mütherich said pleasantly, "is to be careful with the man and his art."

I thanked her and decided I would most surely be careful. For one thing, I'd never mention any of what I had heard to Jim Rorimer.

Early the next morning, before driving to the airport, I stopped at the photographic laboratory to retrieve my developed Minox film.

"I say, is this *all* of it?" I said to the technician incredulously.

"Sir, acute attention was paid to the job. Your instructions were followed precisely."

"But just *four* prints? And looking like *this?*"

"Unfortunately, that is all we were able to develop. Perhaps, sir, there was a minor malfunction. The focus."

"There *was* no focus," I insisted.

"But surely you set the distance precisely. May I look at your camera?"

"You cannot *set* the distance with the Minox I have," I all but shouted. "It's the kind with only the measuring chain."

"Ah. Too bad. That explains the problem," the clerk muttered.

"Can you print them again?" I pleaded. "Sharpen them somehow?"

"There is nothing we can do. I am sorry. Next time, you should perhaps practice a little more with the measuring chain. Or, better, trade your model in for one with the focus."

"There will never be a next time," I muttered. I shuffled through the four fuzzy prints of the cross, again and again, as if by my moving them, gazing at them, they would miraculously become sharp. All I saw were four barely perceptible shadows. My clever espionage activity had resulted in utter failure.

A chilling rain pelted the city of Paris for the two days I was there, deepening my sense of loss. I had to force myself to make the rounds of art galleries. I found half a dozen works worthy of consideration for The Cloisters, but they really didn't ignite my excitement. None of the dealers, and none of my colleagues in the medieval sections of the Louvre and the Cluny Museum, had ever heard of Ante Topic Mimara or his cross.

London was dark, cold and gloomy, enclosing me in a cocoon. I dutifully visited the antique shops, not really appreciating anything. I made the customary rounds of the medieval collections of the Victoria and Albert and the British Museum. And there my spirits began to rise for the first time since Munich. I came across half a dozen ivory carvings which, if not identical in style to the cross, like the Aaron plaque were at least comparable in style. They were all labeled English. I carefully noted their acquisition numbers, so that I could write for photographs and specific information later.

I wondered if I should seek out my friend John Beckwith at the Victoria and Albert, and grill him about Topic and his collection. When we did meet, I held back, sensing danger. At lunch I casually asked if he had come across anything grand on the market.

Beckwith glanced at me with the supercilious look he affected and spoke like a schoolmaster chiding an unpromising student. "Tom, Tom, Tom, no, no, no. I have seen nothing of *court* quality. If I had, would you actually expect me to tell you, my *only* . . . *informed* competition? Well, Tom, you know I would tell *you*. But there has been nothing! So discouraging. Nothing of *court* level."

Anything Beckwith believed had not been created in a court or palace workshop was beneath contempt, hardly collectible. I made a few more gentle probes, hoping he would mention the cross. Beckwith seemed deliberately to be avoiding my inquiries. I sneaked around the British Museum like a fugitive, as though Bruce-Mitford or one of his assistants might pop out of a musty corner of the place and seize me. I toyed with the idea of introducing myself to the man described by Harold Parsons as my archrival. In the end, naturally, I did not go near Bruce-Mitford.

I examined for hours the illuminations in the great Bible of Saint Albans. It was dated around 1120. That had been the very first work of art to come to mind when I first laid eyes on the ivory. The painted Saint Albans figures were obviously related to the style of the cross. The cross was definitely ten, possibly twenty years later in date, perhaps 1140–1150, or even 1160. I began to think I was getting somewhere.

It was late afternoon, and I decided to partake of an old British custom. I descended for tea into the cafeteria hidden in the bowels of the British Museum. And there I saw, purely by chance, one of the eminent medieval scholars in the world, George Zarnetski, a Polish emigré attached to the prestigious Courtauld Institute. I had met Zarnetski several years before and found him not only a brilliant scholar but a genuinely decent human being. He was pleased to see me and invited me to join him.

Since Zarnetski was not associated in any way with the British Museum or the Victoria and Albert, and since I trusted his sense of discretion, I brought up the subject of the ivory cross.

He breathed a small sigh and then averted his eyes momentarily. "Ah, I suppose I should not be at all surprised that you have asked this most unusual question. Yes, I am well acquainted with this work of art. I have studied it at considerable length here at the museum. We have a set of photographs. Now that you have broached the subject, I cannot hold myself back from telling you what I think."

My eyes never left Zarnetski's face.

"The British Museum is avid and determined to bring the cross into their English medieval collections. The keeper, Ruppert Bruce-Mitford, has brought together a group of experts in English medieval art and history to study the cross and advise him."

"You mean there are really photographs available?" I asked hoarsely.

"Why, yes. Large and impressive black-and-white photographs."

Those sons-of-bitches, I thought. "Can you tell me who the specialists are?"

Zarnetski looked slightly pained. "Perhaps that would not be ethical."

"Of course, I am sorry," I told him, cursing to myself.

"But I *would* be able to inform you of my opinion of the object."

"Please," I said eagerly.

"All I can say is that the institution that acquires that object can consider itself the most fortunate in the world!"

CHAPTER THIRTEEN

A Game of Chess

JAMES RORIMER GREETED me with the warm eagerness, tinged by regret, of a retired hunter about to peek into the bag of a younger colleague who had just returned from a bountiful safari.

"Well, out with it! Tell me, what did you find? Anything great?"

"I'll start with London and work backward, hitting the highlights," I said languidly. Just months before, I would have plunged directly into my tales of Zurich and the cross, but now I moved the elements in my story of the cross toward Rorimer like pieces in a chess game.

"London was uncannily empty," I opened. "There was nothing at the auction houses, and apparently little coming up in the next few months, only two ragtag sales of medieval objects. Barling on Mount Street has a wooden, unpainted Madonna. It's French, early thirteenth century. The condition's fine except for recarved folds on the lower right-hand drapery. At eight thousand four it's an attractive purchase, but it's not for us. *Unless* I can convince some private collector to buy it for us."

Rorimer nodded, his eyes glistening.

"Paris, as usual, offered a hell of a lot of fascinating pieces," I went on. "It may please you to know that Ryaux told me he'll come down five thousand dollars on that Lorraine Virgin you've wanted for years."

"Still not low enough. Go on."

I then described an abundance of objects at a half-dozen Parisian dealers I hoped would interest Rorimer, concluding with a spectacular bronze gilt reliquary bust of a young female saint. "The face of this girl is painted so delicately that you'd think it was a pastel in three dimensions," I told Rorimer. "I have made arrangements to have it sent out for study at our expense if we don't buy it, and at the dealer's if we do."

"Fine work. I know the piece, of course. I have admired it for years," Rorimer observed.

"The dealer just obtained this one last month," I commented dryly, not bothering to play to his game.

"So it isn't the German head reliquary?"

"No. This is Italian," I said quietly.

"I see. Please continue."

"Rome," I went on. "Pico Cellini, with Parsons in tandem, has a fascinating little marble head which he thinks is a twelfth-century portrait of Frederick the Second. I want to study this one and think further. If I think it's desirable, and if I get the price down, I'll recommend it to you. Parsons also mentioned something about a large marble sculpture by Giovanni Pisano, apparently from Siena. I didn't see it. Have you ever heard of it?"

"Never. And how was Harold Woodbury Parsons?"

"You were right. I didn't much like him at all."

"Interesting."

"Other than that, Rome was disappointing. But Florence was sensational."

"What makes you say that? Anything decent among the dealers in Florence is on the government's list and can't be exported. The dealers sit those pieces on their shelves to entice you."

"Not Salvatore Romano. He has an angel by Tino da Camaino which is out of this world."

"Do you have photos?"

"They're coming."

"Good. We shall study them together and make up our minds. How is Romano?"

"Fine. He sends you his best. Spain—Jim, that gilded cross I wrote you about is exceptional, but it'll never get out of the country. The painting by the Master of the Cubells Altar is better than the one we have and absolutely *not* a product of our Junyer brothers' workshop. I think you'll be impressed with it."

"Dammit, Tom! The ivory cross. What about that? That was the purpose of your trip, after all!"

"Of course," I said evenly. I hesitated for a moment. "I've been pondering how to convey to you my feeling about the significance of this piece. Jim, you can take all the objects I have just discussed and triple, even quadruple their value. The ivory cross is *much . . . more . . . important.*"

Rorimer grunted and stared at me, his black eyes seeming to penetrate my skull. I said nothing. Formerly, I would have pursued the issue, multiplying my expressions of praise, as though by the simple medium of superlatives I could sway him. Instead, I decided to interrogate him. "Were you able to find out what our competitors are doing about the cross?"

"What?" Rorimer retorted impatiently. "Wait a minute. You were really so taken by it? Did you really have a chance to study it?"

"For hours. Unhindered. With Carmen. She agrees with me."

"Did you get a set of photographs?"

"Topic Mimara still refused. But Parsons assured me he would obtain them. My strong impression is that we will get them. Of course, the pictures I wrote you I took with my Minox are only—well, I'd call them *concept* photos. I expected that. The Minox is somewhat overrated."

"Did this guy have anything else interesting?"

"Oh, yes. Medieval objects. Decorative arts. Loads of paintings. There is even a large Raphael which he showed me only in photographs and for a few seconds. But Randall was right about one thing. Topic also has a number of forgeries."

"I see. But you believe the cross is that fine?"

"It is the finest. Something of the most exalted stature."

"I hope you realize what you are saying," Rorimer commented gravely.

"What?" I reacted as if pricked. He smiled thinly.

"Cleveland is not interested," Rorimer said quietly. "I heard through secret contacts."

I just gazed at him.

"I have reason to believe Sherman Lee thinks the cross is a forgery. He's got a *very* good eye, don't you agree?"

"Sure. But if Lee thinks the thing's a fake, all that proves is that he *and* Dick Randall are both nuts," I said without raising my voice. "The cross is unquestionably genuine. You recall the ivory I wrote you about—the Aaron plaque I found in the Bargello? That's proof. And—"

"Sometimes one can't be sure until one examines an object in hand."

I could scarcely admit that I had broken into the case in Florence. I held my tongue.

"I have managed to glean, from yet other sources, that Boston is a very unlikely candidate for your cross."

"And their reason? Also fake?" I had to be careful Rorimer would not discover that Swarzenski and I had talked.

"No. They seem to be chasing an exceptionally expensive wooden Madonna and Child of the early Gothic period, said to have been discovered just after the war in a belltower of a small church near Chartres. I saw it once—don't ask me under what circumstances, my boy. I suspect it is either fake or a mediocre original, greatly recarved. Boston is so eager for this Madonna, it's unlikely they will drive for the cross." Rorimer paused briefly. "And what is Topic Mimara's current price for . . . your obsession?"

I had intended to tell him the truth. But after that crack, spendidly timed and ringing with truth, I played a juvenile game. "With great difficulty, I succeeded in bargaining the price down." I lowered my voice. "From eight hundred thousand to six."

"Madness," Rorimer muttered. "Here, let me have a look at your pirated photos."

I laid the wretched prints on the table, asserting again, rather weakly, that they were but "concept" photos. He just grunted. Nervously, I tried to point out who the figures were—the Brazen Serpent, Moses, the prophets,

Isaiah. But he fingered the photos like discarded playing cards.

"Madness," he whispered to himself.

"If Boston is out—and I presume we are, too," I put in acidly, "I will talk to Swarzenski about the cross. I have a responsibility to scholarship—"

"No. Don't do *that!*" Rorimer burst out, surprising me. "Keep silent on this," he hissed. "Stay away from anyone in the museum field. Talk only to people I approve of in advance."

"I have already discussed the cross with a few people," I replied coolly.

Rorimer leaned forward, his eyes locked to mine. "Who?"

"Steingräber. Theodore Müller."

"They're all right . . . I suppose."

"And George Zarnetski."

"Goodness, why?" He shrugged. "Well, he's trustworthy and very learned. I hope you took the precaution of seeking his confidentiality."

"I couldn't," I replied. I hesitated. Now was the time. In my game of chess, I moved a piece into check. "You see, Jim, George Zarnetski is on a blue-ribbon committee of top scholars gathered together by the British Museum to endorse the ivory cross. The British Museum is not just serious. They have definitely made up their minds to buy it."

"Are you sure?" he said and leaned forward.

"Positive. Somehow they obtained a set of photographs. They're examining them at this moment. Now. Every day."

"I wonder if I should find out their plans right now. No. I don't want to alert the British Museum yet about our interest. The director there, Sir Frank Francis, is a man of honesty, integrity and also—damn it all—a man of fierce determination. This cross will be immensely appealing to him."

"Do you know what Zarnetski told me?" I said excitedly. "He said the institution that gains this cross can consider itself the most fortunate in the world."

"He *did?*"

"Nothing less."

"Fritz Volbach thinks the same way." Rorimer's remark astonished me. He was even cagier than I had thought. "I talked at length with Volbach when he was here in New York. Peg Freeman put me onto him."

"What did you find out?" I asked.

"He said the cross is a masterpiece of the eleventh century, and its owner a somewhat curious but bona-fide art collector, a wealthy man. I have learned from other sources that Topic Mimara is an *armatore*, an arms manufacturer, like Bofors and Skoda. Not a wholly savory profession, perhaps, but . . . Did he strike you as man who could be trusted?"

"Hard to say. When he was head of the Yugoslavian mission at the Collecting Point, I heard—"

"Really!" Rorimer cut in. "Now that is interesting. It tends to confirm that he's bona fide. Only the most important and trustworthy people were selected to be heads of missions. You know, I was deeply involved in the Collecting Point myself. Helped formulate the program. Even wrote a book about my experiences, called *Survival*. Those days were unbelievable!"

I sat back, crossed my legs, and let his memories waft over me.

"My active period as monuments officer was between April and December 1945. I started as a second lieutenant, eventually became captain, serving with the advance section in Normandy, Paris and Germany. I did what I could to preserve cultural properties in that vast area. From the start I had *two* enemy armies to contend with. One was the Wehrmacht and the other our own troops, who in the fierce struggle didn't give much of a damn about châteaux, cathedrals or church spires where the Nazis, more often than not, placed snipers.

"The closer we got to Germany, the harder it was to save things; it was like clearing the woods of acorns. All I could do was to pick out the examples of architecture most worthy of saving and give quick advice on repairs. You cannot imagine the extent of the destruction! When I got to a château at Fontenay-sur-Mer, our bulldozers were about to push down the last wall of the chapel containing two handsome eighteenth-century statues. Being a mere staff officer, I had no authority to order people around. When I told the lieutenant in charge that the place was historic and should be protected, he was slightly

profane. That got me mad. I told him I'd taken photographs of what was left for my official report and that if
he went on with his destruction I would see to it that he
would have to answer to the report all the days of his
life. 'What a helluva way to fight a war,' he muttered.
But he backed down and stopped his wrecking.

"I dashed up to Mont-Saint-Michel to regulate how our
troops would be billeted in the spendid monastery. I had
no real authority to do so. But, you know, you can't get
anything done without breaking a rule or two along the
way."

I smiled.

"Curiously enough," Rorimer continued, "until our
armies got to Paris, no policy existed for the return of
Nazi-appropriated works of art to their rightful owners.
The Roberts Commission, named for a member of the
Supreme Court, set up in 1942, had charted guidelines
to deal with the fate of art in the path of war. But no
one had reckoned with the wholesale rape, pillaging and
appropriation of treasures by the Nazis—from state collections, private collections, both Jewish and non-Jewish.
Sadly, but true, the seizure of art by the victors from
the vanquished is as old as time itself. Yet nothing in
recorded history equates with the actions of certain
Germans in the last war. Their work was based on a
highly organized psychological and racial policy controlled
by a certain Dr. Alfred Rosenberg, a self-styled philosopher who played a huge part in the Nazis' propa-
gation of anti-Semitism. To Rosenberg the works of art
in Jewish hands were considered ownerless, since Jews
were 'legally' stateless. All of the treasures were shipped
to Germany. There Hitler and Hermann Goering decided
what to do with them. The magnitude of the operation
was almost beyond imagining—at least thirty-five shipments, consisting of over a hundred and fifty freight-car
loads. Train after train.

"The wealth of treasures we found in repositories all
over the Western Zone was incomparable! In one mine
near Bad Ischl, I came across the very best from the
museums in Vienna—Rembrandts, Titians, all the Ve-
lásquezes, the Breughels, four Dürers plus forty-nine sacks
of tapestries and countless chests of smaller objects.

"I finally got to Munich in May 1945. There were

precious few reminders of the Munich I had known in the early twenties when I first visited the place with my father. The important museums were gutted! Ironically, only two structures had survived without much damage. One was Hitler's own office building, the Führerbau, and the other the party headquarters. They had survived the bombings because they had been well camouflaged and were surrounded by fire-fighting equipment.

"It was my idea to make the Führerbau the central Collecting Point for the works of art looted by the Nazis. From 1945 to around 1951 over five hundred thousand looted works of art were returned to their rightful owners throughout Europe. Goodness, how some of the art of Eastern countries had suffered—Poland, Czechoslovakia, Rumania, Albania, Yugoslavia. I find it most intriguing that our Topic Mimara was chief of mission. No, I never did meet him in Munich. You see, I left for home in December of 1945. Imagine that, chief of the mission."

"Jim, did you ever run across someone at the Collecting Point by the name of Edgar Breitenbach?"

"I recall that name from somewhere—but not Munich. Who's he?"

"Breitenbach is an art historian, trained by Panofsky. Apparently he works at the Library of Congress. I'm told he was an acquaintance of Topic Mimara at the Collecting Point and has certain information about him."

"At some point you may want to get in touch with him. I suppose we'll need a few references on Topic for the Purchase Committee, when we get to the point of formally presenting the cross."

I was elated. "What do you think you'll do about the cross? We should get moving."

He paused for only a moment. "I want to pursue this object with all deliberate speed and tenacity. I'd like to examine it myself. I will make immediate arrangements to get over to Zurich. If I like it, I will ask Mr. Topic Mimara to ship his cross here. I insist the members of the Purchase Committee see it on the table before them. The price, of course, is horrendous! But if this work is as good as you say—and I do trust your eye, you know that— it is perhaps worth such a high figure. Anyway, leave it to me to get the price reduced. I would like to get it down to around two hundred thousand. Six is insulting."

"Do you want me to prepare the forms for the trustees?"

"Not yet. It's too soon for that. I want Kurt Weitz-mann to see the piece to back us both up. After all, Kurt is the preeminent ivory expert in the world. I shall talk to him about going to Zurich—at our expense, naturally. The interest by the British Museum worries me deeply. I do want to proceed vigorously."

"Great!" I said. "I'll prepare a memo for you explaining the deal."

"Get cracking," Rorimer said. "I'm becoming excited about this."

"You won't be able to stop me."

Rorimer was silent for a moment. "*That* I know," he said laconically.

The next day I composed a crisp memorandum to Rorimer outlining what Topic Mimara wanted. His reply came back within hours, hand-delivered from the executive suite. He had obviously been in a playful mood. After I read his comments on each one of my points, I made a silent little victory dance around my office.

TO: JIM RORIMER
FROM: TOM
   1. The cross is owned by Ante Topic Mimara of Tangier and the object is on deposit in the vault of the Union Banque de Suisse, Zurich.

[Rorimer's comment: *I'm planning an interesting with-drawal soon—from Topic's bank account—and an interesting deposit.*]

   A. The conditions for its sale are the following:
      1. Price, 600 plus insurance and shipping expenses.
         a. Commission to Parsons is to be paid by Topic.

[Rorimer: *600 a problem—BUT, If we buy it, I will insist Topic give you the commission instead of Parsons.*]

   2. No photos are available for study except when Topic is present.

[Rorimer: *If both of us raise our not inconsiderable voices, we will, I'm certain, obtain a set.*]

3. On no condition will the cross be sent from Zurich for examination.

[Rorimer: *I said I would insist; but let's not cause too many problems.*]

4. Any individual interested in purchasing the cross must examine it at the vault with Topic present at all times. We can bring anyone we want to study it with us. Any responsible means of examination may be used on the thing.

[Rorimer: *I have drawn up a list of the team of experts we'll take with us to help study the object. I hope you approve of my choices. They are: Sherman, Bill Wixom, William Milliken, Hanns, Dick Randall, John Pope-Hennessy, B-Mitford, Frank Francis. Who do you want? I am glad Topic will allow me to bring an ultraviolet lamp. But more equipment than THAT is needed. Please make ready and pick up the following: X-ray, infra-red light, spectographic equipment, carbon-14 and a kitchen sink.*]

5. The purchaser may pay for the object over a number of years without interest. A suitable agreement will be drawn up, if necessary.

[Rorimer: *Perhaps the payment plan SHOULD BE: first year, 23 cents; second, 58 cents; third, $1.51; fourth, 38 cents; fifth, the rest totalling $4.95. That's a decent price! Although perhaps great things are worth great prices!*]

6. No information on the provenance of the cross will be given until either a part or total payment is given.

[Rorimer: *I have a suspicion he found it in Saint Patrick's. Why the devil can't he just come out with it?*]

7. The authenticity is guaranteed by the owner. At any time, if proof should be forthcoming from experts that the cross is of doubtful authenticity, the owner will take the object back and give full recompensation.

[Rorimer: *If we have to return the thing because of its "lack of authenticity" part of the "recompensation" will*

*be the appropriate anatomy of one of my fondest assist-
ants; perhaps you know him, his name is—"Tomic"
Hoving.*]

8. The cross will not be sold prior to February 1962.

[Rorimer: *I have set firmly aside from my hectic schedule
four, possibly five days, around the twenty-fifth of
January, when, together, we can go and study the vault,
the Topic, the Mimara, the cross. I shall enjoy this. And,
equally serious, please communicate with T.M. immediately letting him know (1) we shall be arriving in
Zurich, week of the 25th January. (2) Ask him when
his publication of the cross is coming out and (3) Emphasize yet again that we MUST be able to bring back
photos.*]

I prepared the letter to Topic and promptly telephoned
Rorimer to thank him for his support.

"Flattery with me, my boy, will get you nowhere—
only to Zurich. I cannot wait to see this obsession and to
put it under my ultraviolet lamp. That will authenticate
it."

"Perhaps it will," I replied.

The theory of the use of ultraviolet was simple. If an
ivory was modern, the rays of the black lamp would make
the material fluoresce bright lavender. If the ivory was
ancient, it would appear buttery yellow. The older a material, the more the sun's rays had penetrated over time
and the more muted and yellow the surface would show
up under ultraviolet. That was the theory. In practice the
ultraviolet had major flaws. Ultraviolet worked effectively
on hard stone or porcelain, indicating immediately and
vividly where recutting, repairs or patching had taken
place. But ivory was different, and Rorimer didn't seem to
realize it. It was easy for a forger to age the surface of
ivory so that the lamp would show what appeared to be an
authentic buttery yellow. Smoking the ivory by burning
pine needles soaked in fresh oil would do it. Or wrapping
the piece in a freshly killed animal's skin—preferably
rabbit—and then burying it until the pelt had rotted away
was another technique. A wash of peroxide was quick and
worked well, too. The only true way to test ivory, whether
elephant, hippo, mammoth or walrus, was to make a cut-

ting as deep as possible where two pieces joined, so that the scars would never be seen. No faker had ever concocted a way of simulating the natural, slow aging of ivory through to its core. It was hardly time, however, to tell Rorimer of my views.

"You're still confident Topic Mimara is kosher?" Rorimer suddenly asked. "Did you reach the person who knew Topic from the old days?"

"Yes," I lied. I had not even tried to contact Edgar Breitenbach, so concerned was I that he might impart bad news about Topic. "The man doesn't remember Topic. Anyway, if anything is fishy about Topic, you will readily see it."

"What's that?" Rorimer said sharply.

"Just turn the ultraviolet light on him. If he comes up lavender, no good. But I'm sure he'll fluoresce buttery."

James Rorimer laughed heartily.

In early January 1962, just three weeks before our departure for Zurich, I received an encouraging letter from Topic Mimara, which an associate at the museum translated from the German:

Thank you for your friendly letter of 12, 12, 61 and herewith I answer to your question.

The work of the manuscript will be ready in the course of this month, January 1962. Just when the publication will appear I cannot tell you right now other than saying however that I hope it will do so in the next few months.

When you, with Mr. Rorimer, come to Zurich and when Mr. Rorimer expresses genuine interest for the cross and some of my art objects, then I shall *not* deny Mr. Rorimer a copy of the manuscript and in addition a good photo of the cross.

Also I would be willing to send you some photographs of some of my other works of art which I have in Tangier and if they interest you I can arrange to bring them to Zurich.

When I showed this to Rorimer he cried out, "Wait a minute, does this chap really think I intend purchasing a number of works along with the cross?"

"Oh, no," I tried to assure him. "Topic is being gracious. He wants to let you know that *if* you're interested in other pieces, he'll oblige." I uttered not a word about the loan arrangement I had proposed to Topic Mimara.

Ten days before our trip, Rorimer told me to come up to his office. He had a far-off look in his eyes.

"Jim, anything wrong?"

"Nothing at all. Just a minor change of plans. I have to postpone our forthcoming trip to Zurich. Probably until March."

"Why? It was all set. I informed Topic. You said yourself we've got to move on this cross."

"Yes, yes, and it still *is* all set," Rorimer insisted. "But a number of sensitive issues pertaining to the museum's budget have arisen. It would be better for me to make our trip in March, just after the meeting of the Purchase Committee. Then I will be completely free to move."

"But why can't we go now, just for a few days? You were so positive before. Have you some second thoughts?"

"I have no second thoughts, although I have indicated many times to you that I've never felt happy about the price. Why can't the owner just send his cross here on approval? We'll pay all expenses and the insurance. Why is this man acting so peculiarly?"

"Jim, you know Topic Mimara will *never* send the cross. To ask is to anger him and to risk losing it. The thing is the only grand possession in his life. Part of the allure for him is for people to come to him, visit his shrine and bow down before his unique work of art. And you know the deadline is February."

"The deadline for what?" Rorimer casually asked.

Without thinking I said, "For the sale."

"Young man, it is decidedly *not*. You have a disconcerting talent to bend the facts for your own benefit. You told me in your memo—I have it right here—that the cross would not be sold *before* the first of February. For me there will never be a deadline. No museum on earth will buy this cross under these circumstances. Have you lost your senses? I was impressed with your mature state of mind when you returned from Europe, but now, under the slightest pressure, you seem to be falling to pieces. Be careful. You are losing a hold on common sense. You simply have to learn that running a vast art museum does not require me to hold hands a hundred percent of the time with a youthful curator who has an irrepressible urge to acquire an impossible work of art."

What had gone wrong? It was as though all our past discussion about Topic and the cross had never occurred.

"I don't want to overstate the case," I began cautiously, "and I agree that we should not rush out and purchase it by making a flamboyant offer. But we should start serious consideration as soon as feasible, realizing that we have a long, difficult road to travel. Careful study is mandatory. Weitzmann should see the piece. But your seeing it is critical. So can't we, somehow, just slip over? It will take two days, maybe just one."

"My years of experience in bargaining tell me that this cross is not going to be sold to anyone in the near future," Rorimer answered. "I think we would be making a great tactical mistake in acting too hastily with Mimara."

"Months have gone by," I said. "I saw the letter from Bruce-Mitford saying he wants the cross at any price. And I know he's going to Parliament and is looking for a donor —which I think he'll find. Topic prefers to sell to England. At this precise moment England may not have a hard option, but they might next week. Right now we are in the lead. Next comes Cleveland, no matter what you heard. My gut feeling is that Sherman Lee wants the cross. Who the hell else has the purchase power?"

"I know all of this. Please—" Rorimer said impatiently.

"The whole situation has changed," I pressed on. "The point is that before, when no article was about to be published, there was little danger the cross would be sold. Now things are a lot more volatile. I'll bet Parsons is pushing Cleveland hard. With a good set of photos and the article in hand, Lee might be able to drum up interest from his board. He just might want something fabulous now. The same is true with England."

"Your main point is . . . ?"

"If you don't go now, and offers begin to move and suddenly you have to go at the last moment, your bargaining power is destroyed. What the man wants most is an indication of your personal interest. Unless I read the situation wrong, you should make that gesture now."

Rorimer promised to give my arguments "the attention they deserve." Two days passed, and when I called him to find out his response I learned he wasn't in the museum

at all. He had flown to Palm Beach to spend some time
with a wealthy trustee. On January 15th I received from
his office a copy of a letter he had sent Ante Topic Mimara without telling me a thing about it!

DEAR MR. TOPIC MIMARA,
    I am most certainly going to be in Europe in June. I
may be making a trip in the meantime. When am I going
to see your cross?
Yours sincerely,
JAMES J. RORIMER
Director

Topic Mimara answered within days, saying it would
be difficult but he would be delighted to leave Tangier
and meet Rorimer in Zurich. He suggested mid-February.
    Rorimer did not deign to reply himself. Instead, his
executive secretary informed Topic that Rorimer could
not possibly travel to Zurich until the end of March,
adding, "Mr. Rorimer asks that you send the object to
the museum on approval at our expense. It would be very
helpful if you could send the object since even the
March trip will be difficult. . . ."
    With that, I abandoned the cross to my competitors. I
was bitter. For the first time in my life, my anger did
not fade within a few weeks. Why Rorimer had decided
to scuttle the purchase, I did not know. He never said a
word about the matter and seemed to avoid me.
    I could not comprehend how Rorimer could have
chosen to go to Florida and romance a favorite trustee
rather than pursue a treasure of unique importance. I
felt certain that, were Ante Topic Mimara a rich count or
lord with a château gussied up by a fashionable interior
decorator, or his collection published in glossy volumes,
Rorimer and his trustees would have flown to Zurich at
once.

CHAPTER FOURTEEN

A Litany of Hatred

PERHAPS IT WAS because of my dejected state of mind, perhaps it had something to do with the cross itself; perhaps it was pure chance. But one evening I found myself standing near the bookshelves in my living room, looking into space. Suddenly a volume caught my eye. It was old; the blue leather cover had completely dried out and was flaking away. I opened the book and smiled. The Bible had been given to me by a governess when I was ten years old.

I sat down and started to read my old King James Version of the New Testament. After a while, overwhelmed by the beauty of the words, I leaned back, somewhat shocked to realize I had never really read the Gospels before in my life. I had, of course, studied them, picking out events and phrases having to do with works of art I was involved with. But I had never really read the Gospels or thought about Christ other than as a symbolic or artistic phenomenon.

Within a few hours I had finished both Matthew and Mark. As I became more caught up by the meaning of these Gospels, I referred from time to time to a modern-language text. Now I glanced over my pages of notes:

The point I hadn't realized is that virtually everything in the New Testament has already been referred to in the Old, which foreshadowed every act and utterance of Christ. Another persistent refrain is the occurrence of miracles—healings, the driving out of devils, raising people from the dead. With each miracle, Christ admonished those whom he cured not to say a word. Yet they all did. I find it ironic that Christ never performed a miracle in his own land. Perhaps, being the son of a local carpenter, he felt that no one would believe. He said himself, "A prophet is not without honor, except in his own country."

I was impressed with how human Christ was. He could be angry, afraid, petty, contrite, confused. The miracles, and even the Crucifixion, seemed less relevant to me than Christ's words and parables. They shone with a bright light. Those I found particularly compelling I committed to memory:

Blessed are they who are persecuted for righteousness' sake . . .
You have heard that it has been said, you shall love your neighbor and hate your enemy. But I say to you, love your enemies . . .
When you pray, enter into your closet . . . and pray to your Father in secret.
Oh, you hypocrites, you can discern the face of the sky; but can you not discern the sign of the times?
He that is not with me is against me.
Whoever shall confess me before men, him will I confess before my Father.

Incredible words! But still I was troubled by some claims in the Gospels, especially that Christ is the sole redeemer and that by merely confessing to Him one would gain salvation. "In the old time," to use a phrase often attributed to Jesus, only God could be the redeemer, and God was harsh. Salvation through confession seemed too easy.

I decided to read more and learn more. But during the next few months, as I reflected upon the Gospels, I found my thoughts returning with lingering sadness to my lost ivory cross. One morning toward the end of May, that melancholy was unexpectedly replaced by hope.

I bumped into James Rorimer for the first time in weeks.

"You may not believe this," he said with a sheepish smile, "but I am going to be meeting Mr. Topic Mimara on the twenty-fourth of July. In Zurich. I have decided to take Peg Freeman with me, since she hasn't been to Europe for years and deserves the opportunity. You've already seen the cross."

I suppressed my annoyance that I had not been chosen to accompany him and wished him well. I was intrigued, but I realized it was not yet time for my hopes to be fully revived. I suspected that Rorimer would make a hurried examination of the ivory, decide that the piece was too expensive or that it posed too many problems, and go on his way.

But on the twenty-sixth of June Peg Freeman wrote me from Zurich:

DEAR TOM,

James and I are really quite excited about *that object*. (I am not to mention it by name even in a sealed letter.) We spent a good part of yesterday trying to borrow an ultraviolet lamp. James finally secured a lamp this morning and we studied the piece again under ultraviolet. I must say that it looks *very good* . . . although there are a few questions still remaining. We do want Weitzmann to see it when he can. James says to tell you not to talk about it because of the interest that the British Museum has in it.

I have Mrs. Topic Mimara's list of all the inscriptions, some of which I checked on myself. I have also read part of her article, noting down her comparative material. . . .

I read her letter again and again, my feeling of joy rekindled each time I did. I forgave James Rorimer for his obtuseness, his deviousness, his games. I even dispatched a telegram to him: "Peg sends great news about that unmentionable. Glad you liked it. After Kurt Weitzmann, or even before, I hope we can move!"

Then I dashed off a letter to Peg:

Thrilled by the news. I really do think we should move fast. Anyway I have a suspicion James Rorimer thinks the same. Do you think it might be possible for me to get photos of 'that object' . . . ? I would be delighted to nibble on those inscriptions.

Within a week, to my pleasure, I had in my hands what I had been trying to obtain for more than a year—photographs of the cross. Receiving those black-and-white photographs from Peg Freeman—there were six of them, and they were excellent—was one of the most exciting moments in my career. Seeing them was almost like touching the glistening smooth surfaces of the object itself. They brought back all the emotion, that shivering down my spine, I had experienced when I first laid eyes on the cross. The figures seemed even more delicate and feathery than I remembered. They also appeared to be imbued with a greater sense of spiritual fervor than I had recalled.

With the photographs, Peg had enclosed a couple of typed pages summing up what Mersmann was going to publish in her article. Initially, I resisted even glancing at her conclusions. I was afraid she might have found all the answers, leaving nothing for me. But as soon as I scanned the pages, I recognized she had made what I believed to be a fundamental error in dating the cross to a time just before the Norman Conquest, around A.D. 1050. In my opinion, her date was precisely a hundred years too early.

But her work was invaluable nevertheless. For she had identified almost every one of the highly abbreviated inscriptions by author, chapter and verse in the Bible. She had missed out on just four, the large ones engraved on the sides and front of the vertical bar. It was marvelous to be relieved of the strenuous task of searching every book in the Scriptures for single phrases and lines. I whispered a warm blessing on Frau Topic Mersmann.

When I started to delve into her list, I was confident that within days I would be able to come to grips with the typology of the cross, the basic parallels between the Old and New Testaments. I was even hopeful I might uncover evidence about where and when the magnificent

object had been made. After six weeks of probing, I knew
I had been wrong. What the cross bore was far from the
simple and direct typology I had believed months before.

It had taken me that long to crack the code of the inscriptions, but at last I knew the messages buried deep
within the cross. Mersmann had identified each inscription accurately, yet had made no observation about their
significance as a whole. She had apparently failed to perceive that the inscriptions on the cross were not isolated,
merely single lines standing alone, but that they constituted a beginning, a middle and an end. Moreover, the
story was complex and could be interpreted on more than
one level. On one, it could be construed as a powerful and
beautiful tale of the Passion of Christ expressed through
the testimony of the Evangelists and the predictions of the
ancient prophets of Israel. On another level, the cross
seemed to proclaim the glory of Christ and issued a
fervent appeal to nonbelievers to convert to Christianity.
On yet a third, an almost chthonian level, one was forced
to interpret the cross as the harshest diatribe against the
Jews ever to be found on a work of art.

The full realization of the complexity of the inscriptions
and the cruel intent behind some of them came to me
gradually. I started off for a second time with the writings
on the tiny scroll held by the five individuals in the
central medallion on the front of the cross. I fully expected to follow a clear-cut typology, step by step, and
figured the most appropriate place to begin would be with
the serpent coiled around the forked stick in front of the
crowd of Israelites gazing upon it in awe.

I familiarized myself again with the passage in the Book
of Numbers about the Brazen Serpent. The Israelites had
escaped Egypt and were making their way through the
wilderness. When they began to murmur against Moses
and then against God, punishment came swiftly. God
sent hordes of fiery serpents among the Israelites. Those
who had dared to complain were bitten. Many were
afflicted, some died. The survivors came to Moses, confessed their sins, and begged him to persuade God to
rid them of the serpents and cure their afflictions. And
God instructed Moses to fashion an image of a serpent in
bronze and to hang it on a forked stick. And it "came to

pass, that if a serpent had bitten any man, when he
beheld the serpent of brass he lived."

The passage was a classic typology, an often-quoted
parallel to Christ, who had been hanged upon the cross
and who had suffered to bring eternal life to mankind.
Those who looked upon the serpent and believed in the
power of the image would regain life. The typological
nature of the Brazen Serpent was indeed confirmed by
the words of the dynamic individual standing just to the
left of the creature. He was John the Evangelist, whose
scroll I translated from Mersmann's list as: "Just as Moses
raised the serpent in the desert, so shall the Son of man
be raised up."

But what I had not known when I first deciphered
three scrolls in the medallion was that in medieval typology a phrase or a line from the Bible stood for the entire
passage from which it had been extracted. So I examined
the Book of John further and found: ". . . whosoever believeth in him should not perish, but have eternal life
. . . he that believeth him not is condemned. . . ."

Eternal life with Christ, eternal death without Him.
The meaning was plain. Just who might be singled out
for special condemnation began to become clear within
the context of the next scroll. That scroll was carried by a
stunning little figure, with a daggerlike beard, who leaned
out over the rim of the wheel on the lower left of the
medallion, pointing down with a long, expressive finger.
The meaning of the writing on his scroll, NESPROPHETTE,
had eluded me months before in Europe. Skillfully Mersmann had found them to be the words of Saint Peter recorded in the Acts of the Apostles: *Omnes prophetae
testimonium perhibent,* or "To him all the prophets bear
witness." The Biblical passage from which the phrase had
been taken went as follows:

> . . . God anointed Jesus of Nazareth with the Holy
> Ghost and with power: who went about doing good . . .
> for God was with him.
> And we are witnesses of all things which he did both
> in the land of the Jews, and in Jerusalem; whom they
> slew and hanged on a tree. . . .
> To him give all the prophets witness, that through his
> name whosoever believeth in him shall receive remission
> of sins.

Moses had hanged a Brazen Serpent on a tree, and the Jews had been saved. The Jews had hanged Christ on a tree and were condemned. The message seemed undeniable. With a few misgivings, I turned to the dynamic figure in the center of the medallion.

When I first examined the ivory in the vault, I had believed that this individual who strode across the medallion and who looked up at the Brazen Serpent must be Moses. Now that I scrutinized him more closely, I realized I had been mistaken. Whoever he was, he seemed enraged. He tossed his head back in anger at the Israelites, who were peering in awe at the snake. He jabbed out one hand at them like a boxer and, with the other, brandished his curving scroll almost as if it were a sword.

I searched through Mersmann's list and saw that the words on this scroll had nothing properly to do with the affair of the Brazen Serpent. They were from Deuteronomy, not Numbers, and had been plucked out of context and been made to apply to the episode of the serpent. "Your life shall hang before you . . . and you shall not believe your life . . ."

These were the words of God, not Moses, an enraged God who admonished the Jews for their disbelief and had launched a series of curses.

. . . ye shall be plucked from all the land. . . .
And the Lord shall scatter thee among all people . . . and among these nations shalt thou find no ease, neither shall the sole of thy foot have rest. . . .
. . . ye shall be sold unto your enemies. . . .
Moreover all these curses shall come upon thee . . . because thou hearkenedst not unto the voice of the Lord thy God. . . .

The next scroll in the medallion was tucked under the arm of the prophet Isaiah, who peered down over the lower right-hand side of the rim. I translated the Latin: "Why are you red in your apparel, and your garments like a man who has trod in the wine vat?"

When I first found the lines in my Latin Bible, I had assumed the reference was to the scourging of Christ. But after reading the verses that followed in Isaiah I realized that the lines implied a secondary meaning, one of powerful vengeance. In the King James Version, Isaiah had been sitting alone at the edge of the wilderness, meditating, when a giant of a man, garbed in blood-red clothing, strode out of the horizon and across the sere plain.

Isaiah called out in fear to the awesome apparition, "Who is this who comes from Edom, with dyed garments . . . ?"

The figure responded, "I that speak in righteousness, mighty to save." It was God.

Isaiah then asked, "Wherefore ART THOU in thine apparel, and thy garments like him that treadeth in the wine vat?"

God responded, "I have trodden the winepress alone; and of the people THERE WAS none with me: for I will tread them in mine anger, and trample them in my fury; and their blood shall be sprinkled upon my garments. . . . For the day of vengence IS in mine heart. . . ."

The scroll carried by the fifth individual, Jeremiah, who reclined across the top of the medallion, lent itself to several interpretations. "Why should you be as a man wandering, like a mighty man who cannot save?" On one level, the phrase obviously referred to the mocking of Christ on the cross by the onlookers, "He saved others; himself he cannot save. . . ." On another level, the scroll's phrase was also linked to vengeance. For the adjacent verses in Jeremiah stated: "Thus saith the Lord unto his people, Thus have they loved to wander . . . Therefore the Lord doth not accept them; he will now remember their iniquity, and visit their sins. . . . I will consume them by the sword, and by the famine, and by the pestilence."

The message within the medallion on the front had become all too clear. Christ would be hanged on the cross for the remission of sins. Those who believed in Him would be saved. Those who refused to believe, especially the Jews, would be destroyed. Even though I was well aware that the Scriptures contained a number of comments against the Jews, I was amazed, not so much by the vehemence of individual quotes as by their juxtapositions. It was as though someone, inspired by an inexplicable malevolence, had deliberately chosen to manipulate passages from the Scriptures into a litany of hatred.

As I turned to the writings on the reverse of the object, my misgivings about the spirit of the cross were confirmed. But some of the scrolls were actually benign, being parallels from the Old Testament events to Christ's life. The scroll held by the eagle, symbol of Saint John, on top of the cross, proclaimed, "They shall look upon him whom they have pierced." And David, just below the eagle, mirrored the words exactly from the Psalms. Solomon, whose quotation I had found and translated so long before, voiced a direct reference to the Crucifixion: "I shall ascend into the palm tree and will take hold of the fruits thereof." And at the very bottom of the vertical bar, Saint Mark and Jonah were paired. Mark called out, "For as Jonah was three days and three nights in the belly of the whale, so shall the son of man be three days and three nights in the heart of the earth."

But other scrolls and other prophets did not placidly foretell the deeds of the Savior. Instead, they cried out for vengeance, destruction and death to the Jews. Some of them deviated from the Bible, substituting harsher words. A phrase or single word had been interpolated and used with evil intent without reference to the original Biblical context.

[Amos] . . . they sold the righteous for silver.

[Joel] The sun and the moon shall be darkened . . . The Lord also shall roar out of Zion, and utter his voice from Jerusalem; and the heavens and the earth shall shake . . . for the violence AGAINST the children of Judah, because they have shed innocent blood in their land.

[Nahum] Though I have afflicted thee, I shall afflict thee no more. . . . and the Lord will take vengeance upon his adversaries . . .

[Malachi] Will a man afflict God? Yet ye have afflicted me. . . . Ye are cursed with a curse: for ye have afflicted me, EVEN this whole nation . . .

[Zephaniah] I will kill all those who have afflicted you at that time. . . .

[Hosea] O Israel, thou hast destroyed thyself. . . . I gave thee a king . . . and took HIM away in my wrath. . . . O death, I will be thy plagues; O grave, I will be thy destruction . . .

To the man who chose the inscriptions for the cross, all the prophets did bear witness. Grace, salvation and eternal

life for believers; vengeance, destruction and death for
those who did not believe. From beginning to end; from
Genesis to Apocalypse. This harsh testimony was brought
to a climax in the second medallion, on the reverse of
the cross, which depicted the Lamb of God from the
Apocalypse. If the Brazen Serpent was the first chapter on
the cross, the Lamb was the last, expressing deep love
and joy, and bitter hatred at the same time.

Jeremiah was portrayed twice in the Lamb medallion
—once reclining on top, and a second time just under the
body of the Lamb. His two scrolls were intended to be
read as one: "But I was like a Lamb . . . brought to the
slaughter; and I knew not that they had devised devices
against me, saying, Let us destroy the tree with the
fruit thereof, and let us cut him off from the land of the
living, that his name may be no more remembered. But,
O Lord of hosts, . . . let me see thy vengeance on
them. . . ."

By the time I translated Jeremiah, I had become accustomed to the expression of vehemence on the cross.
Still, I must admit to having been astonished by the
viciousness of Jeremiah's diatribe. What was even more
startling, Jeremiah was engaged in a physical attack too,
one which left no doubt that, on the cross, his adversaries
were the Jews. His second scroll, like a weapon, was thrust
directly at the pathetic figure of a woman standing off to
the left on whose enigmatic scroll I had so long before
recognized the word *maledictus*, "cursed." She was
hooded; her head was bowed. Her eyes were closed; she
seemed almost blinded. With a lance, she was attempting
to pierce the breast of the Lamb. Frau Mersmann had
identified her as the personification of Synagogue. The
writing on her scroll amounted to a twofold sign of contempt: "Accursed is he who hangs upon a tree."

The Old Law prescribed that anyone who had committed a sin worthy of death should be hanged on a tree
and cursed. But Saint Paul, in his Epistle to the Galatians,
had refuted the Old Law, saying, "Christ hath redeemed
us from the curse of the law . . ." Paul had turned the
phrase around and said, in effect, Cursed are those who
say, "Accursed is he who hangs upon a tree."

After vanquished Synagogue, I had come down to the
four last figures on the cross: the Lamb, a magnificent

angel, John the Evangelist, and a figure which was a total mystery—the only one without name or writings among the sixty-four populating the ivory. He was a monk—that I saw from the distinctive monastic hood. He floated horizontally just above the angel, threw his head back in exaltation and raised his clenched right fist high into the air. His position between Jeremiah and the angel was so prominent, I knew from other works of art that he could only be the man who had commissioned the cross. I wondered if I would ever find out who that man was.

Saint John was grieving; his scroll carried the phrase "And I wept much." But the magnificent angel dispelled John's sorrow for all time, quoting from the Apocalypse: "Weep not: behold . . . Worthy is the Lamb that was slain to receive power, and riches, and wisdom, and strength, and honor, and glory, and blessing. . . . Blessing, and honor, and glory, and power BE unto him that sitteth upon the throne, and unto the Lamb for ever and ever."

With that paean of triumph I had gotten down to the last four inscriptions, the large ones carved the entire length of the sides and front of the vertical bar. Fully three times the size of the inscriptions on the scrolls or the placard, they were not abbreviated in any way. Their style was bold, emphatic, wholly unlike the sometimes crowded letters of the other writings. For a moment I had the impression they might even have been added to the cross years after the inscriptions on the scrolls.

The pair of inscriptions on the sides were: CHAM RIDET DUM NUDA VIDET PUDEBUNDA PARENTIS/IUDEI RISERE DEI PENAM MOR . . .

The pair of inscriptions on the front of the cross read: TERRA TREMIT MORS VICTA GEMIT SURGENTE SEPULTO VITA CLUIT SYNAGOGA RUIT MOLIMINE STULTO. Mersmann had neither identified nor translated these verses. They were not quotations from the Bible. It took me several days to decipher them.

The first verse referred to Cham, who "laughed at the shameful nakedness of his parent." Cham was the third son of Noah and, traditionally, the symbol of the Jews. His story was from Genesis. After the Ark landed and the waters subsided, Noah planted a vineyard. He became drunk and fell asleep naked in his tent. Cham looked upon his father's nakedness, laughed and rushed from the tent to tell his brothers, Shem and Japeth. They were shocked. Walking backward into the tent, they averted their eyes and reverently covered Noah with a shroud. When the patriarch awakened and learned what Cham had done, he accused him of blasphemy and punished him with an everlasting curse.

The second couplet in the verse about Cham was the cruelest I had ever contemplated on a work of art. Combined with the first, the entire verse read: "Just as Cham laughed at the shameful nakedness of his parent, so the Jews laugh at the death agony of God."

I turned to the pair of inscriptions on the front of the cross with a sense of foreboding. I found they described what had happened at the exact moment when Christ had died, with his eyes closed, when his head had collapsed in death: "Earth trembles, death is conquered and bewails, from the opening grave life surges forth and the synagogue collapses after vain and stupid effort."

Again I was amazed at the vehemence of the words. Who had invented them? What kind of typology was this? To find out, I had to search through the works of hundreds of ecclesiastic writers from early Christian times down through the end of the twelfth century.

I knew from graduate school that the writings of both Latin and Greek church fathers had been compiled in the late nineteenth century by a team of scholars headed by a brilliant encyclopedist, the Abbé Migne. They were published in two sets of volumes, the *Patrologia Latina* and the *Patrologia Graeca*. Both were on deposit in the library of the Institute of Fine Arts, where I had made my first contact with James Rorimer. I found them in a dark corner of the dusty stacks on the second floor. I walked slowly down the long rows of thick books comprising the writings of the Latin church fathers, elated by the thought that somewhere inside lay the key to unlocking the secrets of the inscriptions on the cross.

The material was vast. Two hundred and eighteen volumes for the Latin authors, each containing over two thousand pages printed in double columns of such small print that one needed a magnifying glass. The Greek ecclesiastic authors had been published in over four hundred volumes. Not a word of a modern tongue had been utilized by the Abbé Migne and his cohorts.

As I gazed at the rows of books, I uttered a quick
prayer to the memory of the abbé and his colleagues.
They had possessed the common sense, and the awesome
tenacity, to prepare faultless index volumes for each
series. Every author, every subject matter, every line
quoted from the Bible had been indexed, cross-referenced,
by date, place, Biblical phrase, verse and chapter.

I seized the six volumes of the Latin index and, hugging
them to me, took them to a desk in the deserted library.
I decided to look first into what the church fathers had
written about the episode of the Brazen Serpent. The
earliest author I encountered was Saint Caesarius of Arles
of the mid-fifth century.

Caesarius' words were fresh and vibrant, almost like
those of a contemporary preacher, passionate with faith:

> We heard about the time when the people were de-
> stroyed in the desert by serpents, because of the pride
> of the Jews and their murmuring against the Lord.
> Moreover, the Lord commanded Moses to make a brazen
> serpent and hang it on a tree, so that anyone who had
> been struck might look on it and be healed from death.
> Although this serpent seems to be quite fanciful . . . still
> it prefigured the Incarnation of the Lord. . . . The brazen
> serpent was then hung on a pole, because Christ was to
> be hung on the cross. At that time whoever had been
> struck by a serpent looked on the brazen serpent and
> was healed. Now the human race which was struck by
> the spiritual serpent, the devil, looks upon Christ with
> faith and is healed. . . . So it is, brethren: if a man does
> not believe in Christ crucified, he is slain by the poison
> of the devil. Then, a man looked at the dead serpent
> in order to escape the live one; now if a man wants to
> avoid the devil's poison, he looks on Christ crucified.
> Death receives its name from a deadly bite, and it befell
> the human race because of the bite of the ancient
> serpent. Moreover, death could not be conquered except
> by death; so Christ suffered death in order that His
> unjust death might overcome the just death. By dying
> for them unjustly, He freed those who were rightly
> guilty. . . .
> By suffering death unjustly, Christ paid what Adam
> justly owed. The latter stretched out his hand to sweet
> fruits, the former extended them to the bitter cross. . . .
> The one lifted himself up against God and fell, Christ

humbled Himself in order to raise up all men. Adam
brought death to everyone, Christ restored life to them
all. . . . The brazen serpent which was put on a tree
overcame the poison of the living serpents when Christ
hung on the cross and died, He suppressed the ancient
poison of the devil and freed all men who had been
struck by him.

As I read my translation I suddenly recognized why
Adam and Eve had been depicted at the base of the ivory
cross, embracing the living wood, their eyes fixed to the
place where a figure of Christ had once been suspended.
Christ would have to be crucified upon the descendant
of the ancient tree which had flourished in the Garden
of Eden. Christ would die, he would descend into the
underworld and would burst asunder the gates of hell and,
in doing so, would defeat death. The tree of Eden and
the cross of Golgotha were in a sense the same. I marveled
at the fitness of the analogy.

I next turned to the Greek writers. In the early eighth
century John of Damascus had written poetically: "The
tree of life which was planted by God in Paradise pre-
figured the precious cross. For since death was by a tree,
it was fitting that life and resurrection should be bestowed
by a tree."

Again nothing harsh. I eventually found commentaries
by a wide variety of Christian authors on ten of the same
Old Testatment quotes that appeared on the ivory cross.
Their comments were, like those of Caesarius and John
of Damascus, simple and without rancor. I began to
think I might have misinterpreted the inscriptions on the
scrolls. Perhaps only the large inscriptions along the front
and sides of the vertical bar, which had not come directly from the Bible, were truly wicked.

But I continued to search through the index for more
ecclesiastic writers and their interpretations. Suddenly I
discovered, in the writings of the tenth-century theologian
Walafrid Strabo, an observation that corresponded to the
interpretation of the cross as an anti-Jewish diatribe: "No
more severe accusation must fall upon the Jews, and with
good reason owing to their arrogance, than that they saw
their life, that is the Son of God, hanging upon the wood
and they disbelieved Him."

Although I had little stomach for the task, I forced myself to search further. Soon I found from the Latin index that eight quotations on the cross, including the one about the Brazen Serpent, were foundation blocks of an essay composed by Saint Cyprian in the late fifth century. When I read the title, I was chilled. It was "Tract Against the Jews." And I was appalled when I read the content of the tract: "You Jews who murdered Christ, you who looked upon him and did not believe, will be cast aside through all of time, punished and destroyed."

For days I hunted inscriptions commented on by Latin church fathers. I found fully twenty in an especially ugly broadside denouncing the Jews, written during the seventh century by Saint Isidore of Spain, entitled *Concerning the Catholic Faith from the Old and New Testaments Against the Jews*. After reading Isidore, I realized that my search could be simplified. I went in the index to one word, *Iudeos,* Jews, and encountered a large body of literature I had not realized existed. The titles differed, but they all embraced the same theme: *Against the Jews; The Perfidiousness of the Jews; Sermon Against Jews; Jews as Persecutors of Christ; The Second Coming of Christ Against the Jews.*

I was saddened but not really surprised to discover that my favorite Christian writer, Tertullian, had written a *Book Against the Jews.* And the author of the most respected and learned history of the early Christian Church, Eusebius, had written in the fourth century a number of anti-Jewish tracts and essays. In one of them he even said that he possessed clear proof that Jews of every community of the world kidnapped a boy every Easter and crucified the child in a "ritual killing."

Even Saint Augustine, the creator of one of the most benevolent books of philosophy of all Christianity, *The City of God,* had issued a *Tract Against the Jews:* "The true image of the Hebrew is Judas Iscariot, who sells the Lord for silver. The Jew can never spiritually understand the Scriptures and forever will bear the guilt for the death of Jesus because their fathers killed the Savior." To Augustine the Jews were cursed for all eternity and fit to live only as slaves, if they were to be allowed to live at all.

Under the same index heading, I encountered another

category of anti-Jewish writing with a large number of quotations identical to those on the cross. These writings were called *Disputations* or *Disputes,* and in them a Christian and a Jew discussed their faiths. Some *Disputes* were gentlemanly throughout. Most, however, started reasonably but soon degenerated into vituperation, with the Christian vanquishing the Jew. The violent sentiments appeared over and over in patristic literature, like a sword hitting flesh. Nowhere could I find a single reference to Christ's own words that He had been crucified because of His own free will or that He had come "to fulfill the Torah of Moses and not to destroy it." Nowhere did I find a reference to Christ being a Jew Himself.

Each anti-Jewish sentiment was like a blow from a sword never to be sheathed. The thrust of Saint Melitus of Sardis, writing in the second century: "Thou slewest the Lord . . ." Or the blows of Saint John Chrysostom, Patriarch of Constantinople, writing in the late fourth century: "The Jews are the odious assassins of Christ, and for killing God there is no expiation possible. . . . Christians may never cease vengeance, and the Jews must live in servitude forever. God always hated the Jews, and whoever has intercourse with Jews will be rejected on Judgment Day. It is incumbent upon all Christians to hate the Jews."

But what was the ivory cross? Was it a sword, an evil tract against the Jews? Or was it a typology to be used to convert Jews to Christianity? Did the phrase "King of the Confessors" call for conversion? Or had the artist of the cross—or whoever had formulated the inscriptions— chosen the word "Confessors" because he could not bring himself to think of Christ as King of the Jews? I did not know what to believe. How such a beautiful work of art could carry such an embittered message I could not fathom.

CHAPTER FIFTEEN

Confessions

WHEN JAMES RORIMER returned from his trip to Europe toward the end of July, he was ebullient. He was, he said, "totally committed to win the superb cross for The Cloisters. Nothing will deter me." He was contrite at having spurned my earlier entreaties, assuring me that he would conclude the matter within weeks. I begged him to call an emergency meeting of the Purchase Committee of the Board of Trustees, vote the six hundred thousand dollars and send me to Zurich to complete the transaction. It could be done in a fortnight.

Rorimer was sympathetic but had promised several trustees not to make the presentation to the committee until Kurt Weitzmann had examined the ivory and given it his blessing. Although I was impatient to move, I didn't dare protest.

Rorimer asked, rather casually, if I had gleaned anything from the inscriptions. I was afraid that if I revealed everything I had discovered, he might back away from the purchase. Many works of art had been turned down in the past for possessing far less controversial characteristics. Yet if I did not tell him I might never be able to prove to him that the cross was authentic beyond question. At length, burying my misgivings, I decided to conceal what I knew he would find offensive—at least until after we had acquired the treasure.

So I just read the scrolls, one after another, without interpretation. It was easy to pass them off as a simple typology. I said not a word about the four large inscriptions, nor did Rorimer ask.

I asked Rorimer what he had found out about Ante Topic Mimara. Had the Yugoslav turned buttery yellow or fresh lavender under the ultraviolet lamp? Rorimer chuckled and told me that he had "fully enjoyed the old boy and totally believed his life story."

"But to be certain," Rorimer added, "since with this cross there must be no hint or suspicion of anything untoward, I mentioned Topic's name to a special source of mine in the FBI. Two days ago I was assured that, in FBI documents at least, there is not a trace of Topic Mimara. And those documents, of course, are unquestionable."

"When will Kurt be able to see the cross?" I asked.

Rorimer paused for several moments and then muttered, "That happens to be a small problem. Mersmann has already shown him the photographs. But he cannot leave his lectures at Bonn University for a month and a half. The twentieth of September will be the earliest possible day he can travel to Zurich. We shall have to wait until then."

Watching the weeks go by, waiting for Weitzmann to examine the ivory, was unnerving. My affection for him slowly began to turn to anger. I could imagine Weitzmann just sitting at Bonn University, hatching theories. Why couldn't he fly to Zurich for a couple of hours and carry out the job he had pledged to do? What was wrong? Why the silence? Was it that he refused to commit himself to an opinion from photographs alone—or, worse, did he have doubts? Damn! What was I to do? The weeks slipped by until it was mid-September. I became frantic.

The twentieth of September came and went with no word from Weitzmann. Four more days slipped by. And then, on the morning of the twenty-fifth, Rorimer called to ask me to come immediately to his office. "I have some news."

"What?" was all I could say.

"Get moving!" he roared. And I took off.

When I entered his office Rorimer motioned me to a chair and, pacing the floor, began to speak slowly. "I have just talked to Kurt on the telephone. He has met with Topic Mimara in Zurich and has a very firm opinion about this cross." Rorimer lapsed into silence.

"What is it, for God's sake?" I blurted out.

Rorimer's face became grim, and he shook his head. Yet I had a feeling he was acting. He sat down, leaned back in his swivel chair, and reached for one particular pipe, black and cracked. A good sign. He always seemed to reach for that one when life was going well.

"We have serious problems," Rorimer began, and stopped to suck away at his pipe. I just waited. Rorimer shot his eyes upward, looked at me and smiled. "It seems we will have to buy the ivory cross," he intoned.

I almost jumped into the air.

"Weitzmann has blessed the thing," he said excitedly. "Listen to what he told me. As you recall, Kurt had seen the photos in Bonn. Mersmann had brought them to him and had attempted to convince him the cross dated to the eleventh century. Weitzmann does not believe that: He staunchly believes the cross is high Romanesque. One fascinating piece of information Kurt gleaned is that Mersmann has made all editorial arrangements to publish the ivory in the prestigious yearbook of the Wallraf Richartz Institute in Cologne. Weitzmann talked to the editor in chief, Hermann Schnitzler. Now, Schnitzler doesn't accept Mersmann's early date, either, but he thinks the cross is so important that he plans to publish it anyway. The article is already in print and will appear sometime in January. And that is good for us."

"You see," I said calmly. "Topic was telling the truth."

Rorimer looked at me coldly and raised his eyebrows. "Weitzmann took his turn in the vault," he said, "and spent hours looking over the cross. His immediate and lasting impression is that it has to be genuine. The iconography has no flaws. No faker would possibly have concocted those inscriptions."

I quickly interrupted Rorimer. "What did he mean? Did he actually decipher them?"

"No. He meant no forger would have dared to inscribe so many."

"Ah."

"And Kurt made another key observation," Rorimer continued. "Something which eluded me—and you too. He examined with special care the bottom of the cross about four inches above the broken-off base. He saw something only *he* would have detected. He noticed a certain polished area around the ivory, just where the priests would have grasped an altar cross. A shininess which could only have been made by hundreds of pairs of hands, working away, over centuries. This wear is almost invisible to the naked eye. It is clearly something no forger could have put there mechanically."

"Why didn't I think of that!" I burst out.

"The upshot," he said, glancing at a note pad, "is that Kurt has convinced himself the piece is genuine. He just can't conceive of a faker not making a single slip in such a complicated program when he obviously had no model in front of him. Much of the cross he cannot explain, but he is convinced that eventually the full story will out."

"Jim, it all sounds great!" I said.

Rorimer became serious. "There are three problems, though. God knows, each one might become insurmountable. Did Topic show you a large blue-glass reliquary vase with painted enamels on the rim?"

"Sure. Dick Randall saw it, too. I didn't like it. Topic has illusions the glass is an English reliquary of the tenth century. He wasn't willing to sell it, or so he said. We wouldn't want anything to do with it, Jim. The price he mentioned was a quarter of a million. The thing is wrong —maybe modern Venetian doctored up by Topic."

"Topic said nothing at all to you about selling the cross only if we buy this glass first?"

"Nope."

"He did to Kurt. I quote, 'I will sell the cross only together with my great glass.'"

"What next?"

"Problem number two," Rorimer muttered. "Topic showed Weitzmann a letter from Bruce-Mitford saying that he will formally present the cross to his trustees in

November. That's only a month and a half from now. So time may be a fatcor. Kurt thinks the British Museum may have secured an option."

"Oh, God!" I moaned. "Maybe that talk is just pressure. If I were Bruce-Mitford, I'd probably conjure up the same smokescreen."

"I am beginning to think it's true," Rorimer said gloomily. "There's something I had not gotten around to telling you. The British Museum is very serious. Sir Frank Francis was in town a few days ago. He's a straightforward, cards-on-the-table sort of fellow. We discussed the cross openly. His trustees have already approved the purchase in principle, and now they have to raise some money. Since their normal purchase funds are meager, they have to appeal to the Chancellor of the Exchequer for the shortfall. They are positive they can get the money. I told Sir Frank we had the money in hand, but I also told him I am profoundly concerned about the price. Young man, you do recognize that six hundred is ridiculous! Never in all of art history has an object fetched anywhere near that. Ah, well, perhaps by the time the Purchase Committee meets I shall alter my opinion."

"Jim," I said with a sigh, "Topic won't take a penny less than six hundred thousand."

"I suppose you're right. He seemed adamant to me too. Maybe I can persuade the committee."

"It comes down to a question of time," I said. "When does the committee meet?"

"October seventeenth," Rorimer replied.

"Are you certain you can't hold a special meeting?"

"No! The trustees would look askance at such a precipitous move."

I could only sigh again. I didn't have the nerve to tell Rorimer how irresponsibly I thought he was acting. To think that one of the most significant acquisitions in the history of the museum might be lost because four or five trustees and a punctilious director could not manage to get together for an hour in the next couple of days! But I was powerless.

"The seventeenth of October will give me plenty of time," Rorimer added hastily. "Anyway, we have yet another problem to solve before that."

"Which is?"

"Our president, Roland Redmond, with whom I discussed the matter at length, is in favor of going ahead.
But he insists Topic give us a clear record of where he
got the cross and, in addition, full proof of his legal title
to it."

I looked at Rorimer dumbly. He must have been reading my mind. He seemed a little embarrassed. "I know
what you must be thinking," he said, "but the Annunciation relief was different. It cost only fifty thousand dollars.
Without firm title or a provenance for the cross, I cannot
go forward with it. Write Topic and get the information."

I wrote the letter at once and sent it to Topic's many
addresses by registered mail.

Mr. Rorimer has asked me to communicate with you
regarding your cross that Miss Gómez-Moreno and I saw
just about a year ago today. Now that we have had the
opportunity to study the cross in great detail and now
that we have received information about it from Professor
Weitzmann (who incidentally was my teacher for my
Doctorate at Princeton) Mr. Rorimer is planning to
submit the cross to the Board of Trustees for consideration. I recall that you said that whereas you would give
no information on the provenance of the cross until you
received payment, once a contract had been negotiated
you would tell the buyer where you had acquired the
cross. Is my recollection correct?

The very day I sent my letter off to Topic, I received one
of those typically breezy, and troubling, letters from
Harold Parsons, whom I hadn't heard from in months.

This is just a line to tell you that I heard, in a very
roundabout way, that the trustees of the British Museum
have given their sanction for the purchase of the early
English ivory cross and that all that now remains to be
done is to raise the money. That may not be as difficult
as it sounds, as the recent purchase of the Leonardo
drawing . . . would seem to indicate.

Having been at considerable pains to do what I could
to save it for one of our American collections to which
it would add the greatest kudos, either the Cleveland
Museum of Art or The Cloisters, I would doubly regret

its going to the British Museum; but between the apathy
of the trustees of the former and the ineptness of Mr.
Randall of the latter, we may all have missed the bus.
I am told that the matter will probably be accomplished
at the British Museum before the end of the month of
October.

When I last saw that strange but highly perceiving
collector Mr. A. Topic Mimara he told me that Kurt
Weitzmann had placed his seal of approval not only on
the cross and the fabulous glass reliquary but also upon
other early English objects in the collection. . . . I do
believe that among the twenty or more objects in ivory,
glass, wood, bronze, and silver which he possesses and
believes to be early English, a large percentage of them
actually are; and that the museum fortunate enough to
secure them, in toto or in part, will have a group of early
English objects of great importance, in fact unique.

Mr. Topic Mimara assured me that he would lend all
of his collection of early English objects to whichever
museum purchased the cross, for an indefinite period;
and would cede any other pieces that that museum
decided to acquire in the future at prices which would
be reasonable in terms of payment at their convenience.
I think that like many collectors he hopes to keep the
fruit of his labors largely together. He told me that
whichever of the two museums to which the objects are
now offered is first to meet his terms regarding the ivory
cross will be given the opportunity to acquire the other
English treasures. Needless to say, I hope it will be The
Cloisters.

Topic was amused that J.J.R.—to whom, please, my
warmest regards—had thought him a "merchant of death,"
like Bührle of Zurich who manufactured precision anti-
aircraft guns. *Armatore*, in Italian, means an owner of
cargo ships, like Onassis, et al. The Topic family are
rich *armatore* with their base at Monte Carlo. . . .

Parsons' letter was followed, within the week, by a
communication from "Topic Mimara"—of Boston!

DEAR THOMAS,

I hear you are working on a small $300,000 enamel.
Having a good time?

What happened to the 1 million dollar cross? The
world awaits reports and retorts of the supposed summer

visits of a certain important gentleman to a bank vault in an international country.

How's your beautiful wife?

Yrs. (in secrecy)
Allah Ben Ahmed
Grand Mogul

The letterhead was that of the Museum of Fine Arts. Good old Dick Randall! The joke eased my tension. But not for long.

Meanwhile Topic himself remained utterly silent. Rorimer kept pushing me to obtain the "facts, the cold facts on provenance and proof of title." The Purchase Committee was scheduled to meet in only ten days. And Rorimer was muttering about canceling the cross from the agenda if word did not come from Topic.

Abruptly I hatched an idea which I hoped would solve Rorimer's—and Redmond's—insistence on the issue of provenance. Rorimer liked the idea, although he did call it a "sort of charade." He urged me to write Topic again. I did, immediately.

Dear Mr. Topic Mimara,

In my letter of September 25 to Tangier I spoke of an imminent meeting of the Purchasing Committee to consider your cross. The time is growing very short and I have become a bit concerned in not hearing from you regarding terms. I realize, of course, that it is possible that you have been away from Tangiers and that is why I am attempting to contact you again in various places.

There is at this final moment one *very difficult* problem regarding the purchase of the cross. With such a large price involved, the Trustees are going to be extremely hesitant unless proof of title is forthcoming. A solution to this problem would be if you told Mr. Rorimer, and Mr. Rorimer alone in strictest confidence, where you purchased the object. If you did this, Mr. Rorimer would give his word that no one else would learn this information—not me, not any of the trustees. All we ask is indication of former ownership or title that would hold the Museum harmless in the event of a claim, however absurd, by a third party. . . .

P.S. This information would be placed in a sealed envelope in the Museum's safe and would not be opened for X number of years.

Topic's answer, addressed to Rorimer, arrived in five days. I had to laugh. The wily old character had not succumbed to my ploy.

. . . You again raise the question about the provenance of the Cross. Of course I can understand your hesitations. But I have answered this question already and will never be able to give you a different answer.

In a few weeks the publication of the Cross will come out. This fact alone should give you a complete assuredness.

In the case that one should reach further negotiations, a way doubtlessly could be found, which would protect you against any third party claims of which you seem to be afraid.

But, should you have any fundamental hesitations to buy anything from my collection, it would be better not to have any dealings at all.

But when James Rorimer read the letter, he did not laugh. In fact, he was so annoyed that he removed the cross from the agenda of the board meeting. I worked on him for days to get it back on. When he finally consented, I casually asked what he would suggest I do to prepare for the meeting.

"Fill in the standard form. Make it short and to the point," he said.

"Fine," I replied. "And what about my presentation to the committee? What would you advise me to say?"

"You don't have to worry. I'll handle that."

We were alone in his office. Without hesitating, without even thinking, I shot out of my chair, leaned over his desk and, outrageously, screamed in his face, "Who the hell do you think you are? What are you doing? *I* got this institution—and *you!*—this close to the cross, and I'll be damned if you're going to cut me out now. Don't you know what it means to me to go before the board? Are you jealous of me, because *I* have done the work, because *I* found the thing, because *I* brought it back from oblivion? I deserve the credit and the opportunity. It would be rotten not to let me show up before the committee. You would be destroying a sacred trust!"

James Rorimer just sat there, pale and silent, his eyes wide open in astonishment. I stopped, and just stared at him. He placed his face in his hands and remained still for what seemed like eternity. I began to tremble.

Finally he looked up and spoke in a soft, hoarse voice. "Forgive me. I was insensitive. Please believe it—I mean it. I was just trying to . . . really trying to take the trouble away from you—take the pressure off you."

He got up awkwardly from his desk, looking old for the first time since I had come to know him. He walked over and gently put an arm around my shoulders. It was a spontaneous gesture, full of compassion.

"I apologize. Will you accept the apology?" he said.

I nodded; I was unable to speak.

"By all means, you should make the presentation. You are the only one who can."

"Jim, I admire you enormously," I said at last. "I respect your eye, your courage, your love for the museum, which I share. I must . . . apologize to you for my outburst. But I couldn't stop myself. I'm mortified by my behavior. I guess I've been captured by the dark side of the cross."

"You have no need to apologize," Rorimer commented softly. "I admit it again, I was insensitive. Sometimes my fondness for the museum makes me forget human beings. The place is more to me than life itself. But the work and the pressures never end. I adore being director, but sometimes hate it, too. And there are times when I'm terrified. I wait for myself to make a blunder—a real one—and have to resign or be removed smoothly, and so cruelly, by the board. The pressures, the everyday demands, can be frightening. Take Redmond. He's been drilling into me for years. Ah, well, if I had to leave the directorship, what then? What would I do? At times . . . it sounds silly, but the specter of humiliation surrounds me and threatens to choke me. It is that occasional fear which makes me so unfeeling. Someday you will feel it and be unfeeling, too."

"Jim, maybe you shouldn't be telling me these things."

"Not at all. I'm glad this happened. I've watched you more closely than you realize. I think you're going to make it."

"The cross?" I asked.

"No, not that!" Rorimer replied sharply. "I mean, I think you'll get what you want. You will succeed, after me, in this job."

Before I could reply, Rorimer turned a little from me and spoke in a whisper. "Yes, I suppose I was jealous of you. Not in a personal way. It's just that I sometimes see a part of my life gone—the curatorial life, the search, the capture, the thrill of the chase for a work of art. Gone. And I become saddened.

"But now my mind is made up about the cross. I won't move slowly any longer." He stopped and looked at me squarely with his incredibly penetrating eyes. "You've changed a great deal in a year and a half. It began when you started out on this quest of yours. Don't take this wrong. I admire your dedication. That's how people acquire great things for this institution. But what I see in you sometimes worries me. The fierceness. Is it ruthlessness? Well? What if you lose this object? What will defeat do to you? You've pegged your future on this cross. What if you lose? The chances are not so good. They're less than fifty-fifty. If you lose, will that destroy you?"

"God, Jim, I don't know."

Then he paused and said, "Tell me something. Are you holding something back about this? What do you mean by the 'dark side'? Is there something you know that you haven't told? Should *I* know?"

Assessing the man more carefully than I had ever done before, I addressed him with utter candor. "Jim, I have been holding back. There are more problems about the cross than you know. I've lied to you. The cross does have a dark side. Some of the inscriptions on it constitute a vicious denunciation of the Jews. It's as though the cross had been used as a Crusader's sword."

He listened, stunned, as I conducted him through the message, inscription by inscription. I spilled out everything: my meeting with Swarzenski; what I had really said to Parsons; the incriminating rumors about Topic Mimara I had gleaned from Albrighi and the people at the Collecting Point. I even told him about opening the case in the Bargello and plucking out the Aaron plaque.

"So I suppose," I said at the end of my confession, "you will want to think again about whether you wish to commit The Cloisters, and yourself, to this unique work of art."

"Maybe you shouldn't have told me," Rorimer whispered. "I'm not certain I should have become privy to this information. Confession isn't . . . well, isn't always the best way to attain one's dreams. How to proceed now?"

"It's your decision," I said quietly. "But I'll tell you what I'd do. I'd go for the thing. It's one of the most extraordinary objects in history. Part of its message, only part, is vile. But visually the cross is superb. Think of it! This cross stands for the whole Middle Ages—beauty, intolerance, passion, cruelty and love. Jim, go for it!"

Rorimer was hesitant. And then, after a moment's pause, he spoke firmly. "The contents of this message, as you call it, must never be revealed to the members of the Purchase Committee—or to anyone else. Certain members would be outraged. As you know, we are a city institution. How to deal with the problem of legal title I just don't know. What problems! If anything . . . anything damaging comes to the surface about the cross or the man, I will have to terminate the negotiations." Then his face broke into a grin. "You had better prepare yourself for the meeting," he said. "There's not much time."

CHAPTER SIXTEEN

Going, Going . . .

I HAD LESS than ten days to prepare for the meeting of the awesome Purchase Committee. My first move was to approach Ted Rousseau for advice and a few votes. He promised to recommend the cross to several of his special friends on the board, notably Robert Lehman, an influential art collector who was then vice-president of the museum. I asked Ted how, if he were doing it, he would handle the presentation of the cross.

"Be brief as hell. Stress the good points, bring up a couple of minor negative points, just for credibility. And, absolutely vital, justify the price. That ought to do it."

After talking with Rousseau, I actually began to believe it might be possible, after all, to persuade a cautious director and a wary Board of Trustees to set aside six hundred thousand dollars for a partly damaged and incomplete ivory cross of unknown origin and mysterious provenance, engraved with a series of viciously intolerant verses, and then to hand the money over to a suspicious Yugoslav who worked out of Morocco and concealed his art collection, of which ninety percent was fake or misattributed, in a bank vault in Zurich.

But after listening to another senior curator, I began to have severe second thoughts. "What I'm going to tell you, Hoving, may be only one man's opinion," he began. "Yet it's the truth. Purchasing a work of art in this place is more a charade than a scholarly procedure. That Purchasing Committee meeting is a farce, an ornamental 'show and tell' thoroughly manipulated by Jim Rorimer. The trustees who come are usually so confused that their decisions are capricious. Or they are so unsure of themselves they just vote along with Rorimer and Roland Redmond.

"Political maneuvering, gracious manners, the ability to flatter the director and the board members—those qualities are more important than connoisseurship or intellect. But remember, sometimes staff members *other* than curatorial have a tremendous influence over Rorimer. I mean the treasurer, or even the operating administrator. And it's happened more than once that an outsider, a personal friend of a trustee, has killed a purchase by making an offhand remark against it at a fashionable soiree.

"The meeting of the Purchase Committee usually takes place over dinner. There's a cocktail hour. We curators are invited to both—'summoned' would be a more accurate word—and we are treated with immense tolerance. Wine is served at dinner, followed by more drinks. So you can expect to face a group of tired and tipsy trustees. After the dinner, each curator makes a presentation. You'll be interrupted continually by the director, urging you to hurry up. The way to assure victory"—he smiled—"is to suck up to everyone in sight."

But what the cynical old curator did not know about was the very thing we searched for in graduate school—a gimmick. To persuade them to approve the cross, I had to find one that would hook the trustees, lift them out of their seats. Yet that gimmick could not be truth. "Gentleman, I offer you a unique and thrilling cross. It is a genuine, honest-to-goodness neo-Nazi cross, dripping with medieval venom, something so extravagant that it will curl your hair, bankrupt your museum, and cause an international scandal!"

I thrashed around, hunting for days, before I chanced upon the quintessential gimmick. My basic problem, other than its astronomical price, obscure provenance and ambiguous ownership, was that the cross itself could not be present to make its own argument. Topic Mimara's photographs were excellent, but they were for scholars, and were too small to make a striking impression. I seized upon the idea of constructing an authentic-looking model of Topic's cross. Taking photographs of his photographs, enlarging them to the exact size of the object, I pasted them on a scale model of the cross in wood I arranged to have built in the carpentry shop at The Cloisters. The effect was dramatic.

To distinguish myself from other curators at the meeting, I restrained myself from uttering a word about the cross during cocktails or dinner. I let my colleagues chatter on about their works of art. I sensed what the trustees really wanted was small talk, not a sales pitch. I tried to be charming, confident, fascinated by the interests of each trustee. I had, in fact, been briefed on each of them in detail by Ted Rousseau.

But I appeared to be in trouble from the start. Robert Lehman, with whom I chatted about his "splendid medieval bronzes," seemed uncomfortable, even wary of me. Arthur Houghton, president of Steuben Glass, whom I tried to impress by talking informatively about his "beautiful crystal sculptures," seemed distant and disinterested. I turned then to Walter Baker, vice-president of a leading New York bank, who had a choice collection of Greek and Roman antiquities. Initially he was amiable, but gradually he turned glacial. I approached Henry Luce, founder of *Time* and *Life*, armed with information about his interest in Oriental art. Luce gave me the impression he was not listening to a single word. And Roland Redmond, who at first boosted my spirits by congratulating me on my maiden appearance before the committee, crushed me by observing that he had a "host of serious questions about this cross."

At last dinner was cleared away and the moment came for me to make my presentation. I was finally where I had yearned to be. But the situation had none of the glamor I had been dreaming about. There was just a bare conference table surrounded by seven groggy men: Rorimer, who impatiently waved his hand for me to get going; five bored trustees; and the heavy-lidded secretary of the museum, Dudley Easby.

"Gentlemen," I began in a strong voice, "my story is brief, for the object I have to offer is the greatest of its kind in existence."

My approach worked. Although Rorimer leaned far back in his chair, with one finger held skeptically to his chin, every one of the trustees sat up. Henry Luce started to fiddle with what looked like the volume control knob on his hearing aid.

Casually I spread Topic's photographs, like a fan, across the end of the table. "I thought of passing around for you these photographs of the work of art. But they are small. Since the object is two feet high, majestic and carved from spectacular golden glistening ivory, I will not. I have something better."

Rorimer leaned forward with a faint smile on his face.

"The object I offer is the fullest summation of medieval civilization I know of—a magnificent English altar cross dating to the middle of the twelfth century. It is far too rare and valuable to have been shipped to this meeting. But, in a sense, I have it and will show it to you nevertheless."

With these words I took several quick steps to a cupboard and brought forth my model, which was concealed under a cloth of deep-red velvet. "When I first saw this great work of art, deep in the heavily guarded sanctuary of the Union Banque de Suisse in Zurich, my heart stopped for an instant. When the cloth was pulled away and the great altar cross was revealed to me, I marveled."

I swept away the cloth and, in rapturous tones, continued my discourse. "Fifty-six magnificently carved figures. Each only about an inch high. A half-dozen scenes from the Bible. Incomparable! Dozens of inscriptions—mostly Latin—proclaiming the eternal power and glory of the Christian Church."

Henry Luce, Robert Lehman and Walter Baker got out of their chairs and moved closer to examine the model.

"My reaction was just the same as yours, gentlemen. I couldn't take my eyes off the piece. I too wanted to find out at once everything to be known about this incredibly complex masterpiece. But I knew that would take months, even years. I hope there will be opportunity for that. Think of the thousands of crosses that must have been

made during the entirety of the Middle Ages! This one
is the most imposing ever to have survived.

"But don't take my word for it. Let our chief rivals
speak. The British Museum wants to acquire this monument more than anything in its recent history. That august
institution has assembled a team of the most learned
scholars in England to support the purchase. A key
member of the team told me, in confidence, that 'the
institution to acquire the cross can consider itself the
most fortunate in the world.'"

I paused to let that sink in, and then went on. "Our
own director has personally examined the cross and established its authenticity." Rorimer beamed.

"This is my first appearance before you. I have been
advised I am supposed to say that the price of this
masterpiece is justifiable, citing comparable prices of
similar works of art. I can't do that. There has never
been anything comparable to this cross in world history.
What is the price? It's six hundred thousand dollars.
Amazing! The British Museum is being asked to pay a
little less—five hundred and forty-six thousand dollars.
Why? The owner prefers to sell it to England. Can the
price be negotiated? Never! In fact, after the beginning
of the year the price will rise if no one has purchased
the cross.

"I could try to ease your minds on the price by com-
paring the cross to a superior painting. But that would be
nonsense. To me, the incredible price is a point in favor
of this unique work of art. I am not wasting your time
with a second-rate medieval bauble. I bring you universal
excellence. We have more than double the amount needed
in The Cloisters Fund. John D. Rockefeller gave his
generous endowment because he wanted us to house the
greatest works of art in medieval history. This is it, the
very best!

"Where did the owner obtain the cross? We don't know.
He refuses to tell. No matter. A lengthy article by his
wife—a recognized scholar—will be published within two
months in a world-renowned art-history journal. The cross
will be described as coming from the owner's collection.
If there were any difficulty for him or for us on provenance, I ask you, would the owner allow his wife to publish

such information? For that reason there is, I maintain, no risk to us at all.

"As for proof of ownership, we don't yet have that. But we are working on it. An appropriate document can, I am sure, easily be drawn up."

At these words Dudley Easby snubbed out his ever-present cigarette, glanced at me sharply and gave me a conspiratorial smile.

"For my conclusion, I have been told I should be a trifle emotional. Someone even told me to let the tears flow. But if the cross does not come into the collection of The Cloisters, there won't be any tears. Just laughter. Joyous laughter from the British Museum. If we fail to acquire this transcendentally beautiful work of art, future generations will look back and say that those responsible were looking at the mud at their feet and not the shining horizons."

Arthur Houghton glanced at Rorimer. "Jim, may I have the first question? Thanks." He turned toward me. "I must say your presentation has been innovative. Crisp. It woke me up. I liked it. Tell me, how does the cross compare in quality to all existing crosses, not just those on the art market?"

"Sir, there is only one comparable cross existing," I said. "You may have seen it. It's the ivory cross of about the same dimensions made in the eleventh century for King Ferdinand. It's in Madrid, in the Museo de Arqueologia."

"Hardly like to be sold off, either. Eh? Thank you, Mr. Hoving."

Henry Luce spoke up. "Do we have the money?" Seeing Rorimer nod affirmatively, Luce went on. "I say we buy it. Why not vote now?"

Rorimer gently reminded Henry Luce that a vote would have to wait for the executive session.

Walter Baker smiled broadly before weighing in with his questions. "Is provenance really a vital issue? There are few Greek or Roman objects whose provenance we know. Who is the present owner?"

"Mr. Baker," I answered him respectfully, "the man is a painter, collector and businessman by the name of Ante Topic Mimara. He's wealthy, I'm told."

"Does he have any pieces in my field?"

"Not that I saw."

"Thank you. Well, Jim, I'm impressed."

Finally Roland Redmond rose from his chair. "We are grateful for your invigorating talk. Our executive session will now begin. I must say personally that there are serious problems to be discussed on price and ownership of this unique object."

As I retrieved the model and the photographs, Robert Lehman grasped my arm, gave it a friendly squeeze and whispered, "Good presentation. One of the best I ever heard. Good luck."

I retired to Rorimer's office to await the verdict. But I couldn't sit down. I just paced around and around the circular conference table, clapping my hands together silently with excitement and pleasure. After half an hour, I could hear Rorimer outside the open side door, laughing as he conversed with the departing members of the committee. I heard the words "promising" and "able young man" and "No, he will not be disappointed." I had won!

Rorimer burst into his office, tossed his papers on the desk, collapsed in his chair, propped up his feet on the desk and reached for a pipe. He smiled broadly. "Excellent job. Quick, to the point. I have the necessary votes to proceed as I see fit. And I have signed the purchase blank."

"Great! Oh, great!" I cried out. "Jim, I'll never forget this. Never! What do we do next?"

"We must obtain a legal bill of sale and guarantees from Topic Mimara that no third party can lodge a legitimate claim for the cross. I've drafted a telegram to Topic which will be dispatched this evening. Here, read it."

A. TOPIC MIMARA C/O DR WILTRUD TOPIC MERSMANN, KÖLN-BOCKLEMUND, ARNOLDSHOF, GERMANY.

AM NOW IN POSITION TO MAKE DEFINITE OFFER TO PURCHASE YOUR OBJECT. BELIEVE INTERVIEW IN NEW YORK IN NEAR FUTURE HIGHLY DESIRABLE, ALTHOUGH TRANSACTION WOULD BE COMPLETED IN SWITZERLAND. PLEASE CABLE ME WHEN YOU ARE ABLE TO MEET ME AND OTHER MUSEUM REPRESENTATIVES HERE.

JAMES J. RORIMER

"He'll never come," I pointed out.

"I know," Rorimer said. "But I've given him an out by mentioning Switzerland. So, we are finally on our way."

Two days later, Topic answered Rorimer's request with a telegram of his own. "Because of recent illness I cannot travel to New York. Letter explains."

When the letter arrived, after two weeks, it contained two time bombs.

I do understand your need for security. Therefore I am proposing to you—after you have bought the cross— to have other important English objects in my collection, as a loan and for your security, exhibited in your museum for a period of time to be agreed upon. Their value, according to the evaluation of experts, amounts to $2,500,000.

Furthermore, I must insist on your buying, besides the cross, several other objects from my collection, because otherwise one cannot find a justification in connection with the promise I have already given the British Museum. Should the payment for the additional objects be impossible for you at this moment, I will agree to a later payment as well.

"The man is a blackmailer!" Rorimer roared. "I refuse to knuckle under. This impertinent Slav is already asking nearly fifty thousand dollars more from us than the British Museum. I absolutely reject this nonsense. I'll be damned if we will exhibit his junk at The Cloisters. If we did, we would be authenticating his fakes and establishing astronomical prices for them, to boot! I'm going to throw some cool water on your friend Topic!"

Rorimer's letter was icy.

You certainly have left me in a position where I cannot possibly make the next move.

Perhaps we will be meeting in Europe next spring, after you have reconsidered the fact that we are prepared to discuss a proposition which would make it possible to pay the kind of substantial sum you were talking about, and still have what our lawyers would consider adequate title. You only complicate the whole program by inviting us to buy other pieces, and thereby confuse the transaction.

It is not your good faith that troubles us; it is the

actual lack of knowledge by at least one of us as to
where and how the cross was acquired.

Two months went by. Finally, as we approached the
end of 1962, on the twelfth of December we heard from
Topic. He had shifted course. He wrote that he had "only
brought up the idea of loaning a substantial amount of
the English collection to The Cloisters because a year ago
in Zurich Mr. Hoving had suggested the possibility."
Plaintively, he added, "To suggest a loan was obviously
an error. I meant well and have been falsely understood."
About the provenance and title of the cross, Topic would
add nothing. "I have said all I will ever say." Once more,
however, he remarked that we must purchase something
else with the cross. He concluded by suggesting that
Rorimer meet him no later than February the fifth.

"I can't go then," Rorimer growled. "That is when the
Mona Lisa will be arriving at the museum and I am
expecting a million visitors. I can't possibly leave my
desk! Write your 'pal' and convince him I mean business
about proof of ownership. Tell him we're not about to
buy anything else before the cross."

My letter was, I hoped, a masterful combination of
politesse and hardheadedness.

I hope you do not believe there was a misunderstand-
ing on our part about your offer to loan us a number
of your English objects. We do realize this offer is a
mark of good faith in the negotiations.

However, certain confusion on our part does arise on
the point of whether you wish to offer certain objects as
loans or as purchases. Perhaps you would be willing to
clarify this point for Mr. Rorimer and myself. After the
negotiations on the cross were concluded we would, of
course, be more than willing to discuss buying certain
other pieces in your collection. But at this moment the
cross is our primary interest. . . .

What our lawyers and trustees might consider adequate
title is still a problem. We are not, we believe, being
difficult in this regard. You must understand that, as an
internationally famous institution, the Metropolitan Museum must act with circumspection. . . .

The very day I sent out the letter to Topic, I learned
that our British competition had become an actual menace.

Harold Parsons wrote to convey what Topic had told him: "'The English have made great strides in their program and have already fifty percent of the funds in hand to purchase my cross. *All* the English scholars are completely enthusiastic about it and *all* have signed a letter to the Finance Ministry for the acquisition. Too bad that Mr. Rorimer walks with feet of lead.'"

Seeing the cross gradually slipping from my fingers made me frantic. I dispatched three more express letters to Topic, imploring him to sell the cross alone and to reveal something, anything, about its provenance. Rorimer, meanwhile, wrote Sir Frank Francis at the British Museum, pointing out: "I have not heard from you about the cross since your return to England, as agreed. A certain confidential letter suggests that we are still in violent competition. . . ." At the same time, Rorimer arranged for the Metropolitan's curator of Western European Art, John Phillips, who was about to go to Italy for several months, to change his plans and visit Sir Frank in London at once.

A long week went by. I received a letter from Parsons saying that Topic had backed off from his insistence that we buy something with the cross. Topic's final advice was, "The suitor who comes first with the money gets the girl." I rushed to tell Rorimer.

"Forget that. We are in grave danger," he said. "I just got off the telephone with Jack Phillips, who has just seen Frank Francis and Ruppert Bruce-Mitford." James Rorimer looked more distracted than I could remember ever having seen him. "The British Museum has applied to the Exchequer for the money and may receive funds by the end of this month."

"Christ," I muttered.

"Phillips told me quite a tale. Apparently, Bruce-Mitford was rude as hell. Phillips said his wrath was *immense*. He kept shouting that both Cleveland and the Met had already had their chance years ago and had rejected it. Now was his chance. He paced his office—didn't even offer Phillips a chair. He shrieked, pounding his desk, swearing he would get the cross."

"What are you going to do?"

"I'm not going to do anything," Rorimer snapped. "*You* are!"

I stood there, uncomprehending.

"You're going to Zurich tonight," he ordered. "That gives you six hours to prepare. I've had you booked on Swissair leaving Idlewild this evening. You land tomorrow morning in Zurich. I suggest you book lodgings at the Hotel Central. It's good, cheap, and only a short walk from Topic's hotel, the Limmathof. I will supply you with three documents and the name of a lawyer in Zurich with whom you may consult. One of the documents is this letter from me to Topic."

I read it rapidly.

DEAR MR. TOPIC MIMARA,

Mr. Thomas P. F. Hoving will be bearing this letter by hand as the Museum's emissary and representative because, alas, I cannot get away from an over-burdened desk. Mr. Hoving is also the bearer of certain documents which he will be able to explain in detail and of course he can always be in communication with me by mail and telephone.

It would be my proposal, in view of other options the Museum has, that an elegant solution to our problems would be that we send money to a Swiss bank and you transfer the object to Mr. Hoving. With this thought in mind I send you best wishes.

I was reeling with excitement and pride.

"Secondly," Rorimer said, "Dudley Easby has prepared a bill of sale which you must get Topic Mimara to sign in the presence of the American consul in Zurich. *Must!* Third, I have supplied you with another document for Topic to sign if we buy the cross, promising he will never reveal the selling price."

"Jim, this is the most splendid moment in my life! I can hardly believe it's happening." I let loose a muted but exuberant cheer.

"Don't cheer too soon. It won't be easy. And by the way, you've got more to do than buy the cross. I've received information in recent days that a private collector in Orléans wants to dispose of a spectacular collection of twelfth-century Limoges enameled caskets. I want the two caskets in this photograph. I persuaded the trustees to vote ninety thousand dollars for the pair. When you have the time, get to Orléans and work out a deal. Now, on the cross, be firm but gentle. Oh, be anything, but get it!"

"I'll get it," I said hoarsely. "I have only one question. Do I take the check for the six hundred thousand with me? Or will it be deposited in our Zurich bank?"

"No check yet. We can make a deposit later, if necessary."

"If necessary? What do you mean? If I get there before the British, we have the cross. I may need the money tomorrow."

"Maybe not. You're going to have to bargain with the man. In the executive session of the Purchase Committee I asked for and received board approval to spend no more than five hundred thousand dollars."

I felt as if I had been sandbagged. I could scarcely believe Rorimer had been deceiving me all these months. And after his apparent enthusiasm those last few days, it seemed incredible he was still holding back on the price.

"What kind of a game are you trying to play?" I shouted. "You don't really want the cross, do you? You're sending me over just to cover your tracks and show the trustees you 'tried.' You know damn well Topic will never come down."

Rorimer looked at me coolly. "Do you want your precious cross or not? You don't have to take that plane this evening—or any time, young man."

"You're sending me on a futile mission. You know it. The British will win."

"Have it your way. But stop wasting my time. I have a great deal else to do. Are you going or not?"

"I'll go," I said dejectedly. "But I'll fail."

"Do you have any glimmer of understanding how much half a million dollars is? Do you realize how difficult it will be for the British to raise half that sum? Go!"

I shook Rorimer's hand weakly and left in a daze.

CHAPTER SEVENTEEN

The Stroke of Midnight

THE FLIGHT TO ZURICH was a near-disaster. All of Europe was being battered by the most severe snowstorm in decades. My plane was diverted to Barcelona, then to Nice. Eventually, we were on our way to Zurich hours late. Then on the final approach in the winter's darkness, the snow whipping by our landing lights, the pilot, still unable to see the runway seconds before touchdown, pulled up abruptly. I had thought we were going to crash.

I was thoroughly unnerved. After another hour, the jet finally landed in Geneva, normally a flight of twenty minutes. Chaos. Dozens of aircraft from all over Europe were parked in confusion on the snow-swept tarmac. Thousands of passengers milled throughout the small terminal. I managed to place a call to Topic Mimara at his Zurich hotel to say I was on my way. He only grunted. I bulled my way through crowds of passengers jamming the railroad station and boarded the last available train to Zurich.

After a five-hour trip, I walked into the Hotel Central. Topic Mimara was waiting dolefully in the lobby.

"Signor Topic," I said, managing somehow to smile, "I have arrived to purchase your magnificent cross for the Metropolitan Museum."

He scowled. "You are late, Signor Hoving. Too late. The Metropolitan always walks with feet of lead. Your museum has no real interest in my great cross. I have decided to give the British Museum an exclusive option until February tenth to raise the money. Only after that will you have the chance. The price is still two hundred thousand pounds for the British and six hundred thousand dollars for you."

My face simply collapsed. Then, from somewhere deep within me, I found a renewed sense of strength. "Come," I said, guiding him toward the bar of the hotel, "let's have a beer and talk it over. I have no idea why you have made this precipitous decision to give the British Museum what amounts to a lifetime to decide on your cross. You knew I was on the way. You knew of the Metropolitan's interest, and my personal commitment to your splendid object."

"Ah, Signor Hoving, you are young and keen, and I do like you," Topic Minara remarked. "But I prefer England because my wife, who has finished her great study, believes the cross is English—as do all the distinguished art historians and museum connoisseurs who have seen it. You see," the man went on softly, "it would be convenient for me and my wife to visit London, but the long trip to New York for me to pay homage to my cross from time to time would be intolerable."

"Signor Topic, perhaps that's a good enough reason for your decision. But I have a problem, too, which involves your deadline. We have a long list of works of art we want to purchase, including a great collection of Romanesque enamels. James Rorimer doesn't want to wait too long."

"Rorimer," Topic Mimara rasped. The name was spoken with startling anger. "He toys with me. I do not like him. He is shrewd and, I think, not wholly honorable. When he was here, he made light of my honor. I had explained to him that I had given my word to the British Museum. And he said, 'Oh, forget your word. What's a word these days, anyway?' He told me he would give me half a million dollars and I should hand over the cross to him. I was angered. No. I have decided to allow the British the period of time until the tenth of February to raise the money."

I was inches away from the brink and slipping toward the abyss. I knew that if my English rivals were given an option until February, they would win. I had to say something to gain Topic's sympathy. He might be an enemy of Jim Rorimer, but he might be persuaded to become an ally of mine.

"Signor Topic, you are a man of honor," I intoned. "Forget about Rorimer. You don't have to like him. But please understand, I have to carry out his wishes. When you were young, you must have experienced the same. I adore your cross. I want it more than the British, more than Bruce-Mitford. I have fought harder. I had to fight Rorimer. You must give me a chance. I am a man of honor. In that regard, we are alike."

"I do know of your passion for my treasure," Topic remarked with gravity. "I have seen it myself. And Harold Parsons described your yearnings for my great cross."

"And as a man of honor," I slipped in, "you will want to give me an equal chance."

"What would that be?"

"Give the British just a week. Why should they have until February tenth, anyway?"

"The funds are already in the Exchequer. Bruce-Mitford told me there is to be a meeting of all the directors of the British Museum with the Chancellor of the Exchequer on the ninth of February."

"If they really want your cross, they can have their meeting earlier. I got here first. Where are they?"

"They are coming soon. In fact, tomorrow. Bruce-Mitford is coming with an assistant. Why don't you join us for dinner? It might amuse you."

Nothing Topic might have said could have surprised me more.

"But why are they coming now?" I said, my voice rising. "They won't have the full amount. Are they coming to bargain?"

"No one will be allowed to bargain," he said curtly.

"What if they can't raise the full amount?"

"No bargaining," Topic said, and paused. "You do have all the money, Signor Hoving, don't you?"

My mind raced. What could I say to the man? I was

edging even closer to the brink. I could not lie to him and tell him I had the full amount. What if he called my bluff? What a quandary! I needed something to say that would instill in Topic total confidence that I could pay his full price, perhaps even more. Topic leaned over his empty beer glass, staring at me, his face a hard mask. At that moment the perfect ploy came to mind.

"Do I have the money?" I repeated. "Signor Topic, I, Thomas Hoving, know your full price to us is six hundred thousand dollars. I swear and pledge to you, on my honor, I *know* that."

Topic Mimara relaxed and smiled.

"Signor Topic," I went on hurriedly, "when you wrote to Parsons you said, 'The suitor who comes first with the money gets the girl.' And here I am! The British may be coming, but they aren't here yet. I am!"

"What do you want, Signor Hoving?" Topic asked. "Are you suggesting that right here and now you will give me a banker's check for six hundred thousand dollars and tomorrow I shall hand the great cross over to you?"

"Much as I would like to suggest that course of action," I replied quickly, "it would not be honorable to my rivals." I almost choked on my words.

Topic sat staring at me. Finally he spoke up. "I have the solution. You are persuasive. Things must be fair and equal. I shall inform Bruce-Mitford he has a clear option to raise the two hundred thousand pounds. But that option will expire January thirtieth—at the stroke of midnight. If the British withdraw before then, you must pay me in a day. Otherwise, the price will rise. That is fair."

"Agreed!" I said quickly. "Except for a minor detail." Topic cocked his head. "You must give me a signed document stating you own the cross. It is one of Rorimer's requirements. Remember, I begged you to put the information about where you obtained the cross in an envelope only for Rorimer's eyes."

"Signor Hoving, if you were Rorimer what would have been the first thing you would have done when you received the envelope?"

"In all honesty, I would have opened it and placed a long-distance call to—" I smiled innocently—"just tell me where, Signor Topic."

He roared with laughter.

"But you don't have to do that," I hurried on. "Just sign this bill of sale and warranty of ownership. Here, I brought it in English and in German." I handed him the document garnished with a long red ribbon underneath the gold seal of the Metropolitan Museum.

Topic read the pages slowly, his lips following each word. His forehead seemed to furrow deeper with each paragraph. When he finished, he looked up, puzzled. "All it really means is that I must swear before your consul here in Zurich that I am 'the sole owner and know of no impediment which will prevent conveyance of absolute title to the Museum.' True?"

"Yes, that's all. Very simple."

"If you had sent this document months ago I would have signed and you would now have the cross. Instead, you and Rorimer wrote so many difficult letters."

What an exasperating man! I could have strangled him. But calmly I added, "The contract also states that our price includes any commission to Harold Parsons."

"Of course. I will pay. I've always said so."

"And the agreement also says," I persisted, "you must promise never to reveal how much the museum paid."

"Agreed." He scrutinized the documents again. "Wait. There is something amiss. See here, where it says 'in consideration of the sum of'—there is a blank. The figure, six hundred thousand dollars, is not written in. Why?"

"A detail," I assured him. "You see, my instructions were to take this contract to a lawyer in Zurich to obtain the . . . precise language for what the American consul must sign."

"Perhaps a good solution would be to have the correct figure typed or written in right now and then I shall sign," Topic remarked.

I felt dizzy. "But, Signor Topic, legally I must obtain your signature only in the presence of the consul."

"And there is still the option of seventeen days for the British," Topic observed. "Much as I like you, Signor Hoving, and hope that you acquire the historic cross, I do not think you have much of a chance. But you are clever, you have persisted. You did arrive first—barely. And you have managed to extract from me the most valuable concession. The British will be angered, but if their dedication is equal to yours, then they will raise the money."

I dragged myself up to my tiny, cold room and lay back on the bed, utterly drained. My entire body quivered, my head thundered with pain. I had not slept in over thirty-six hours, but my mind refused to relax. Much as I tried to slumber, I could not. I took a sleeping pill, then a tranquilizer. Still no sleep. Midnight. Bells on a nearby church sounded as though they were ringing inside my skull. One o'clock. I dozed for what I hoped was an hour. My watch showed that not even ten minutes had passed. I dozed off again, only to be awakened by the sharp clang of a trolley bell. Two o'clock. Sleep, please come. I tried all the systems—counting sheep, counting prophets, relaxing every muscle from the toes up. Nothing worked. I just lay there, thinking about defeat. I had lost. The full bitterness of the realization penetrated my troubled mind.

In the middle of that hopeless night, distressed to the bottom of my soul, I got up, splashed frigid water on my burning face, and placed a call to Rorimer. I didn't even care if I sounded incoherent. But when the call clicked through and the phone on the other side of the Atlantic began to ring, I discovered to my surprise that I was absolutely lucid.

"I've tried every argument and means of persuasion at my disposal, Jim. It went on hour after hour. Topic is obdurate about the six hundred thousand. He simply will not break. However, I did win two major concessions. He was about to give the British Museum until February tenth to come up with the money, but now they have only until January the thirtieth, seventeen days. He will also sign the bill of sale. If I had come with the whole nut, I think he would have made a deal. He kept asking if I had all the money. I couldn't lie, but at the same time I felt I had to avoid the truth. Right now, anyway, he thinks we're stronger than the British. If he ever suspected the truth, we'd be cut off."

When I had finished, Rorimer congratulated me for what I had been able to achieve. "But," he said, "I too am obdurate. I'm not going to give in so easily. I sincerely doubt the British will be able to raise the money. I think they will try to bargain him down. Topic may get furious with them and turn to us. Then we can offer four hundred thousand! Think about it. If the British already have the money, there's nothing we can do that would make the difference anyway. Good luck."

More discouraged than ever, I fell into bed and slept. Nothing stirred me, not the clanging of trolleys, not even the cautious visits by a few hotel maids. I awoke at four the next afternoon, thoroughly refreshed, famished, prepared to vanquish the British, ready to subvert Topic, and eager to do anything to persuade James Rorimer to send along one hundred thousand dollars more.

At seven-thirty that evening, four of us met in the lobby of the hotel. Bruce-Mitford turned out to be tall and silver-haired, an elegant character dressed in a mackintosh and a long knitted scarf. He reached out his hand, shook mine firmly and said, "Well, Hoving, I imagine you must feel something like Paul Revere!" I had to laugh.

At first I mistook Peter Lasko for an acquaintance of Topic Mimara's. He was a rotund little man, all in black —black overcoat, black suit, black hair and eyes. He resembled a caricature, the archetypal anarchist. But his looks were deceiving. He spoke with the greatest of voices in an impeccable Oxonian accent.

Our dinner was at Topic Mimara's favorite restaurant, the Rebe on the Schützengasse. With a flourish, Topic positioned himself at the head of the table. I sat to his left, Bruce-Mitford and Lasko to his right. The affair developed into a Balkan version of the Mad Hatter's Tea Party. I spoke Italian to Topic; Bruce-Mitford and Lasko could not understand. Lasko conversed with Topic in German and, from time to time, in what I took to be Croatian; neither Bruce-Mitford nor I could understand. Invariably, when anyone addressed one word to Topic, another would interrupt in German, English or Italian to Topic, I would ask Topic in Italian what he had said, which would cause Bruce-Mitford to demand to know what *I* had said.

There was little substance to the meeting. I managed to throw in a few comments about the formidable purchase power of The Cloisters. Bruce-Mitford countered by reminding me of his option. We parted company warily, but cordially.

The next day, January 15, was my thirty-second birthday. It arrived on the coldest day I had ever lived through. The city was shrouded in a dark-gray and yellowish freezing mist. I spent the morning huddled against the lukewarm radiator in my room wearing my long underwear, wrapped in two blankets. Thirty-two years of age! I was hardly the modern counterpart to Alexander the Great, was I? He had died at thirty-three, having conquered the whole world. I was in danger of losing the only conquest I had ever pursued.

I badgered Topic Mimara into having lunch with me that gloomy day and then stuck with him almost until dinner. What a birthday! I tried to cajole him into revealing what had occurred in his discussion with Bruce-Mitford and Peter Lasko. He edged away, changing the subject amiably, and launched into anecdotes about various episodes of his life.

"Collecting is the spice of life, don't you agree? I remember the first work of art I ever found," he rambled on, "the one which converted me into an avowed art collector. It was in Italy. I had just been released from prison." Seeing the look on my face, Topic laughed. "Or I should say a prisoner-of-war camp. You see, I had been in the Austrian Army during the First World War and was captured in Italy. Luckily, the armistice came soon after. I was released and decided to remain in Italy to become a painter and a restorer of paintings. One day in the summer of 1922 I found myself in Tivoli, painting a landscape of the ancient ruins of the Villa of Hadrian. I could hear two peasants singing as they dug away at the base of an olive tree. Then suddenly they stopped. Alerted, I got up, left my easel and walked over to them. 'What have you found?' I asked. One of them handed over a small object, caked with dried clay. I cleaned off part of it with my finger and saw a bronze sculpture. It was the image of a young athlete. Not Roman, original Greek. I bought the bronze from the peasants for a few lire. They were happy, so was I. It was the beginning of my life of collecting."

I blinked hard and did not say a word. Topic Mimara had just told me the story of his first acquisition in virtually the same terms he had used to describe his adventure to Hanns Swarzenski. But in telling the story to Hanns, he had claimed his first collecting triumph was the early Christian glass chalice.

Topic kept on reminiscing. "Works of art. How much better they are than human beings! Great works of art transcend even the great men of history. I am a close friend of Tito, who is a great man, even if he is a Communist. I met him in Paris in the 1930s during the Spanish Civil War and we have been friends ever since. He has said on more than one occasion I should come back to Yugoslavia to become the head of culture and run all the museums. I always tell him, 'Never!' And I mean it. My dream is to build for my country a museum to contain the best pieces from my extensive holdings."

It was hard not to laugh. Think of that! A museum of forgeries! Poor Yugoslavia.

"Leaders!" Topic added disdainfully. "The world seldom gets true leaders. Perhaps they don't exist. Most leaders are fools or maniacs. I once met the greatest maniac of them all—Adolf Hitler. It was in the Hotel Regina in Berlin, in 1928, long before he came to power. I happened to hear the end of a speech in which he ranted on about vanquishing Europe and the world. I went over to him afterward, introduced myself, and asked how he thought he could win such a war. Hitler said, 'I have the German people.' And I told him he was truly insane, for the rest of the world had the Chinese, the Russians, the French, the Americans—the entire force of population and what those populations could manufacture. I told him he was doomed. Hitler just laughed. He wasn't angry at all. But I think he never forgot my words, and in a peculiar way respected me for them. Later, years later, during the last war, I believe he protected me even though I was an avowed anti-Nazi."

"How's that?" I asked, more than a little dubious.

"Ah, that is another story," Topic said, lapsing into silence.

After considerable effort, I persuaded him to tell something about what progress the British had made.

"Ah, it is difficult for the British to raise the money," he said. "I have learned that their government, their Exchequer itself, is willing to go to that amount. But it is not voted. That means the British Museum must raise fifty thousand on their own."

"I see. And what of their new deadline? What did he think of that?"

"Bruce-Mitford asked for more time, of course, but I said no. He also said that if the British do commit the funds it will be the first time in history they have done so without the trustees of the museum examining a work of art."

"Would you take the cross to London to be examined?" I asked anxiously.

"I don't know," Topic responded.

I telephoned Jim Rorimer and reported the information I had managed to glean. Once more I pleaded with him to recommend the extra hundred thousand. But Rorimer told me he was sticking at half a million. He did say, though, he would consider my plea with care. Before hanging up, he urged me to take some time off.

But I could not relax and would not leave Topic. I dispatched a quick note to Margaret Freeman. Writing, talking, reading were the only activities keeping me from cracking—and I was getting closer and closer to that point with the passage of each hour.

PEG—Please *push* Jim. But don't annoy him. We *must* have this thing! We must go to $600,000. Use any idea you might have that will influence the raising of the $100,000—But *don't* say you know that's the difference.

The next day I stayed so close to Topic Mimara I was practically in his hip pocket. I was with him from eight-thirty in the morning until six at night. We went over the old territory time after time. My head was splitting from the effort of speaking Italian.

Again, as on the previous day, he sought to divert me by telling me a story. This one stunned me. It had to be true. I had been trying to humor him into revealing when and where he had found the cross. "Why can't you tell—just me," I wheedled. "I'll keep it a secret. I won't tell Rorimer."

He threw up his hands in mock alarm. "Perhaps one day, Signor Hoving. Not now." Then, very casually, he said, "When I saw the cross for the first time in 1938, it was in pieces and black with dirt. When I was handed the square block with the Bull of Saint Luke and the scene of the Three Marys at the Tomb, I knew I had seen something very much like it before. I sat there thinking. Where, when? Then it came back to me. It had been in a small jewelry and antique store near a butcher shop and blocks off the main square in the town of Mons in Belgium, a few kilometers from the border with France. That had been in the fall of 1931. I had a missing block from the cross. No question. On one side there was an angel, like the one sitting on the sarcophagus in the Three Marys."

"Yes, yes?" I said. "That's right. That would be the symbol of Saint Matthew, the missing Evangelist. What was carved on the other side? Please, it's incredibly important."

"It was so long ago."

"*Try* to remember."

"Well, there was Latin writing on the narrow sides . . . but I do not know or remember what."

"Can't you remember anything? What about the other side?"

"On the side opposite the angel was a crowded scene, divided horizontally across the middle. There was a group of little figures above the line, and more figures below. It was complicated. A scene on two tiers."

I stiffened. There was no doubt Topic had seen the block missing from the bottom of the cross. I knew instantly it had to depict the Harrowing of Hell, that episode when Christ descended into hell, smashed the gates and brought out the blessed, including Adam and Eve. The scene almost always was divided into two halves. Chronologically, the subject fit perfectly with the carvings on the cross, between the Lamentation and the Three Marys. Moreover, proof existed on the cross itself. The inscription on the scroll held by the tiny figure of Saint Matthew referred specifically to the scene: "For as Jonah was three days and three nights in the belly of the whale so shall the Son of man be three days and three nights in the heart of the earth."

"Where is it now?" I demanded.

"When I saw the block," Topic said, "I knew I had to have it for my collection. I was poor in those years, so poor I had to cinch in my belt because of hunger. The little money I had I spent not on food, but on art! I haggled with the dealer. But he refused to come down a franc. I left. That was that."

"Is it still there?"

"After I found the cross in 1938, I went back to Mons as soon as I could. It was still before the war. I became excited, as you can imagine, when I walked down the narrow street toward the shop. I turned the corner . . . the shop was gone. No one knew where the proprietor had gone." He paused. "Perhaps if you are lucky, Signor Hoving, and are able to buy my great cross, you will find this piece."

I walked home through the lightly falling snow. I was elated to think that the fourth block, obviously one of great beauty, might still exist. Were would I start the hunt? Then, I thought, what difference did it make? I would never get the cross anyway. I fell into a depression.

After a lonely dinner and far too much wine, I trudged through a bitterly cold and deserted city. During that fierce winter—some said it was the most severe in a century—the streets were empty after nine o'clock. Disheartened, my shoulders hunched against the snow which had begun to thicken, I walked by the Landes museum and was startled to see a huge figure marching awkwardly along its facade. But it was just my shadow, enlarged gigantically. Shivering, I made my way back to my dismal room, bowed down by the weight of defeat. I sat on the bed, holding back tears.

The next morning the sun was shining, and my depression of the evening before evaporated. I decided to stop brooding about the cross, its pieces, Topic, the British, or Rorimer. I telephoned the collector in Orléans, Guy Cranier, whose Limoges caskets Rorimer coveted, and asked if I could visit him to study the objects and begin negotiations on their purchase. Cranier, a soft-spoken individual, urged me to come right away, saying that he sought a resolution to the matter of sale promptly. I was keen to see his material, for I had learned from our researcher in New York that Cranier's collection of medieval artifacts had not in fact been assembled by him, but by a legendary art collector named André Lorrain.

Fortunately, the poisonous weather which had been hanging over Zurich since I arrived lifted temporarily. My plane actually landed in Paris on time. I made the train connection at the Gare Montparnasse at dusk, ten minutes before its departure for Orléans. There were only three other passengers aboard the car I happened to choose. I moved as far away from them as I could and snuggled down into the seat to stay warm. We started off, and as we picked up speed I scraped some ice off the window and gazed out at the depressing signs of deep winter. Iced-over streams flashed by, illuminated by the dim reflection of a rising moon.

I dozed off and dreamed myself into a chain of sweet triumphs. The British had surrendered, sending me a telegram with warm congratulations on my success for America and the Metropolitan! Rorimer and Roland Redmond had flown to Zurich to throw a party in the bar of the Hotel Central. A hundred Swiss had been invited. I was called upon to speak, but was too overcome. I smiled modestly while the audience showered me with applause. My reveries were shattered by a conductor shouting, *"Station Orléans!"* I awoke to the frightening realization that I was back once again in the cold world of reality, with no ivory cross. As I jolted myself into consciousness, my brain was stabbed by a sharp thought. I knew suddenly what I had to do to gain the cross. And it had to do with the man I was about to encounter.

I left the train and walked hesitantly down the platform looking for my host. Soon the handful of commuters had climbed into their cars and had driven away. The waiting room was closed. Where was Guy Cranier? Then I noticed a trim, slight man approaching me cautiously. He wore a tailored black coat with a discreet fur collar and a neat gray hat. He looked like a rich collector.

"Dr. Hoving? I am your host, Guy Cranier. It is a distinct pleasure to meet such a distinguished and learned representative of the famous Metropolitan Museum of Art." The man spoke English immaculately.

"Meeting you is a pleasure for me too," I answered. Cranier took me to his car, an impressive chocolate-brown Mercedes. He chatted animatedly about the brutal winter, my journey which he hoped was comfortable, his eagerness to hear my views concerning his collection.

"I hope you will enjoy what I have planned, Dr. Hoving. First we will stop by your hotel. It is modest-looking, but excellent. Then, if it is agreeable with you, I propose driving to my home, where we shall see my collection. We can talk. Tomorrow we shall meet again. And for lunch, in honor of my guest from America, I have ordered something special—Maine lobsters."

"What a surprise, I love them," I exclaimed. "But alas," I added, "I'm afraid I won't be able to eat them. I may have to return to Zurich very early in the morning. I have other works of art to examine."

"How sad for me," Cranier remarked. "But in that case we shall have the lobsters this evening. It may be possible to complete our work even in this short time."

After I had checked into the hotel we drove to Cranier's home. I asked him to tell me about his collection.

"My story is very simple," he replied. "I am a teacher at a technical high school here, but my real life is art collecting. I am an amateur, a lover of art, especially the glorious art of the Middle Ages. Over the years, I have managed to assemble a nice little collection. I have been lucky. Some of my· Limoges enamels are jewels. And I was able to obtain them at the right time."

"Sounds promising," I commented, wondering why the man had not mentioned the name of André Lorrain.

"My collection, Dr. Hoving, is not just promising, it is magnificent, especially considering that Limoges enamels are so rare."

I wondered what the man was trying to do. He must have realized that, as a medievalist, I knew that during the twelfth and thirteenth centuries Limoges had turned out tens of thousands of enamels. There was hardly a cathedral, monastery or even parish church that had not acquired two or three of them. Some Limoges might be jewels, but they were certainly not rare.

Cranier's home, like his handsome car, appeared at odds with his station in life as a schoolteacher. His library was filled with classics, beautifully bound, well used. Fine furniture abounded; two fireplaces were ablaze, a dozen candles illuminated the dining room. A small but good collection of French academic painters graced the walls. I wondered if the house had once belonged to André Lorrain. He conducted me into an oak-paneled oval room with a series of cabinets fitted out with gleaming brass hinges and locks. In the center was a round table covered with felt the color of burgundy.

For nearly two hours, Cranier presented works of art for my examination. All were well above average in quality, and the two that Rorimer desired were exquisite. They were obviously worth a fortune. Cranier kept badgering me to appraise the quality and value of each piece, which was bad form. He persisted. I tried to avoid offering an opinion, but he was adroit in getting me to talk. Everything I did say Cranier would write in a small notebook. I was annoyed. I began to suspect he had gotten me to come all the way to Orléans for my expertise and a stamp of approval from the Metropolitan. How ironic! He might queer the deal himself.

Finally we halted the examination and sat down to our lobsters. "Well," Cranier said, "I imagine you would like to have my whole collection for the Metropolitan."

"I won't deny that it's a decent collection of Limoges enamels," I told him, "but ours already is extensive. No, I'd say I would consider only two large caskets. They're above average. What's your asking price for the pair?"

"Dr. Hoving, I am afraid there has been some confusion. I am not at all sure I want to part with those caskets or any of my holdings."

I pressed one hand against my face to keep from smiling. "Look, Cranier," I managed to rasp, "didn't you tell me on the phone you wanted to sell?"

"If that was the impression I gave, I do apologize," Cranier replied. "What I meant was that I wanted to resolve in my own mind, and with your help, of course, whether I should sell at all."

"I can't believe this," I said harshly. "Do you realize you got me all the way here from Zurich on false pretenses? You won't sell the caskets?"

"Well, I have not really made up my mind," he said. "I am so attached to the collection I have built up over the years."

I looked directly into his eyes. "Everything you have is from André Lorrain's collection. How did you get your hands on it, anyway? Are you a relative or something?"

Cranier was astonished. "How did you recognize that the pieces were his?" he asked. "Well, it doesn't matter," he recovered quickly. "André was a dear friend of mine in his late years. He passed his collection on to me."

"Can you prove you have legal title?"

"What a thing to suggest, Dr. Hoving. As I said, I don't know if I even want to sell."

"If you did, Cranier," I went on happily, "what would your price be?"

"What would you be prepared to offer?" he countered.

"It's not customary for the Metropolitan to make an offer, but in this one case . . . my offer is eighty thousand dollars."

"I see," Cranier remarked, his face brightening. "It is interesting that we might not be so very far apart. Eighty thousand dollars. Well, I might be induced to sell one."

It was time to make my escape. "My price, Mr. Cranier, is for the pair."

"The pair? Only eighty thousand for both my jewels? Ah . . . I see, a jest."

"Not at all," I replied. "But I am willing to increase my offer to ninety thousand for the two."

"But that's nowhere near . . . That's preposterous!" he cried out.

"Thank you, Mr. Cranier," I said with a relieved smile. "Oh, thank you. . . . And, by the way, feel free to use my remarks about your collection wherever you want for whatever reasons."

A look of sheer incredulity crossed his face.

I telephoned Rorimer as soon as I reached my hotel room. "Cranier is nuts, Jim. His prices are double what you were prepared to pay. But there's a silver lining. With the caskets out of the way, now you have the extra hundred thousand dollars for the ivory."

"That's beside the point," Rorimer replied reflectively. "But I still have a yearning for those enamels. Perhaps I shall instruct you to make Cranier yet another offer. Under no circumstances would I want to drop something like the caskets, even for something else. I am a spoiled boy. You can be that, later on, when you grow to be my age."

"You mean you've decided not to go to six hundred thousand?" I shouted into the phone.

"I have not decided," Rorimer answered sharply. "Sorry, Tom," he added quickly, "I realize all this has been a strain on you. My advice is to take a few days off. Why don't you go skiing? I'll let you know my final decision by cable."

"All right, Jim," I said with a sigh.

When I returned from Orléans I called Topic Mimara to find out what, if anything, the British were doing. He had not heard a word and told me he did not expect to for a week. My rivals, I assumed, were scratching around trying to raise money, just like me. There was nothing I could do in Zurich, so I decided to get out of town. Jim Rorimer had been dead right; I did need some time off. I recognized that I was coming close to the breaking point.

After consulting some guidebooks, I made up my mind to go to a certain locality named Engelberg—literally, Angel Mountain. The resort had the advantage of being only two hours from Zurich by train. Even more attractive, Engelberg was the site of an ancient monastery high up on the Joch pass. In the treasury of that monastery was a famous Romanesque altar cross made of wood sheathed with gold plates worked in relief. So, I rationalized, I could combine work with relaxation.

The farther my train went south toward Engelberg, the better the weather seemed to become. By the time I got off the train and ascended the cog railway car which would take me halfway up the Joch pass, the sky had become a bank of gray clouds with wide bays of blue. By the time I boarded that means of conveyance to the monastic and sporting town, the sky had become a pulsating blue, so clear you could see silver bands where the azure collided with the snow-swept peaks.

At the end of this breathtaking journey, attendants helped me off, grabbed my luggage and asked what they could do to make my visit more pleasurable. Was I really in Switzerland? Or had I actually been transported right up to heaven? "Here am I!" I cried out euphorically upon landing. "The Ascension of Tom Hoving into Engelberg as written on the cross of Topic."

"Please, I am sorry, but I do not understand you, and I speak good English," the attendant told me without a smile.

"A personal joke," I said lamely.

It was all so perfect I couldn't stand it. The hotel recommended by the attendant was adjacent to the monastery. Since there was no possibility of skiing the first day, I passed the time leisurely organizing my equipment, drinking a cup of tea in the attractive hotel restaurant, and strolling around the village.

I approached the visitors' entrance of the Benedictine monastery when the clock in the tower began to strike five. A black-robed monk admitted me. I entered a vast rectangular hall, a sort of library and treasury combined. The interior, Baroque in style, shone with the colors of muted crimson and tarnished silver. A glass case housing the Engelberg altar cross dominated the hall. It was smaller than the ivory cross, and far less sophisticated or powerful in style. I studied the Engelberg cross for the greater part of an hour. Although the gold sheathing dazzled the eye, the etched figures were uninspired. On the back there was a ladder of prophets, but none had scrolls or identifications. Engelberg's cross was no competition. There was nothing better in the world than the ivory cross of Topic Mimara.

I was the first person on the chairlift at nine o'clock the next morning. The weather was perfect, dry and cold. I made one lazy run over the well-tracked *piste*, to limber up; on the second I began to let myself go. Is there anything in the world like skiing on perfect snow on a nearly deserted mountaintop in Switzerland? I started off slowly, skating to gain speed over some flat terrain. Suddenly I heard a sound, like flags snapping in the wind. Startled, I looked up and caught a glimpse of a great creature, garbed in a black robe, standing straight up, knees locked, arms akimbo, hurtling down the mountain. It was one of the monks, skiing like a statue! I pulled up, laughing so hard I almost fell.

When he had disappeared, I continued on my way and entered some fresh deep powder snow. Powder isn't everybody's delight, but I adore it. Soon I was slamming easily through knee-deep fluffy snow, shouting exuberantly. Halfway down I overtook another skier, and, without a word, we fell into a pattern. I would ski ahead, making half a dozen turns, then wait for him to catch up. He would pass me, carve some turns and wait for me. It was one of those chance meetings, the harmonious encounter of strangers who would probably never meet again. For the next three days we skied like a team, even touring back mountains. My friend's name was Willi, and it happened that he was the assistant chief of police of Zurich.

One evening at dinner, after a perfect day, I regaled Willi with the harrowing tale of my thwarted chase after the "great, unique ivory cross owned by the most peculiar collector in world history." He was intrigued and pressed me for details, particularly about Topic Mimara.

The next day, when racing down an icy chute, it suddenly occurred to me that I might break a leg and miss the deadline. Much as I hated to leave Engelberg, the incredible skiing, the companionship I had fallen into by chance, I forced myself to return to Zurich. Before departing, I had a last drink with Willi, who lowered his voice as he told me what he had found.

"I shouldn't tell you this—it's contrary to regulations. But I called an associate at headquarters this morning, and your man Topic has a record of unusual length and complexity, including at least one arrest and many suspicious dealings. Listen. The record includes an arrest for blackmarket activities after the war, suspicion of conspiracy to steal from the Collecting Point in Munich in 1948, a suspected art theft in Czechoslovakia in 1961, and possibly more."

I couldn't utter a word. Willi looked at me and spoke quietly. "My advice is not to buy anything from this man Ante Topic Mimara. By the way, he has some other names."

"What are they?" I moaned.

"Maté Topic, Popic, Popic Mimaru, Mimara, Matutin-Mimara."

"Willi, do you or your associates have any record about his works of art—the ivory cross in particular?"

"No. Nothing. I can only tell you the man has sizable cash and art holdings in a bank. But he seems like a bad one. I cannot possibly imagine how or why an institution like the Metropolitan Museum could consider doing business with him. Don't have dealings with this man."

All the way back to Zurich the wheels of the train seemed to clack, over and over, Willi's refrain—"Don't have dealings, don't have dealings." I knew I had to telephone Jim Rorimer and give him the bad news. I had no reason to doubt Willi's information. The Metropolitan probably had no business buying a work of art from Topic for a hundred dollars, much less six hundred thousand. I speculated on whether he had stolen the cross and wondered if that was the reason he refused to talk about its provenance.

When I arrived at the hotel I gave Rorimer's telephone number to the concierge. I realized that if I procrastinated one minute I might weaken in my resolve. I hated thinking about it; I feared doing it; I wondered what in God's name I would do afterward. Then the concierge handed me a yellow envelope. It was a cable. I told him to cancel the phone call.

I went into the bar and ordered a double martini.

"Okay, hit me," I said aloud to myself and ripped open the envelope.

REQUEST GRANTED. DETAILS FOLLOW.

RORIMER

I dashed into the hotel to place a phone call to Rorimer; not to tell him what Willi had revealed, but to congratulate and thank him. I had made up my mind the moment I read the cable that Topic's questionable past would unduly complicate the affair. After all, we were going to add the cross, not Topic Mimara, to the collection of The Cloisters.

Having been granted the requisite funds, however, did not ease my anxiety. Indeed, my apprehension increased tenfold those last few days before the thirtieth of January. Staying in the race did not mean I was destined to breast the tape. From what Topic had told me, the British were inches away from the finish line. I had called him just after speaking to Rorimer.

"Signor Hoving, welcome back to Zurich," Topic began.

"Any news from England?" I asked impatiently.

"Yes, there is some news," he replied. "Yesterday I was invited by a representative from the Office of the Chancellor of the Exchequer to travel to London for a few days with the cross."

I was numb.

"The man begged me to come, even without my cross if I could not bring it on such short notice. He said the authorities in the Chancellor's office had a few routine questions about the provenance of my treasure and wanted to discuss how to establish my title of ownership in writing. Similar to your document. He told me that the money is available from special funds for the transaction to be concluded."

"What are you going to do?" I asked, on the edge of panic.

"I said to the man, 'Why should I come? *You* come to meet me, then we can arrange a deal. You have Scotland Yard, the Royal Army, Navy, and Air Force. Parliament can pass a law preventing the departure of my cross from England. I am just a humble restorer and art collector. If you wanted the cross, you can fly over to me!'"

"You told him that!" I exclaimed, and laughed.

"I did," Topic replied. "And I am confident the official representative will come here to me."

"When? You will let me know, won't you?" I pleaded.

"Assuredly."

My spirits plunged. My journal entries for the following days were clouded and confused.

I have this firm feeling the British will pounce in a few days. Topic doesn't lie. I spend too much time in my loathsome room barely dozing, steadily deteriorating in mind and soul. I know I shall lose; my depression is profound. I have to force myself to be active, to venture out into the bitter cold. I find the city so unfriendly, so unremittingly cold and gray. But I walked for two hours on the surface of the lake of Zurich. That great body of water is entirely frozen over for the first time in several decades, I'm told. The determined Swiss are commuting on foot into town from the far side, miles away. Ten thousand seagulls are sitting on the expanse of ice. Their white forms make the surface look as if it had been littered with marshmallows.

From the moment I learned of the impending arrival of the British, I made it a point to meet with Topic at least twice a day. During one of our desultory encounters I put caution aside and asked, "Where did you find the cross, anyway? I am so near to owning it or losing it, surely it doesn't matter now if you tell me. Knowing where it had been in recent years might give someone a clue to its origin."

"I did not find the cross in England, Signor Hoving, I

assure you," he answered with a chuckle. And then he smiled broadly, throwing his arms out wide. "I shall tell you how I found the cross. Why not? What is the harm?"

I leaned forward in my chair as the words began to pour forth.

"It was in the summer of 1938. I recall the circumstances well." And he proceeded with his tale. "I was making my way back to Germany through the eastern countries, searching through antique shops, examining the contents of churches and monasteries. Part of my success in collecting, you see, is that I have always avoided the well-known places. I prefer to go where treasures might have been overlooked, even by scholars. I had little money—my wealth was my skill as a restorer. I would make repairs and be compensated with works of art.

"I had gone up to a small monastery hidden in the hills above a still, hot valley. The shape of the belltower indicated to me Romanesque times. There was a large oak door embedded in the plastered stone wall of the monastery. Suddenly I heard a voice calling out in a language I did not understand. It was perhaps Latin. And I waited. Soon I heard three bolts being drawn. The great door opened. A monk or priest was standing just beyond the threshold. He was garbed in a dark-gray habit, a hood casually tossed back on his shoulders. He seemed to me surprisingly young. His eyes were attentive, composed. I knew at once he could be reasoned with."

The monk allowed Topic to explore the works of art scattered throughout the monastery and the chapels. Topic found nothing of interest. The objects were all provincial, dating for the most part to the nineteenth century. But he had a strong feeling that this monastery did possess something far older. Topic called it intuition. So he kept asking the priest if there were not works stored away, "old things, broken things." After a while, the priest admitted that there were.

"He took me down a narrow circular staircase, into a small chamber pervaded by the odor of dampness and straw. The monk pointed to a large cupboard leaning against a wall, and I felt drawn to it. He reached in and pulled out a package wrapped in old paper which crumbled and fell away. He handed me what looked like a sheath made out of chamois. Inside was a black object about a foot long and three inches wide, slightly curving. For an instant I thought it could be a human bone, the relic of some forgotten saint, a bone blackened and split at one end."

When Topic took hold of the bone he was astonished at its weight; it was heavier than human bone. He rubbed the object with a soft cloth, and some of the dirt brushed away, revealing a golden-yellow, glistening surface. It was not bone at all, but walrus ivory. It was the bottom bar of the cross.

"Soon there were five pieces on the table before me. I knew I was looking at one of the masterpieces of world history. The priest was reluctant to sell, but the monastery was in need of repairs and had no money. I reasoned with him. I showed him how he could restore the monastery if he sold the cross. I was poor in those days. I had to purchase it piece by piece, over a period of time. But finally the cross was mine." Topic Mimara leaned back in his chair and sighed.

"But *what* monastery?" I asked. "What country?"

He shrugged. "The place was in the eastern sector. I have told you enough for now."

"Will you ever tell me?" I asked.

Topic did not answer; he just looked at me expressionlessly.

"Listen," I said, "why don't you write down the information and put it into your vault with instructions to have it sent to me or the British Museum—whoever buys it—upon your death?"

"I will consider that," he replied.

On the twenty-eighth of January, Topic, true to his word, informed me that a group from the office of the Chancellor of the Exchequer would arrive the next morning. I spent the day preparing myself for the inevitable. I managed to rationalize that my career would continue, my life proceed, without the cross. Other works of art were bound to come my way—works which, if not as superb as the ivory, would console my days.

To my surprise, I slept deeply and long that night. I awoke more refreshed and more at peace with myself and the world than I had been since coming to Zurich. We had made a great try. I lay there stoically, wondering when I would hear the dreaded news. It was then that

I heard for the first time the sounds of salvation, heavy sleet pelting against my window. Another violent storm was sweeping across Europe. The airport, I soon discovered, was closed. The weather report predicted that the storm might last for as long as three days.

And miracle followed miracle. I heard on the news that same afternoon that Charles de Gaulle had vetoed Britain's entry into the Common Market. I was certain the Chancellor of the Exchequer and his aides would have more important tasks to perform during the crisis than chase after a work of art.

And finally January 30 arrived. I remained in my room all day, huddled up in my blankets, hunched over the tepid radiator. The snow continued to fall. I passed the hours turning the pages of, but not actually reading, three Simenon mysteries. Had I really won? I could not be sure. Topic was capable of changing his mind at the last moment in favor of my rivals. I hoped for the best, but expected the worst.

At eight-thirty in the evening I joined Topic for dinner at the Limmathof. It was crowded, noisy and smoky. We ate slowly, waiting for the stroke of midnight.

One hour to go. Suddenly someone from the hotel desk came over and whispered into Topic's ear. He rose from his chair. "The British—Peter Lasko wishes to speak with me on the telephone," he said.

"Do not extend the deadline," I said tensely. "It is a matter of honor."

"I must listen to what they want. Perhaps they have the money but cannot get to Zurich because of the storms."

"The deadline is sacred. You promised, remember?"

Topic looked at me, shrugged, then disappeared.

I could scarcely draw a breath. Every muscle in my body seemed to quiver. Half an hour went by. Oh, Jesus, I kept saying over and over to myself as another fifteen minutes passed. What the hell was the bastard doing? It was eleven-forty-five. I became convinced he'd given in to the British. I got up from the table, went into the hotel lobby and asked for him at the reception desk. The concierge had no idea where he was. There was nothing I could do but return to my table and wait for midnight.

A few minutes later, Topic eased himself into his chair.

"The British have begged for one more week," he said impassively. "They are very close to saying yes."

I sat rigidly.

Then Topic looked over at me and spoke gently. "But it is midnight, and so it seems, Signor Hoving, you have won."

I couldn't move. My hands were locked between my knees. Slowly I began to relax; the tensions began to flow from my mind and body. Seeing I was about to speak, Topic slowly raised his hand.

"You have won, Signor Hoving," Topic told me silkily. "You have won the opportunity to buy my cross—and the unique reliquary glass from Winchester. And I shall make you a very special offer. You deserve it, since you persevered. I will allow you to have the glass with the cross for only two hundred and fifty thousand dollars more. You will be an even greater hero to your colleagues in the museum. For only eight hundred and fifty thousand dollars you will have gained the two most splendid English medieval antiquities in the world."

I reacted as if I were living in slow motion. Very smoothly, I leaned across the table until my face was only inches away from his. In my softest, most carefully modulated Italian, I launched the basest curses at him. *"Caro stronzo, tu sei piccolo buco nero di Dio."* His eyes widened.

"If I hear one more word of this nonsense," I went on pleasantly, "I'm going to get up, walk away without looking back at you, go to my hotel and have a long sleep. Tomorrow morning I'll stroll over to the Union Banque de Suisse, retrieve the museum's check for six hundred thousand dollars, tear it into tiny pieces, gather up the confetti, and stuff it . . . in my pocket. I shall proceed to the airport and, just before boarding my plane for New York, throw your confetti into the air. You will never see me or anyone else from the Metropolitan Museum again. Cleveland is out. Boston is out. England is out, and the Metropolitan will be out as well. I'll bet you a bottle of champagne on that."

Topic Mimara hadn't moved a muscle throughout the entire diatribe. When I had finished, he sat immobile for a moment. Suddenly he thrust out his arm and stopped a passing waitress. "Champagne," he said. "Two bottles, the best of the best!" Then he tipped back in his chair and roared with laughter, rocking slightly back and forth.

"I *like* you," he barked between laughs. "I do like you. You turned out to be just what I thought you'd be. Yes, *you* did it. You won the girl. For now, I shall keep the unique reliquary glass for myself. Beg for it, but you won't get it. Right now you can have only the cross!"

CHAPTER EIGHTEEN

Hugo the Master

I RETURNED TO THE Metropolitan Museum, a conquering hero, three years and twenty-seven days after I had set out on my quest. The golden ivory cross entered the institution without a stir and was quietly logged in at the Office of the Registrar under the number 63.12—the twelfth acquisiton of the year 1963. The night of its arrival it was placed in a special vault available for works requiring the highest security, along with a special visitor, the *Mona Lisa*, perhaps the most valuable painting ever to be exhibited on loan at the Metropolitan. There, by means of closed-circuit television, armed guards watched over the treasures.

That very night, at an unknown hour, a near-catastrophe occurred. Undetected by the guards, the sprinkler system inside the vault mysteriously turned on. For more than eight hours the *Mona Lisa* and the cross were sprayed by a gentle rain. No one was ever able to figure out how or why the sprinklers had triggered. The miracle was that no damage was done to either of these incomparable works.

I still could scarcely believe we had acquired the cross.

The acquisition represented one of the most courageous decisions in the history of the museum. When the race had come down to the wire, James Rorimer found, somewhat to his astonishment, that the members of the Purchase Committee were unanimously in favor of voting the necessary funds. He had canvassed them the day he heard from me in France. Roland Redmond had been quick to respond: ". . . I am in favor of paying six hundred thousand, as I think the cross is an outstanding object. The price is high, but the cross is unique and the owner won't take less."

Amazingly, the museum had spent a record sum on an object about whose history and origin nothing was known. Determining where it had been made, when and by whom became my next obsession. Doing so proved to be an adventure as exciting as the chase and capture itself.

When I began, I knew it would not be easy. A great deal of luck would be required. Tracing a work from the Middle Ages is an incredibly difficult and mostly frustrating task. When one is working with a late-nineteenth-century object—say, an Impressionist painting by Claude Monet—one has access to an abundance of documentation. Thousands of publications, newspapers, archives, memoirs exist. And there is at your disposal an extensive body of signed and dated paintings. You can take the newly emerged Monet and, fairly easily, place it in the proper period of its stylistic progression.

Not so a medieval work. Only a small fraction of all artists who lived during the twelfth century were known by name. Even known artists were seldom mentioned in records, and, when they were, the reference was invariably uninformative. Few works were ever signed or dated. And, to make my chances even less promising, with the exception of illuminated manuscripts, ninety percent of English medieval art treasures had been destroyed after the dissolution of monastic orders carried out by Henry VIII.

I decided to start by scrutinizing the style of the work itself. In art, every period, every country, every artist has an identifiable style. If enough material has survived, it is sometimes possible to date a work by means of style down to the year, the month and even the day. Style is like a signature, but frightfully more subtle and complex.

One defines style not only from single details but from their sum. Faces—the special contours of noses and lips and eyes—are important, but so is the inner spirit. The overall character of the style is revealed by a host of factors—gestures, size, texture, the way in which one figure relates to the next.

The stylistic hallmark of the cross was the distinctive way the artist had formed the draperies, as if the clothing were slightly damp. Shoulders were accented by whirlpools of drapery. On the arms were double swirls, resembling the figure eight. Over the thighs were long, smooth elliptical flows. Draperies, stretched taut, cascaded into fluid chevrons.

The carvings on the cross bore other striking stylistic characteristics. Cloaks and beards fell like daggers. Faces were shaped like wedges. The figures fit into their diminutive environment like tiny actors in a stately play.

In casting out my nets to find stylistic comparisons with the cross, I followed the same general technique which had worked so successfully with the pulpit relief of the Annunciation. But this time, instead of searching through the art of medieval Europe, I concentrated on England in the twelfth century. Soon I had isolated virtually all the English monuments of the period that were illustrated in books and slides available to me. I counted over three hundred pieces, which included manuscript illuminations and sketches, sculptures, enamels, ivories, seals, stained-glass windows and even lead fonts.

Within a week I had examined these illustrations thoroughly. I had expected the normal result, a large group of objects bearing no stylistic relationship to the cross, and another group, far smaller, comprising perhaps a dozen works, bearing general resemblances only. It had not entered my mind that I might encounter specific similarities. To my intense surprise I found one, and only one, work of art which compared in style to the cross. And the relationship was intimate, such as that between identical twins.

That work was a majestic illuminated manuscript, a Bible, measuring almost two and a half feet in height by one and a half in width. I had had no idea that a Bible could be so large. It contained six enormous and lavish illuminations, each vividly painted on a separate piece

of vellum, depicting scenes from Genesis to the Book of
Job. There were also thirty-eight brilliantly colored initials,
including one which extended down an entire page and
was inhabited by a host of phantasmagoric human beings
and animals.

The more I studied this spectacular Bible, the more
impressed I became. Eventually I noted fifty crucial
stylistic similarities to the cross, ranging from the general
spirit to tiny but telling details. The more I gazed at the
Bible and the cross, the more I wanted to believe that
the same artist had created both. It was conceivable.
But, I had to admit, my training told me it was unlikely.
Artisans of the Middle Ages tended to adhere to one
discipline or medium. Painters painted; sculptors carved;
and builders laid stone upon stone. I wondered again if
I would ever discover the identity of my artist. Because
of the paucity of known artists and the sparseness of
records about art, it seemed unlikely.

I plunged into the task of gathering as much information as I could about the majestic Bible. As it happened,
a great deal was known about the manuscript. But the
information was scattered throughout a number of books
and articles published over a long span of time. It took
me days to hunt them down. Most scholars, I found,
considered the book one of the prime manuscripts of
medieval England, one of three so-called Giant Bibles.
It resided in the rare book library of Corpus Christi
College in Cambridge, England, and was called, simply
enough, "Manuscript 2."

The specialists were clearly puzzled by Corpus Christi
"Manuscript 2." It was obviously English. And it owed
a powerful debt to the style of the Saint Albans Psalter.
But the beautiful illuminations were far more sophisticated
and inventive than those in any other twelfth-century
English manuscript, including the two other Giant Bibles.
Some scholars regarded the illuminations as a late mani-
festation of the grand mid-twelfth-century style. Others
claimed it was the creative force which had given birth to
the entire style.

I soon learned that the fabulous Bible had been created
at the monastery of Bury St. Edmunds in East Anglia. It
had been commissioned by one of the monastery abbots,
Anselm, who had enjoyed an exceptionally long tenure

of twenty-seven years, from 1121 to 1148. The date of
the book was probably around 1135. During the next few
days I read through several dry-as-dust scholarly essays
on manuscript illumination in twelfth-century England.
And then I chanced upon some truly vital data about
the Bible and its artist in an excerpt from the *Gesta*, the
contemporary history of Bury St. Edmunds—information
which took my breath away.

For the name of the Bible's artist was actually known.
He was Master Hugo. He was apparently a layman, not a
monk. Moreover, he had been highly praised and highly
paid by the monastery.

> Then Sacrist Hervey, the brother of the Prior Talbot,
> managed to accumulate all the funds needed for the
> creation of a great Bible. And the Bible was painted, in
> an incomparable fashion, by the hand of Master Hugo.
> Hugo was not able to find in our land the vellum of
> the quality he sought, and travelled to Scotland to pur-
> chase it.

I learned that Hugo had been versatile, an exception
to the rule. He had also made works of art in other
materials for the abbey. To my frustration, none of these
pieces was identified, at least in the books at my disposal,
except for a small bell cast in bronze. Yet I had been
astonishingly fortunate to have unearthed in so short a
time three dazzling specific ties with the cross: the Bible,
Bury St. Edmunds, and possibly Hugo himself. Although
I dared not come out and proclaim it openly, I was
beginning to suspect that my cross might be another one
of Hugo's incomparable masterworks.

The next obvious move was to get hold of the *Gesta*
and to read everything written about the Benedictine
Abbey of Bury St. Edmunds. But before I could do so,
something else unbelievable took place.

I was at my desk gazing raptly at the cross in front
of me, soaking up the incredible subtlety of the object,
when I was told that Kurt Weitzmann wanted urgently
to speak with me on the telephone.

"Tom," he began, "I have found something very important here in Princeton—in Adolph Goldschmidt's files
on ivory carvings."

My response was almost flippant. "What is it, the missing block?"

"Not the block, but a photograph of it," he said precisely.

"My God, Kurt," I shouted. "Is it the Harrowing of Hell?"

"No. It depicts Christ Before Pontius Pilate. And it is very dramatic. The style of the figures appears to me to be identical to the rest of the cross."

"I'm driving down tomorrow, early in the morning," I said.

As soon as I examined the little photograph, I had no doubt that the block had to be part of the cross. I was puzzled that the scene was not the Harrowing of Hell. Topic Mimara's description of the double-tiered scene had sounded so convincing. But it was obvious he had been wrong—which would not have been the first time.

Weitzmann and I were able to identify the participants in the drama. On the far upper left were two heads looking straight up. One was a helmeted soldier; the other, a Jew wearing a distinctive conical hat. They were staring up at the Christ, whom "they had pierced." That fit perfectly with the narrative on the cross.

The main scene was not only dramatic but cruel. Just below the soldier and the Jew stood a giant of a figure also wearing the distinctive conical hat. He was obviously one of the high priests. He seemed almost to prance, his long legs crossed like a pair of lethal scissors, and was slapping Christ viciously across the back of his head. Christ, hands tightly bound, was being dragged forward by a soldier toward Pilate enthroned.

Just above the high priest floated a scroll. Its letters, which matched the style of the inscriptions on the cross, spelled PROPHTIZA, meaning either "Prophesy unto us" or "Prophecy and testimony of Zechariah"—possibly both. We found two passages in the Bible which seemed particularly apt. One, in the Book of Zechariah, stated: "They shall look upon Him whom they have pierced." The other, from Matthew, said, "Others smote him with the palms of their hands. Prophesy unto us."

"How did you find this photo?" I asked. "It's a miracle, really."

"Yesterday morning," Weitzmann recounted, "I hap-

pened to look through some of the material Goldschmidt
had gathered years ago for a supplement he was planning
for his catalogue of medieval ivories. I knew of your
desire to find the missing bottom piece, of course. I
wasn't searching for anything special. But when I came
across this photograph I said to myself, 'Here, I have it!' "

"It's magic, Kurt! Maybe this block still exists. But
where?"

"Goldschmidt even provided some leads. See here
what he wrote on the back," Weitzmann observed, turning the photograph over.

Foto produced by Waldemar Titzenthaler Fotothek,
Berlin. Presented by Dr. Vera von Blankenberg; Berlin
West, Lützowuferstrasse, 18.III. Possession of Mrs. Fuld;
Berlin of 1932.
(English XIIth? Walrus ivory plaque, 2¼ x 2¼ inches.)

When I told Rorimer, I was amused to see that his
attitude had not changed. He continued to be secretive
about the cross and warned me not to tell anyone that
the plaque was a missing fragment of the object. He even
ordered me to inform Weitzmann in writing that the set
of photographs of the cross we prepared for him was not
to be shown to a soul until after I had published the ivory.

I began my pursuit of the plaque. At once I saw that
it was an almost impossible quest. I called Berlin information and was told that the Waldemar Fotothek had disappeared. There was no listing for either Dr. von
Blankenberg or a Mrs. Fuld. I made a list of around fifty
scholars, professors and curators in Europe and sent each
a letter with the photograph of the Christ and Pilate
block, giving all the facts Weitzmann had discovered, but
not mentioning the cross.

I had planned to approach half a dozen dealers in my
search, but Rorimer allowed me to contact only one,
Saemy Rosenberg, head of the distinguished New York
firm of Rosenberg and Steibel. Rosenberg had been based
in Germany until the rise of Hitler, when he fled. According to Rorimer, Rosenberg knew the old German private
collections better than anyone else. Saemy Rosenberg told
me he had a close friend who had been acquainted with

several members of the Fuld family in the 1930s and
would make appropriate inquiries.

I tried everything. I even sent a letter to the publisher
of Dr. von Blankenberg's last book, printed in 1943, but
received no response. From the West Berlin telephone
book Marj Baucom, who had conceived the stunning idea
of tracing Topic Mimara through the Austrian police,
found twenty-five von Blankenbergs, including the operator of a fresh-fruit stand, a podiatrist and a policeman.
We wrote or phoned them all, but turned up no leads.
The German police knew nothing.

Two weeks after I had talked to Saemy Rosenberg he
conveyed some vaguely hopeful news. He had talked
with the friend who had once known the Fuld family.
The individual remembered compiling a list for one member of the family, ten years before, in connection with art
claims in Germany. The ivory plaque was not on that list.
However, it did appear in a Fuld inventory of 1932 as
"a Christ Before Pilate." "This must be the ivory in
question," Rosenberg wrote, "but as there are no measurements in the inventory . . . my friend was not able to
identify it for certain. . . . It may be that this ivory is
with some heir of the Fuld estate whom my friend does
not know." Saemy Rosenberg told me he would urge his
friend to keep looking.

The Christ Before Pilate wasn't the only missing part
of the cross I sought. I was searching, too, for other
plaques, plaques portraying ancient church fathers, similar
to the Aaron ivory in Florence. I had come to believe that
the base on which the cross must originally have stood
had been adorned with a series of church fathers. I reconstructed the base as a solid rectangular footing, probably of bronze, decorated with a series of small ivories.

My hopes were soon aroused that I might also have
unearthed the original figure of Christ when I studied
photographs of a fragmentary walrus ivory of the Savior,
lacking head and arms, that was in the Guildhall Museum
in London. The style of the figure seemed comparable
with the cross, and the measurements made the possibility
plausible. To test my theory I suggested to Rorimer that
the Conservation Department make a plastic cast of the
lower portion of the vertical bar which I could either take
or send to the museum in London. He refused at first,

saying that the cast might dislodge some of the green wax inlays in the letters of the two large inscriptions. I kept on insisting and finally wore him down. "All right, go ahead," he said in exasperation, "but be careful." I pointed out that I was patently qualified to supervise what amounted to a routine operation.

I returned now to the history of the Abbey of Bury St. Edmunds and Master Hugo with a high sense of anticipation. I even entertained the hope that I might find his other works of art still surviving somewhere. To my sorrow I learned that all Bury's treasures had been lost. At the once great monastery were only a few paltry fragments of architecture. Within a few years after the dissolution of monastic orders, during the sixteenth century, the vaults of the nave and narthex had fallen. Soon the stained glass had been smashed. Some rare gates of bronze had been melted down. The contents of the library had been dispersed.

How tragic! For the abbey had been exceptionally beautiful. I chanced upon a poetic description written by Henry VIII's antiquarian, John Leland, who had visited Bury around 1530. It was haunting.

> Why need I in this place extol Bury at greater length? This *only* will I add, that the sun does not shine on a town more prettily situated—so delicately does it hang on a gentle slope, with a little stream flowing eastward —not on an Abbey more famous, whether we regard its endowments, its size, or its magnificence. You would say that the Abbey was a town in itself, so many gates has it—and some of them are even of bronze!

Three centuries later, Thomas Carlyle, who had become enamored of Bury and intrigued by one of its abbots, a certain Samson de Tottington, tried to evoke the mood of the ruins.

> Alas, how like an old osseous fragment, a broken blackened shinbone of the old dead Ages, this black ruin looks out, not yet covered by the soil; still indicating what a once gigantic Life lies buried there! It is dead now, and dumb; but was alive once, and spake.

I wondered if I could ever get Bury St. Edmunds to speak. There were, I soon found, certain voices at Bury

which still had the power of speech, a body of histories,
chronicles, ledgers, and even an engaging biography of
one of the abbots, Carlyle's favorite, Samson de Tottington. To listen to Bury's voices I decided to go all the way
back to the very beginning. I found something interesting
almost at once.

Bury St. Edmunds had come into being because of
marauding Danes and a martyred king. The story goes
back to 870, when East Anglia was ruled by King Edmund, who had come from ancient Saxon stock. He was
a most devout Christian. In 870, hosts of Danes, led by
a certain Ingwar, invaded his lands. There are two historical versions of what happened, the secular and the clerical.
The secular held that Edmund fought valiantly but was
vanquished by superior forces. But the clerical view was
that Edmund, when attacked by the Danes, offered no
resistance and, like Christ, gave himself up "like a Lamb
. . . brought to the slaughter."

I was intrigued by the coincidence between the reference to Edmund as a lamb and the Lamb medallion on
the cross, so I went to the clerical version written by a
certain Abbo, a tenth-century abbot of Fleury. In his
preface, Abbo swore to the accuracy of his account. He
had, he claimed, heard the tale in his youth from the
lips of an aged and decrepit man who had told it "in full
faith to King Athelstan, asserting with an oath that *he*
had been King Edmund's armor-bearer on the very day
of his martyrdom . . ."

Abbo praised King Edmund as an uncommonly good
man, a virtual slave to the Savior. But Satan chose to
tempt this devout monarch, not for his lands, but for his
soul. Satan enlisted Ingwar, the heathen Dane, as his
instrument of temptation. Ingwar ravaged the land, seeking good King Edmund everywhere. Ingwar demanded
half of Edmund's land and vassals. Edmund sought the
advice of one of his bishops. The cleric told the monarch
that, like Christ, he should never submit to a pagan. So
Edmund sent word to Ingwar that he should renounce
war and should confess to Christianity. Ingwar responded
by pushing forward with his invasion.

Edmund asked his bishop once more what he should
do. This time, the bishop advised Edmund that he must
yield. Edmund was captured and was brought before

Ingwar, "like Christ before Pilate." He was scourged, shot with arrows and then beheaded. But throughout his ordeal, Abbo wrote, Edmund never veered from his "patient confession" to God and Christ, and therefore "forever saw his life before him."

I instantly recognized these additional parallels between the saga of King Edmund and the writing on the cross. Eagerly, I read on.

Abbo related that the Danes threw Edmunds' head into a forest and left his body on the field of battle. The Danes felt that breaking up the King's corpse would be the final humiliation. But just as Christ's body was destined not to be broken, so was Edmund's spared.

I noted with growing interest still another parallel to the cross. For the scroll held by the Eagle of John read in part: ". . . not a bone of Him shall be broken."

When Ingwar had departed, the King's subjects discovered his headless body. They were horrified to see how cruelly he had been mutilated. But suddenly they heard the Kings voice crying out, "Here, here, here!" The throng rushed into the woods. There, in a small clearing, they came upon an enormous wolf protecting the King's head. The creature allowed Edmund's subjects to retrieve it. The body and the head were buried in a martyr's shrine. A spate of miracles occurred. And when, according to Abbo, the coffin was later opened, another miracle had occurred. The King's head and body had been rejoined. Only a thin red line indicated the decapitation. "Not a bone of Him shall be broken." The King was by now regarded as a saint.

After the chronicle of Abbo, I went on to later histories of Bury St. Edmunds. In 903 the saint's remains were transported from where they had lain to a larger shrine nearby, at Boedricsworth, later to be called Bury St. Edmunds. A young monk named Egelwin was elected to guard and protect the relics. In the year 1010 the marauding Danes threatened again, so Egelwin took the saint to London and deposited him in the Church of St. Gregory. The relics remained for three years, and performed dozens of miracles. When it had been established that the Danes had retired, Egelwin informed the bishop of St. Gregory that it was time to take Edmund home. The bishop would not allow it. Edmund had attracted so many

pilgrims that the bishop had decided to keep him in
London and deposit him in the Cathedral of St. Paul.

But Saint Edmund himself moved against those who
would seek to hold him back from Bury St. Edmunds.
Miraculously, the saint's body became so heavy a dozen
men could not budge the coffin. Egelwin and three
brother monks watched as a crowd of men struggled
vainly, bending beneath the growing weight of the coffin.
When they abandoned the effort, Egelwin and his retinue
approached the casket, lifted it without strain, and carried the now virtually weightless body of Saint Edmund
back to Bury

There Edmund became the patron saint of kings. King
Canute revered him and granted the monastery a charter
unique in England which allowed perpetual possession
of lands and absolute independence from episcopal or
even royal control. When King Edward the Confessor
visited the shrine in 1044, even he became a fervent
votary of the royal saint. William the Conqueror also
looked upon Bury with great favor, giving it more lands
and riches. From William's time on, Bury St. Edmunds
flourished. Walls, churches, choirs, towers, cloisters, sac-
risties were erected. Its incredible expanse of lands was
tilled, bringing wealth untold.

I had the distinct impression, as I continued to read
the history of Bury, that the monastery was stronger in
lands, wealth and influence than in intellectual or artistic
achievements. But all that changed in 1121, when Anselm
became abbot.

From what I gleaned from the *Gesta*, Anselm was a
remarkable combination of ecclesiastic, scholar, administrator and art connoisseur. He had come from Rome,
from the Church of Santa Saba, which enjoyed an alliance
with Bury. And it seemed possible that Anselm had
recruited the great Hugo to travel from Italy to England.
I had found another reference to Hugo in the *Gesta*. It
was even more remarkable than the description of the
Bible, and suggested that Hugo was Italian. Anselm had
commissioned Hugo to cast a set of double doors in
bronze for the abbey. No doubt they were covered with
scenes. Hugo's doors, the very ones which made such an
impression upon the antiquarian John Leland in the mid-
sixteenth century, were known throughout England in the

twelfth. The *Gesta* became effusive in its assessment of those unique doors, "made by the hands of Master Hugo, who, in all his other works surpassed every other artist, in this marvelous work surpassed even himself." Bronze casting on a scale as large as monastery gates was virtually unknown in England during the twelfth century. The art existed only in Byzantium and Italy, where it had survived since Roman times.

Although I could only speculate that Hugo was Italian, I knew him to be a genius and uncommonly versatile. To go from delicate manuscript illumination to casting a pair of great bronze doors to fashioning a beautiful bell was the work of a virtuoso.

Abbot Anselm passed from the scene in 1148, leaving an unparalleled series of works for which he had been responsible. He was succeeded by Abbot Ording, who served until 1156. Ording was described in the history of the abbey as a "staunch defender of the faith and the rights of Saint Edmund." It was said he was an excellent administrator, but not especially learned or interested in art. I had made up my mind to skim over the story of Ording's tenure, when a passage leaped to my astonished eyes. Ording had commissioned two works of art; and one was a miracle to me.

He had adorned the great altar with a silver frontal. On another altar, the one in the choir, he had "set up a cross with little statues of Mary and Saint John, incomparably carved by the hand of Master Hugo."

I shouted with joy. Although the chronicler had not specified the substance from which the cross had been made, he had said it was *carved*. That meant that Hugo's cross could not have been metal. Nor would it have been made of modest wood. To me it was, of course, walrus ivory. And it was standing on the desk in my office.

Euphorically, I sought additional proof in the *Gesta* and other documents relating to Bury St. Edmunds and to Abbot Ording. I discovered no further information. I did learn, however, that Bury had had a famous library whose books had not all disappeared after the dissolution. A keen scholar of the early twentieth century, M. R. James, known also for his ghost stories, had discovered by deft detective work that the medieval library at Bury had contained a staggering number of two thousand five hundred volumes. Among the titles James found were Isidore's *Tract Against the Jews;* a commentary on the Passion of Christ; and commentaries, or "glosses," on every book of the Scriptures.

James had also actually traced all the surviving books from Bury, no fewer than three hundred and two. In one of those supreme strokes of luck history sometimes affords, someone in the fourteenth century had marked each manuscript in Bury's library with an enigmatic *ex libris* which James had deciphered. More than half the surviving Bury books, many still bound in their original deerskin covers, had come to rest in the library of Pembroke College at Cambridge.

When I told an overjoyed Rorimer that I had come within inches of proving our unknown cross was a masterpiece made by one of England's greatest artists, he issued a peremptory—and pleasing—command: "Go to England as soon as you can and look through those books at Cambridge. I'll bet you find the final proof. How lucky you are!"

CHAPTER NINETEEN

King of the Confessors

WHILE MAKING PREPARATIONS for the trip, I kept on searching through the histories for more evidence that Hugo was the creator of my cross. Nothing turned up, but I did find a clue, a most disquieting one, which made me suspect that someone else besides Hugo and Abbot Ording might have been involved with the making of the cross.

For, in the course of perusing these volumes, I was astonished to find a reference to an abbot who, in the year 1190, had expelled all Jews from Bury St. Edmunds. That was perhaps thirty-five years after the cross had been made, it if *had* been made during the tenure of Abbot Ording. Nevertheless, it was the most dramatic link I had yet found between the anti-Jewish diatribe on the cross and the history of the abbey.

The abbot responsible for the expulsion was Samson de Tottington, who had been born and bred in Norfolk and had taught school at Bury for a while before becoming a monk. Samson was portrayed at length in one of the most candid pieces of writing from all the Middle Ages,

a gossipy chronicle composed in the decades from 1170
to about 1200 by a Bury monk, Jocelyn of Brakelond.
Jocelyn had even served as personal chaplain for Abbot
Samson and, as he wrote, "was with him, day and night,
for six years."

There was one part of Samson's life Jocelyn was most
familiar with—his life-and-death struggle with the Jews.
When I learned that, I realized I'd better delve into the
history of the Jews in medieval England.

Although the Jews had first come to England with the
Romans, they arrived in sizable numbers only with William the Conqueror. For several generations their presence
was tolerated, for Henry I issued a strong charter protecting them. In essence, Henry's charter granted the
Jewish community the privilege of being a separate and
protected entity. The continued existence of the community was to the King's economic advantage, since Jews
alone were allowed to lend money. Although Henry's
arrangement was not entirely benevolent, in general the
Jews did flourish until almost the middle of the twelfth
century. But in the year 1144 something happened which
forced a profound change in their status. From that moment on, hatred began to build, reaching a crescendo in
1190 in York and at Bury St. Edmunds.

It was on the eve of Easter, in 1144, that a horrifying
event was said to have taken place in Norwich: a ritual
murder. Late in the afternoon of Good Friday, the partly
decomposed corpse of a twelve-year-old skinner's appren-
tice named William was found in the woods. Modern
scholars think it likely that the child had lost consciousness
during a fit and had been buried prematurely by his
family. In 1144, however, it was thought that William
had been a victim of some Jews who had wooed him
away from his home and crucified him on the second day
of Passover—in mockery of the Passion of Christ. The
ritual killing as first mentioned by Eusebius.

The terrible story spread like wildfire. A wave of religious fervor and anti-Jewish sentiment swept through
Norwich and, in time, through other parts of England as
well. William was entombed in the cathedral. Various
miracles were reported at the time of burial and for years
after, and William was proclaimed a local saint.

Contemporary claims of miracles are preserved in the

literature of medieval England. In 1152, a woman from nearby Bury St. Edmunds, bent double from infancy, heard "Saint" William's voice in a dream: "Come, oh come, to my shrine." She went, came as close to the tomb as the crowd would allow, and was instantly cured. On another occasion a man from Lincolnshire, who had murdered his brother and two nephews with a pitchfork, was making a penitential journey to the shrines of saints. His right hand was bound tightly in a ring he had fashioned from the murder weapon. When he reached Bury St. Edmunds, the ring snapped free and the man's arm became even more pained. Saint Edmund appeared before the man in a dream and instructed him to go instantly to Norwich and visit William. He did as he was told; his arm was healed and his conscience cleared. Contemporaries marveled not so much at the miraculous cure as at the bond between Edmund and William, saying, "the one withstood the heathen raging against the law of Christ, the other endured the Jews, who renewed, in him, the death of Christ."

The death of William of Norwich was not the only supposed ritual murder. There was a second at Gloucester, a third at Bristol, a fourth at Winchester, and a fifth, on June 10, 1181, at Bury St. Edmunds, where a ten-year-old boy named Robert was found dead in a stream.

Someone from the abbey claimed that the boy had been crucified by the local Jews. The horrifying claim of ritual murder was doubtless concocted by monks of an anti-Jewish faction in the abbey who were trying to overthrow the supporters of Abbot Hugh, who had just died, and his former second-in-command, Sacrist William, both of whom had been staunch protectors of the Jews. A book on the life of Robert was written by Jocelyn of Brakelond, as he proclaimed in his history of Samson. "The holy boy Robert . . . suffered martyrdom and was buried in our church, and many signs and wonders were performed among the common fold as I have set down elsewhere." The champion of the anti-Jewish faction was, of course, Samson de Tottington.

As I plunged into Jocelyn's chronicle of Samson, I was transported back through time into the innermost chambers and secrets of the abbey. "I have been at pains to

set down the things I have seen and heard which came
to pass in the Church of Saint Edmund in our days,"
Jocelyn began. "I have included certain evil things for a
warning . . ." When Abbot Hugh, who had come to power
after Ording in 1156,

> had grown old, his eyes waxed somewhat dim. . . .
> Pious he was and good, a strict monk and good, but in
> the business of this world neither good nor wise. Farms
> were casually rented out at small rates, the woods were
> chopped down and from day to day all things went from
> bad to worse. . . .
> Abbott Hugh found but one remedy and one consola-
> tion, and that was to borrow money. . . . Not a month
> went by but one or two hundred pounds were added to
> his debts; the bonds were continually renewed. . . . This
> infirmity spread from the head to the members—from
> the superior to his subjects. And so it came to pass that
> each obedientiary had his own seal and bound himself
> in debt to the Jews as he pleased. . . .

The list of Jews to whom Hugh had mortgaged the
abbey was long. "Isaac, son of Rabbi Joce, four hundred
pounds; Benedict, Jew of York, eight hundred eighty
pounds; Benedict of Norwich, one thousand pounds . . ."
The prime offender, according to Jocelyn, was William
the Sacrist. He had borrow secretly at exorbitant interest
rates.

Eventually Henry II heard rumors about the scandal
and sent his financial examiners. But William and his aides
duped the examiners, who returned to the King, saying
"All is well. The Church is in good state; its rule observed."

Incensed by the incident, Jocelyn, then a novice at
the abbey, went to his mentor, Samson, who was then
the subsacrist in charge of all works, ranging from con-
struction to works of art. "Why are you silent? You who
hear and see things as these, you who are a cloister monk
and have no desire for office and fear God more than
man?"

"My son, a child newly burned dreads the fire," Samson
replied. He told Jocelyn that he had once been imprisoned
for having objected openly to a policy of Abbot Hugh's
and William's. Samson then quoted to Jocelyn from the
Bible and invented a contemporary typology, making

deft parallels from Scriptures to the scandalous goings-on. He started with Luke: "This is the hour of darkness, this is the hour when flatterers prevail and are believed." Then he switched to the Psalms: "Their power is made strong and we can do nothing against it." He concluded with Exodus: "We must, for a time, shut our eyes to these things. Let the Lord behold a judge."

On the ninth of September, 1180, Abbot Hugh fell from his horse, his kneecap jammed into the ham of his thigh. "Physicians hastened to him and tortured him in many ways but healed him not. His leg mortified; he died in a terrifying fit on the fourteenth of November."

At that moment there began a rough-and-tumble contest, between William and Samson, for control of the abbey and its vast lands. William won easily at first by handing out favors. "He gave and spent as he pleased, . . . giving away that which he should not have given, 'blinding the eyes of all with gifts,'" Jocelyn observed, quoting Deuteronomy. Samson dutifully carried out his works and "left nothing broken or cracked or split or unrepaired." He supervised the painting of a vast series of scenes from the Bible, ninety in all, to be placed in the choir. Apparently something of a poet, he "composed elegiac verses for each one."

Instantly I was alerted to a new clue. The editor of the edition of Jocelyn I happened to be reading had noted that Samson's elegiac verses were probably recorded in a certain manuscript, designated "Arundel XXX," in the library of the College of Arms in London. I made a note to examine the verses. It was possible they would bear some relationship to the large inscriptions on the cross.

I returned to Jocelyn's text and learned that good works and poetry did not advance Samson's cause. William the Sacrist, Jocelyn dryly observed,

regarded Samson . . . with suspicion as did many others, both Christians and Jews, who took William's side: the Jews, I say, for the Sacrist was called their father and patron; they rejoiced in his protection, had free entrance and exit, and went everywhere through the monastery, wandering by the altars and about the shrine, while masses were being sung. And their money was kept in our treasury under the Sacrist's custody—and more unseemly still, in the days of the war their wives and children took refuge in our pittancery.

Arguments over who should be chosen abbot by Henry II raged through the abbey. Each "confessor," as Jocelyn referred to the monks, had a perfect candidate. The dispute continued for months. Samson kept quiet through it all, "neither praising nor critcizing." He just listened. Twenty years later he would tell Jocelyn he could still quote every piece of gossip, word for word.

Then the body of little Robert was discovered. It was the crack of doom for William the Sacrist and other supporters of the Jews. I wondered how much Samson had to do with the ugly discovery. At that precise moment, the King's representative stepped in and ordered that a committee of the prior and twelve monks, chosen unanimously by all the confessors, appear before the King with a candidate. Six were chosen from William's camp and six from Samson's.

Just before the committee of thirteen departed for London to meet with King Henry, two confessors predicted, from dreams, the outcome of the contest. One, William of Hastings, had a vision in the night of a prophet, clad in white, who appeared before the gate of the abbey. When asked who was going to become abbot, the prophet replied, "You shall have one of your own, but he shall raven among you like a wolf."

The other confessor said, "Last night in my sleep I saw Roger the Cellarer and Hugh, the third Prior, standing before the altar in the choir. Between them was Samson, towering above them from the shoulder upward and wearing a hood and a long cloak that flowed to his heels. And he stood with his fists clenched and raised into the air like a pugilist."

When I came upon that passage, I laid the book aside and slowly rose from my chair. I proceeded to the vault. I removed the cross and brought it to my desk in the Medieval Department to examine it once again.

I was concerned with one figure, the only one unidentified on the cross, the curious hooded monk floating inside the Lamb medallion, the character who had his fist raised into the air. Could he possibly be Samson? Could Samson's artist, not Hugo, have fashioned the cross?

Could Samson have created the inscriptions and the verses? I remembered the paintings in the choir and his verses. Suddenly it seemed plausible. My only problem was how to explain the clear reference in the *Gesta* to Hugo's "incomparable cross," and how to account for an artist working in the 1180s in a style virtually identical to Hugo's, three or four decades before.

With a magnifying glass I studied the hooded figure. It seemed that the ivory from which it was carved was a separate piece. I decided to perform minor surgery. With a scalpel in hand, working gingerly, I chipped away some restoration material, probably applied by Topic, and saw to my delight that the pugilist *was* a separate piece cleverly inserted into the Lamb medallion. I extracted it and, examining the back, saw that the ivory, although walrus, was distinctly different from the rest of the cross. Who else could it be but Samson? The monk who had the dream had been precise in describing where Samson had stood like a fighter. He had been standing before the altar in the choir—the very altar, I assumed, for which Hugo's cross had originally been made.

I returned to Jocelyn and learned that, after some anxious moments, Samson de Tottington was finally elected by his peers and approved by King Henry. But at the moment of Samson's victory, the King issued a warning: "Have a care, for by the eyes of God, if you do ill, it will be *at* you!"

Samson, unperturbed, fell to the King's feet, kissed them, and then rose and led the brothers to the altar. "His head was held high, and the look on his face unchanged." When the King saw this he muttered, "By God's eyes, this elect thinks himself worthy to be the guardian of this abbey!"

Abbot Samson moved cautiously in his first year. He retained Abbot Hugh's staff, even those who had been responsible for the debts to the Jews. Even William, their "father and patron," remained as sacrist. Then Samson pounced. When he had totally consolidated his power, he deposed William. A conspiracy was hatched to oust Samson. He just watched it develop. Then, days before the coup, Samson pounced again. He called a meeting of all monks before the altar in the choir and showed one and all the fruits of his silent labors—a great sack filled with canceled bonds. All debts to all debtors had been paid. It was the equivalent of tens of thousands of pounds.

But Samson's obsession with the Jews never waned. On Palm Sunday, March 18, 1190, a fiery sermon was delivered in the choir, most probably by Abbot Samson, who frequently preached to the townspeople. After the sermon they rioted against the Jews. Fifty-seven Jews were slaughtered. By that time, at Bury, there was no place for them to go for protection. In the past, the Jews could come to the abbey itself and its pittancery. Under Samson, there was no place to hide.

Immediately after the holocaust, Samson petitioned the King to allow him to expel the few surviving Jews from town, claiming that everything in the town and the vast lands of the abbey belonged to Saint Edmund. The Jews, argued Samson, must either be Saint Edmund's men— that is, "confessors"—or be driven out. Henry gave his reluctant approval, but forbade Samson to seize property and land belonging to the Jews without compensation. The day the Jews left Bury under armed guard, Samson issued an edict that "all those who from this time forth shall receive Jews or harbor them in the town or anywhere at all in the liberty of Bury shall be solemnly excommunicated in every church and at every altar."

Samson de Tottington ruled vigorously for thirty years and died in 1212 on the thirtieth of December. Jocelyn, his biographer, had died before him. The words of an unknown monk formed his epitaph in the *Gesta:* "He had prosperously ruled the Abbey . . . and had freed it from a load of debt."

The time had come for me to go to England. In preparation, I had dismantled the cross and taken it to the conservation laboratory so that a cast could be made of the lower vertical bar to determine if the Guildhall Museum's Christ figure belonged to the cross. I was assured the cast could be made overnight.

Next morning, as soon as I entered the conservation lab, I knew from the ominous silence that something terrible must have occurred. I rushed to the office of the chief conservator, Murray Pease, who was huddled over a table with his assistant. When he saw me enter, his face assumed an expression of profound mournfulness. I looked

down to see what lay on the table. It was the vertical
bar of the magnificent cross. It was no longer golden
yellow. It was a garish kelly green, and looked as though
it had been totally dipped in bright-green paint. Ruined!

Pease sat me down and told me how the disaster had
come about. The technician responsible for the cast, he
said, without anyone's knowledge, had left the ivory
encased in plaster in a drying chamber the previous night.
The intense heat apparently melted the wax impregnated
with green paint which the artist of the cross had used
as inlays for the letters of the two large inscriptions on
the side and the front. This paint soaked through into
the subsurface of the ivory. Pease told me there seemed
to be no way of applying solvents to wash it out. The
paint had penetrated well below the surface and was
trapped. "It would be like trying to clean an old blotter.
I don't think it can be done."

I returned to my office, locked myself in and wept.
After a while I took out paper and pen and composed a
note to Rorimer:

> The cross is ruined. The request for the cast was mine
> and it was an act of impetuosity. You had warned me.
> Instead of a cast I could just as easily have made
> detailed measurements. In doing what I did, I have
> destroyed a significant part of one of the great monu-
> ments of history and in so doing, have violated my
> curatorial profession. Accordingly, I have decided to
> submit my resignation as Associate Curator of the Me-
> dieval Department and The Cloisters effective immediately.

But the cross, my talisman, must have been protecting
me. I was just about to drag myself up to Rorimer's
office and hand over my letter when I got a telephone
call from Murray Pease.

"Tom, I believe I'm onto something. I've been thinking
frantically about how to clean up the damage inflicted
on the cross. I may just have the solution. Give me tonight.
Meet me in the morning—say, nine o'clock. Then, if the
bottom bar is still bright green, do what you believe
you must."

I was pacing nervously outside Pease's office by eight-
thirty. As soon as he arrived, he ushered me into a remote
area of his laboratory. Banks of ultraviolet lights had

been set up, blazing away at the bar of the cross. Pease explained what he had done. "You see, I began to think hard. It occurred to me that ivory always turns whiter when you set it in the sun. So, I thought, under a dozen suns—these ultraviolet lamps—wouldn't the green stain bleach away? Out of aluminum foil I cut a precise little mask for each letter in these large inscriptions, so they wouldn't be bleached. Let's turn off these lights and see if it worked."

Fearfully, I looked down. Then I stepped back in amazement. A miracle had taken place. The bottom bar was a pristine golden yellow, with delicate green inscriptions. There was no hint of damage.

Once in London, I raced joyfully through my tasks. The day after I arrived I took my plaster cast to the Guildhall Museum, where I was allowed to place the walrus figure of Christ upon it. Instantly, I knew I had been mistaken. The fragmentary Christ was far too small, its style too primitive.

Next, I ensconced myself in the rotunda of the reading room in the library of the British Museum and proceeded to make stylistic comparisons with every English twelfth-century monument I could find published in that vast historic repository. I wanted to be certain the stylistic relationship of the cross to Hugo's Bible did not extend to works created at any other monastery. It did not. But I did discover two manuscripts, a few years later than Hugo's Bible, which showed definite similarities. And they, I was delighted to find out, were also from Bury St. Edmunds.

The moment had come, finally, for me to start off on the pilgrimage in my quest for proof that the cross had been made at Bury by the incomparable Hugo—and altered in his day by Samson de Tottington. I made the necessary phone calls to scholars to pave the way, and stepped aboard a train for Bury St. Edmunds.

When I arrived in Bury and walked to the site of the former abbey, I realized that both John Leland and Thomas Carlyle had been right. The remains of the abbey were few, a couple of battered and blackened stone piers sticking out of the ground, surrounded by some of the most beautiful gardens I had ever visited. I found the spot in the old cloister where Samson had been laid to rest. I sat for some minutes quietly gazing at a modern marker on the tomb. I left reluctantly, knowing that at Bury, unfortunately, the voices were stilled.

I now made my way to Cambridge. With some difficulty I had gained permission from the librarian at Corpus Christi College to take Hugo's masterful Bible in my hands. After so many months of poring over the photographs of the illustrations, I believed I had become fully sensitive to its quality. But when I turned the heavy cover and looked for the first time upon the huge illuminations, fresh as the day they had been created, with sparkling greens, lush reds and pastel shades of blue, lavender and yellow exploding from the pages, my hands trembled. "Incomparable" was too pallid an encomium for Master Hugo.

From these aesthetic delights I turned to the drudgery of searching through Latin texts in the library at nearby Pembroke College, where the bulk of the surviving Bury manuscripts were to be found. There were only a couple of dozen which I dated to the twelfth and thirteenth centuries. I cannot say why I reached first for manuscript number 72, a glossed—annotated—Saint Mark. Perhaps it was because I knew it to be late twelfth century.

I carried the thick volume to a desk and cautiously opened it. I marveled at the feeling of age that its stout vellum pages seemed to exude. With the help of my Latin Bible, I could soon interpret the handwriting of the monk who had copied the text of Saint Mark. Between the lines and on most margins was a profusion of notes commenting on virtually every verse in the text.

I leafed through fairly rapidly, scanning the pages for any elements common to both the manuscript and the inscriptions on the cross. I reached the passage where Mark describes the Crucifixion: "And when they had crucified him, they parted his garments, casting lots upon them . . ." I was startled when I read the notes in the margin next to the text. There, in a neat hand, someone had written: "Cursed be all those who hang on wood, becoming a curse, for they who said it are cursed. . . ." The words were amazingly close to those carried by Synagogue on the cross. I could barely contain myself. I knew I was onto something critically important.

I wanted to race forward, but forced myself to resist the temptation. I slowed down and read every word, each individual letter. Next in Mark was: "And it was the third hour, and they crucified him." Adjacent to that passage the annotator had written: "Noah became drunk and was nude under the tent and was laughed at . . . and the wood became stained with Christ's blood."

My mouth was dry.

I read the next verse in Mark: "And the superscription of his accusation was written over, THE KING OF THE JEWS."

There, between the lines, were the most astonishing Latin words I had ever read. The annotator expanded upon Saint Mark:

> That superscription, that placard over His head, called unchanging in the Psalms, was written in three languages; in Hebrew, King of the Jews; in Greek, King of the Confessors; in Latin, King of the Confessors, all carved into the placard of the cross: all of these languages commemorate the perfidiousness of the Jews.

If these unique words existed anyplace in the world other than on the cross and in the Bury St. Edmunds manuscript I was looking at, I did not know of it. In fact, the cross and the annotation contained the same mistake in the Greek word "Confessors." It should have been *exomologesion.* But it was EXOMOLISSON on the cross, *examolisson* in the manuscript.

I hunted through all the rest of the old Bury manuscripts that day, and at twilight came across another startling piece of evidence. In a miscellany which contained some writings by John of Damascus on the sym-

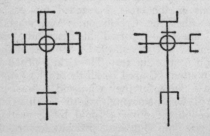

bolism of the cross, I encountered two little drawings in the margin of one page—sketches of two crosses. Both looked like my cross. Near one appeared a Latin text, virtually incomprehensible except for three words, *mirificat fect f*, or *mirificat fecit fieri*, which translated as "caused it to be made marvelously." It had to be a reference to Hugo's cross.

Jubilantly I sped back to London, to the College of Arms, and to the manuscripts identified as "Arundel XXX," in which, around the year 1300, an unknown person had copied dozens of inscriptions from all over the Abbey of Bury, including Samson's verses. With my heart pounding I traced my finger down the page. And found it!

Samson's verse about Cham read: CHAM DUM RIDET NUDA PARENTIS GENITALIA VIDET. The version carved on the cross read: CHAM RIDET DUM NUDA VIDET PUDEBUNDA PARENTIS.

The verses—neither of which was a Biblical quotation—were extremely close, but not identical, although they held the same meaning. The differences involved the substitution of GENITALIA for PUDEBUNDA, virtual synonyms, and an altered scansion. Strictly translated, the verse in the manuscript said: "Cham laughed, the shameful nakedness of his parent to have seen." The verse on the cross said: "Cham laughed to see the shameful nakedness of his parent."

I thought I had an explanation for the variation. The verse in the manuscript had been copied from one of ninety paintings devoted exclusively to Old Testament objects. Those paintings had been placed in the choir under the direction of Samson in 1180 with his verses, before the boy Robert had been killed and before Samson had been elected abbot. The pro-Jewish forces still held sway. After he had been made abbot, and no doubt after he had expelled the Jews in 1190, Samson had had his own image added to the Lamb medallion to commemorate the monk's prophetic dream. And then, in prominent inscriptions, none of them abbreviated, Samson had caused to be emblazoned on the cross a series of sentiments that viciously denounced the Jews.

The first part of his long inscription on the side of the vertical bar, CHAM RIDET DUM NUDA VIDET PUDEBUNDA PARENTIS, Samson adapted from his earlier verse about

Cham. But he transposed the word *parentis,* "parent," so that it would rhyme with the word *mortis,* "dead" or "dying." Hence, instead of the single verse on the painting, CHAM DUM RIDET NUDA PARENTIS GENITALIA VIDET, on the cross it became CHAM RIDET DUM NUDA VIDET PUDEBUNDA PARENTIS, IUDEI RISERE DEI PENAM MORTIS— "Cham laughed to see the shameful nakedness of his parent, the Jews laugh at the agony of God dying."

Samson had invented the additional line to meet the circumstances. The vicious writings fit Samson's character —and his sentiments very well.

Just before I was to return to New York with my precious findings, I received word of yet another marvel. Saemy Rosenberg had found the plaque depicting Christ Before Pilate. He had written from Holland with the news. "The relief is still in the possession of a member of the Fuld family. But, they say it is alabaster and not ivory. I will try to see it and shall report to you. I also enquired whether it may be for sale . . ."

Nothing seemed more fitting than to close out my successful sojourn in London with an elegant dinner at Claridge's with Saemy Rosenberg. Saemy had indeed found the missing piece depicting Christ Before Pilate. It was walrus ivory, not alabaster, and measured two and a quarter by two and a quarter inches. A friend of his, a dealer in Frankfurt by the name of Wilhelm Henrich, had tracked it down to a crusty member of the Fuld family. There was, however, a slight hitch: Mrs. Fuld was rich and did not need money. To her the ivory was unimportant as a work of art but valuable as a personal keepsake. She had insisted on knowing the identity of the institution, why it wanted the piece, and how much it would pay.

Over dinner, Rosenberg raised his hands slowly and asked, "What can I do? You have not told me anything. So I cannot divulge this information. I'm sorry, I have done all I can. But is this little curious ivory all that important?"

"Jim Rorimer will kill me," I laughed, "but so what! Yes, the piece *is* that important. It's vital. It belongs to the most sublime English medieval ivory ever made. Here, look at these photographs."

As the dealer examined the two life-sized prints I carried with me, I filled his ear with my theory about Hugo and Samson. Rosenberg turned to me and in an awed tone of voice exclaimed, "I have never seen anything more beautiful. It is more important even than the entire Guelph Treasure. Your cross is a miracle! I shall do everything in my power to gain for you its missing piece. Oh, I hope I can manage it!"

A week after I arrived back in New York I received a phone call from Rosenberg, who had just returned to the city. "I have done it. I have it. I am looking at the missing ivory right now," he told me in a smooth, unemotional voice.

"What? My God, that's incredible," I cried out and then asked hesitantly. "But will we be able to afford it?"

"We shall discuss the price. The story is most curious—"

"I'm coming down," I yelled, starting for the door. Within fifteen minutes I was sitting in the inner gallery of Rosenberg and Steibel, cradling the little ivory in my hands. It was not the half-inch-thick block I had expected, carved on the back with a vigorous image of the angel of Saint Matthew. The Christ Before Pilate panel was only about a sixteenth of an inch thick and was stained green on the back from being attached to bronze. From that I deduced that the beautiful piece had doubtless been one of a series of panels attached to a bronze base supporting the cross. That meant Topic Mimara had been right about the bottom block, after all. I was thrilled by Rosenberg's discovery. But what price had Mrs. Fuld attached to her treasure—hundreds of thousands of dollars? I barely dared ask.

"When you showed me those striking photographs of the cross in London." Rosenberg began, "I was deeply moved. So I decided to communicate with Mrs. Fuld. I told her that the institution that wanted her ivory, and wanted it more than anything else in the world, was the great Metropolitan Museum in New York. I told Mrs. Fuld that her piece belonged on a spectacular cross for which the museum paid dearly. I suggested that she place any price she wanted on her ivory. I assured her the museum most certainly would meet the price."

"Oh, God, I can't bear to hear the rest," I cried.

"You may be thinking that I have acted irresponsibly. But I risked nothing in saying what I did. If I had said nothing—ah, that would have risked all. You see, I had already concluded that Mrs. Fuld really didn't care for the piece as a work of art—or, in fact, as a memento either. But, like so many wealthy old people, she didn't want to be bothered with the arrangements a negotiation would entail. And I realized that since she is rich, it would never occur to her to seek a fortune from a great museum with this one keepsake." Rosenberg paused.

"And so the price is . . . ?" I asked, and once more lapsed into silence.

"A mere twelve thousand five hundred dollars."

Within a day of its arrival in the United States, the dramatic plaque representing Christ Before Pilate was purchased with Cloisters funds by an elated James Rorimer. "Fine object. Fair price. Good job. What luck!" he exulted.

Rorimer announced the acquisition of both cross and plaque at the annual meeting of the museum's corporation in October 1963, heralding them as among "the most important works of art in all our collections."

A few days after Rorimer's private disclosure to the corporation's members, the London *Daily Mail* broke the story throughout the world.

> The Metropolitan Museum of Art in New York is about to announce the most spectacular art coup for many years—under the noses of the British.
>
> For a rumoured £250,000 the museum has bought a fantastic 12th-century ivory crucifix generally acknowledged as the most important English Romanesque work known. There will be a storm of indignation in Britain, because the crucifix was offered, at a much lower price, to the British Museum.
>
> The crucifix went to the Americans only because the British Treasury finally refused the funds for its purchase. . . . The price was certainly not considered excessive for a treasure of this importance, but the situation was complicated because [the owner] was not able to disclose to British negotiators where he had obtained the cross.

A fanfare of publicity ensued. *Life* magazine published a colorful story about the masterpiece illustrated by lavish full-page photographs. All of the major publications—

Time, Newsweek, the New York *Times*—carried extensive articles about the Metropolitan's newest treasure.

The cross was displayed in a specially crafted glass case in the most prominent place at The Cloisters. The public came in droves.

Once Hugo's incomparable cross was placed in its permanent home, I occupied myself with the task of hunting down the missing figure of Christ and the bottom block which Topic Mimara had stumbled upon in Mons in 1931.

A monumental and splendid walrus-ivory figure which seems to be the original Christ was discovered in the Kunstindustriet Museum in Oslo. It had earlier been in the art museum in Copenhagen and was the same little sculpture I had once been attracted to when, in Florence, I examined its photograph in Adolph Goldschmit's book on medieval ivories. I had dropped the figure from consideration then because Goldschmidt had seemed to suggest that part of the Tree of Life was carved on its back. But I had misinterpreted Adolph Goldschmidt; for Christ's back was smooth.

The Oslo Christ was eventually sent to the Metropolitan on loan. When I held the figure up to the cross. I knew at once there could be no doubt about its origin. The small circles dotting the front of the palm tree stopped precisely at the edge of Christ's loincloth. A peg hole in Christ's head lined up perfectly with a sawn-off peg on the cross just below the Brazen Serpent medallion. The width of the Christ corresponded to the width of the tree.

The Oslo figure provided the ultimate stylistic evidence to support my theory that Master Hugo had carved the cross. To compare the majestic figure to those in Hugo's Bible, almost the same size, was to be convinced that the man who had painted the Bible had carved the cross.

To find the bottom ivory block carved with the angel of Matthew and the Harrowing of Hell, I constructed a wooden painted model of the piece the exact dimensions of the others. On one side I pasted a scaled photograph of the angel of Matthew from Master Hugo's Bible; on the other, a photograph of an illumination of the Harrowing of Hell from an English manuscript of the mid-twelfth century closely related in style to Hugo's paintings.

I sent the photographs of my model to scholars and art

dealers throughout Europe. And soon I received thrilling information. An art dealer in Brussels answered my letter, saying that shortly after the war he had come into possession of a square block "of walrus ivory, medieval in date and exceptionally beautiful," which corresponded almost precisely to my model. He had sold the block to a young French collector in 1956. Regrettably, he had never asked the man's name.

I am still looking for the priceless little block. It is out there somewhere and is bound to appear in time. For it, like the cross, is imbued with magic.

EPILOGUE

Scholars, Rivals and Spies

IN THE YEARS SINCE the acquisition of the ivory cross I
have pursued the missing block and other issues as well.
I have kept abreast of the opinions of scholars who are
still trying to assemble a detailed history of the work. I
probed into the reasons why my competitors failed in
their quest for the object. And I gathered together everything I could find about the mystery man Ante Topic
Mimara.

In the spring of 1964 I published an article on the
cross in the museum's *Bulletin*. Looking back, I realize
what a failure it was. Just before completing it, I surrendered to a last-minute loss of nerve. Instead of forthrightly proclaiming my belief that Master Hugo of Bury
St. Edmunds had carved the incomparable cross and
Abbot Samson de Tottington had later added the verses
and his image, I waffled. I wrote that, although the cross
might possibly have been carved by Hugo around 1150
and the large inscriptions been added by Samson, it was
more likely that the masterpiece had been created in the

decade 1180–1190, a generation after Hugo, by an unknown artist under Samson's direction.

At first I received a pleasing number of letters praising
my article and its conclusions. Then came the brickbats.
My former adversary Peter Lasko of the British Museum
let me know that he thought the cross was definitely
English, but "probably not from Bury St. Edmunds and
most certainly from the decade 1100 to 1120." John
Beckwith of the Victoria and Albert informed me that,
although my efforts to prove the cross was from Bury and
the time of Samson were "gallant," he was convinced
the cross dated around 1180 and had been carved in
York or Canterbury. Neither Lasko nor Beckwith, however, ever came forward with documents supporting
his viewpoint.

A special researcher whom I had hired to come to the
Metropolitan to track down further information regarding
the inscriptions, Sabrina Longland, also entered the fray,
and later she wrote three noteworthy articles about the
cross. One of her conclusions was that all the material I
had unearthed linking the cross to Bury St. Edmunds was
"coincidence." Yet she too never offered any evidence
which attributed the cross to any other artistic center or
any artist other than Hugo.

Sir Kenneth Clark, later Lord Clark of Saltwood, one
of England's great art historians, read my article and sent
it along to Norman Scarfe, the English scholar and specialist on the history of Bury St. Edmunds. In an accompanying note Sir Kenneth observed: "I think the connection with Bury is convincing. But, as you will see, this is
established by comparison with the Bury Bible, which
would put it back to Abbot Anselm: the connection with
Samson which Hoving seeks to prove via the Jews goes
too much against stylistic evidence for my taste."

As soon as I received word of Sir Kenneth's opinions,
I knew he was right. I had made a grievous mistake in
attributing the cross to the time of Abbot Samson. I
realized I should have stuck with my first impression, that
the Bury Bible and the cross had both been made by
Hugo, the Bible around 1135 and the cross around 1150.

In 1974 Norman Scarfe published an article in which
he concluded, convincingly, that the cross and its figure
of Christ had been carved during the tenure of Abbot

Ording by Master Hugo. To Scarfe, the "small" inscriptions had been written not to condemn the Jews, but to convert them to Christianity. He argued that during the time of Ording, before the abbey had fallen into debt to the Jews, conversion of the local Jews rather than expulsion and eradication would have been the desired Christian goal. I agree entirely with Scarfe's theory, except for two vital points: only Samson could have conceived the scurrilous verses in the large inscriptions; only he could have ordered the insertion into the Lamb medallion of his own image. To my arguments Norman Scarfe replied that Samson's couplet on Cham which had accompanied the painting in the choir could just as easily have been inspired by the earlier inscriptions on the ivory cross. I had no riposte. But when I asked him who he thought the monk with the raised fist could be other than Abbot Samson, Norman Scarfe had no reply.

The essential reason why my competitors failed to purchase the Bury cross was that Ante Topic Mimara's dubious manner and his mysterious background left too many questions unanswered.

William Milliken, director of the Cleveland Museum, examined the cross three times during 1956 and 1957. He was overwhelmed by the object, yet eventually chose to give it a wide berth:

"Topic Mimara was *slimy!* On meeting him, I had the *most* adverse impression of anyone I've ever met in my life. He was obviously a peasant, a clod, and he was frightening. The more he attempted to lather me with good-fellowship and what I suppose he equated with charm, the more I was repelled—and frightened. What an awkward personality! The moment I first saw the cross I was bowled over by it. But I was afraid of *him*. I instantly thought, could he, Topic Mimara, possibly have faked it? But then I said to myself, No. If I had had the money on hand, I might have been tempted to buy the piece. But it was my adverse feeling about Topic which was why I didn't proceed."

Sherman Lee, who succeeded Milliken as director, was responsible for Cleveland's final rejection of the cross. Lee was offended by Topic and even more by his price.

At first sight, Lee was, in his words, "wildly enthusiastic" about the ivory, but ultimately he turned the piece down because he could not bring himself to consider spending such an amount of money despite the fact that he had more than enough funds at his disposal. At one point in the negotiations Sherman Lee could easily have gained the object for half a million dollars, significantly less than the amount asked of all other contenders. He let the opportunity go by.

In England, the first to hear about the cross was Timothy Clark, a specialist in ceramics at the auction house of Sotheby's in London. Clark, who informed Peter Wilson, president of the firm, remembers the day vividly:

"Topic Mimara, a most unlikely sort, had sold a number of things through us after the war. He was a furtive type. He had—well, the scent of what I would call the 'spylink' about him. I recognized the type; I served with our intelligence service in Aleppo and played many dangerous cat-and-mouse games with the Sicherheitsdienst, the counter-intelligence section of the Third Reich. Topic Mimara was the kind of person I had to deal with in the war. Everytime he came in, I felt a little reluctant to see him.

"In the spring of 1956 Topic—he also called himself Topic Mimara Matutin—talked with me about selling some porcelains. He was rather amusing. The man knew nothing about porcelains. A third of what I saw was acceptable. The other two-thirds appeared to be fake. I'm sure he wasn't trying to deceive. He simply could not distinguish betwen real and wrong. Suddenly the man laid a series of large photographs of an ivory cross on the table. My instant thought was that, if true, the cross was incredible. And I escorted him right away to Peter Wilson."

Peter Wilson remembers being confronted with a short, gray-faced, clean-shaven individual who maneuvered his way into the office like a crab. Without expression, he introduced himself simply as "Topic Mimara, collector," and handed over two large photographs. Peter Wilson's immediate thought was that the photographs revealed one of the most magnificent works of art he had ever contemplated:

"I tried to get him to sell the piece through us. I assured him that with the proper publicity, we would be able to obtain one of the highest prices ever recorded for a work of decorative art of the Middle Ages. Topic Mimara muttered that he was not convinced an auction would be the best way to sell. I worked very hard on him. Several times I thought he might bend. Eventually he did not. What an absolutely astonishing work of art! Years later I again became involved with it under the most frustrating of circumstances."

Before the cross returned to haunt Peter Wilson, it came to the attention of John Pope-Hennessy, keeper of the Department of Architecture and Sculpture at the Victoria and Albert Museum. Pope-Hennessy would later become director of the V. and A. and then the British Museum. In early October 1957 he heard about it from Sir Kenneth Clark, a long-time friend of Harold Parsons. Sir Kenneth had examined the cross in Zurich and called it "a grand, compelling object of great national importance."

Pope-Hennessy wanted his colleague John Beckwith to examine the piece first, for Beckwith was in Florence at the time. Pope-Hennessy sent several telegrams urging him to make contact with Ante Topic Mimara, travel to Zurich and study his holdings. But Pope-Hennessy never received a response, so he took matters into his own hands and flew to Zurich at the end of October. When Topic placed the cross before him on the conference table in the vault, Pope-Hennessy acted as if impelled by an electric shock:

"I knew I was looking at one of the most marvelous works of art I had ever seen in my life. It was something I knew to be genuine without any hesitation whatsoever. I was deeply moved; I could only think that it had to emerge from the recesses of that bank vault and come out into the open. Which museum in the world would become its home did not greatly concern me.

"I repeatedly asked the man to quote a price. He refused, insisting he would only sell the crucifix with a group of other English medieval objects for not less than half a million pounds. Upon leaving, I asked Topic for photographs. Without the least objection he handed me a set, telling me casually to send them to a Tangier address when I was through. I brought the photographs back to London and showed them to a great scholar in medieval art and texts, Francis Wormald. He deciphered some of the inscriptions and pronounced the cross 'utterly convincing as to authenticity.' "

Pope-Hennessy prepared a memorandum on Topic's collection. He wrote that Topic Mimara was not at all keen to part with the cross but was hoping to use it as bait to sell other items. Pope-Hennessy recommended to his director, however, that the museum keep a keen eye on the object. After that, the memorandum was buried in the official files of the Victoria and Albert.

The reaction to the cross at the British Museum was more complex. On Saturday morning, May 18, 1961, a young specialist on Viking art who would one day become director of the museum happened to be working alone in his office. He was interrupted by a guard calling to say that "a man and woman from the Continent" wanted to see someone in the department about a "significant work of English medieval art." David Wilson, a dutiful scholar with a high sense of adventure, told the guardian to send the couple up at once.

Within minutes Wilson found himself facing a heavyset man clad in an elegantly tailored camel's-hair coat, and a diminutive pale woman who spoke hesitant but clear English. She introduced herself as Dr. Wiltrud Topic Mersmann and explained that her husband, Ante Topic Mimara, an art collector and painter, "not a dealer," had amassed a sizable collection of art. She explained that her husband had decided to put his estate in order and wanted to sell a choice object to the British Museum. Topic Mersmann produced two life-sized photographs of the cross.

When Wilson looked at the pictures, his first impression was one of profound astonishment, instantly followed by a twinge of doubt. The object seemed so grand, so ambitious, he wondered whether it might be an incredibly clever forgery. As he looked more closely, his doubts began to wane. The multitude of figures were carved in such a natural manner that David Wilson perceived he was confronting a rare masterpiece. He told his delighted visitors exactly what he thought and made arrangements for Topic Mimara and his companion to return Monday to meet Sir Ruppert Bruce-Mitford and his associate, Dr. Peter Lasko.

At the meeting, Topic nodded curtly and abruptly began to talk. "This is my object and I want to sell it to you. What is your opinion of it?"

Bruce-Mitford's immediate impression of the curious man was that he looked as pleased "as a dog with two tails." Sir Ruppert turned away and studied the photographs for the greater part of a half hour without uttering a word. Finally he turned back and raised his eyes to Topic. "Your cross is one of the most striking and beautiful works of art I have ever seen."

At the start of the meeting Peter Lasko had been nervous. "Topic was shady," he recalls. "He looked like some sort of Mexican bandit, although of course he wasn't Mexican. To me, the cross seemed incredibly important. But the price was ghastly. I felt sure, however, that Mr. Topic Mimara would bargain. I told Ruppert I was quite excited, and suggested we copy the photographs Topic had left and get right on with the research."

In the first week of June 1961 Ruppert Bruce-Mitford and Peter Lasko flew to Zurich and spent three days examining the work of art in the bank. Confronted by the object, both men were "knocked over." On their return, they submitted an enthusiastic report to Sir Frank Francis, heartily recommending the purchase despite the "astronomical" price. Sir Frank agreed and passed his keepers' findings to the Standing Committee of the British Museum trustees, a body which acted upon acquisitions. The committee was in favor of purchasing the cross for the museum and the nation. But no funds were appropriated, since nothing near the amount asked for the cross existed in the museum's coffers. Amazingly, a full year went by before the trustees even authorized Bruce-Mitford to explore possibilities of raising the money outside the museum. When he tried, Bruce-Mitford was unsuccessful.

In mid-November 1962 the full Board of Trustees authorized Sir Frank to make formal application to the Exchequer. When he did, the Chancellor of the Exchequer asked him for assurances of Topic Mimara's good character. Bruce-Mitford suggested that Peter Wilson of Sotheby's might consent to speak on behalf of the Yugoslav.

Bruce-Mitford met the auctioneer at his home in Chelsea and gingerly discussed how to deal with two seemingly insurmountable obstacles still standing in the way of the purchase—the uncertainty of Topic's title to the cross, and the museum's lack of funds. Within days, Peter Wilson believed he had found ways to overcome both.

"I went to the Exchequer," Wilson recounted, "and vouched for Topic Mimara. Then I approached a friend, a certain art collector, who must remain anonymous, about helping to get up the rest of the funds. I described the cross to my friend and told him how magnificent I believed it to be. The man was enthralled. Interesting! For he was Jewish, and deeply religious. He pledged to lend the British Museum one hundred and fifty thousand pounds free of interest—indefinitely. He also pledged to give the museum fifty thousand pounds outright. So all the funds for the cross had been raised well before Topic Mimara's deadline."

Despite the generous offer and Peter Wilson's *bona fides*, no action was taken. Sir Frank Francis was troubled that Topic Mimara refused to come forward with proof of ownership. Certain aides in the office of the Chancellor of the Exchequer had become even more concerned. Sir Frank, in desperation, sent Bruce-Mitford and Lasko to Zurich in a last-minute effort to solve the problem. The keeper was told by Topic that I had come with a blank check. He flew into a rage. Peter Lasko could hardly control his superior. Bruce-Mitford kept muttering, in English, in the presence of Topic, "Crook! Why doesn't this wretched man just admit he's a crook!" Lasko had to make what he described as "diplomatic translations" for Topic. No matter how hard Bruce-Mitford and Lasko tried, Topic refused to utter a word about where he had found the cross. He did, however, offer the British Muesum a seventeen-day option.

On his return to London, Bruce-Mitford worked gallantly to persuade his director and the officials at the Exchequer to move forward with the purchase anyway. But to no avail. The option lapsed. The sorrow of the moment remains a trauma even now. To Sir Frank

Francis, "The day we lost was one of the saddest of my life. But what could one do?"

Fitting together stray fragments of information about Topic Mimara into a coherent portrait of the man and the nature of his activities has not been easy. Topic Mimara's personal inclination has been to remain forever "the most private of private people." The man seems to have given only one interview to the Western press, the London *Sunday Times* in 1963, a few days after the Metropolitan Museum publicly announced the acquisition of the cross. The headline of the article, written by Antony Terry, was provocative: ART TREASURES WERE NOT NAZI LOOT, SAYS TOPIC MIMARA. The article stated in part:

> In a hilltop castle overlooking Salzburg, Austrian-born art collector Mr. Ante Topic Mimara disclosed to me some of the cloak-and-dagger background to his remarkable private collection of art treasures, and strenuously denied that they were "Nazi loot," taken from the Jews.
> "I handed the photos over to the local police and they were able to reassure Jewish interests that the Nazi loot rumours were false. I am unlikely to help the Nazis as I was their victim while I was living in Berlin during the last war. I spent most of that time in custody."
> The collection was smuggled out of West Berlin with the help of the U.S. authorities over 10 years and after Mr. Topic Mimara had been given a warning from East Berlin that the Russians would kidnap him.
> British and French officials in Berlin balked at the risk of smuggling his priceless art collection out of the encircled city, but U.S. officials told him: "You are genuinely in danger—get out now and we will move your collection after you have gone."
> Piece by piece, the art treasures were secretly shifted. Since then, the collection has been "somewhere in North Africa." . . .

I soon learned that newspapers were not the most fruitful places to look for information on Topic Mimara. The police of several countries and people involved in intelligence gathering proved to be far more revealing.

According to the French Sûreté, Topic Mimara had departed the ravaged city of Berlin in the early months of 1946 and had taken up residence in Säckingen, a hamlet in the French-occupied zone of Germany, on the border with Switzerland. In the winter of 1947, Topic was arrested by the Sûreté for black market activities and for currency violations. He was expelled from the French Zone and vanished for a year.

He surfaced again, somewhat flamboyantly and with a different name, in mid-December 1948, when he arrived at the American-occupied zone to take up duties as head of the Yugoslavian mission at the Collecting Point. He wore the uniform of a full colonel in the Yugoslavian Army and called himself Maté Topic. A U.S. military cable established his credentials and gave him permission to travel freely to a number of key cities throughout Germany.

RFHAM
6/APA
12-141325
2.2 R. FWAD/ OUG - S. UCOM
RE: MATE TOPIC

CLEARANCE GRANTED TO MATE/TOPIC, CMA.
YUGOSLAV MILITARY MISSION FRANKFURT, KARLSRUHE, WIESBADEN, BERLIN AND MUNICH AS EXPERT ON CULTURAL ART. 15 DECEMBER, 1948.

                                           SIGNED, P.D.
Received 15 December, 1948
         M.R.

At the moment of his arrival Maté Topic came to the attention of Edgar Breitenbach, who was at the time an art intelligence officer in Munich for the American mission at the Collecting Point. Breitenbach, a noted art historian who would later distinguish himself at the Library of Congress, was suspicious of the colonel from the moment they met. Breitenbach's wife, Margaret, had a vivid impression of the man as having "very red lips and beady black eyes, definitely not a typical Don Juan." Even so, according to her husband, soon after his arrival Colonel Maté Topic had seduced a young German art historian assigned to the Yugoslavian desk, Wiltrud Mersmann.

Edgar Breitenbach watched the colonel's activities for several months. He became convinced that Topic stole significant numbers of works of art from the Collecting Point for Yugoslavia, and possibly for himself, with the help of his lover. His system was simple and effective. Through Mersmann, Topic gained access to the catalogue cards in the files at Munich, which listed and described works of art stored at the Collecting Point whose origins were unknown. If Topic fancied a certain work of art, he would copy the facts from the card and send the information to Belgrade. In time, the Yugoslavian government would transmit an official request for the restitution of the piece to its "homeland." Topic shrewdly selected obscure churches and monasteries as provenances for the art he spuriously claimed. In time Colonel Maté Topic was able to obtain, and dispatch to Belgrade by train, four sizable "restitution shipments."

Breitenbach also suspected that Topic had been involved with the recovery in Germany of a cache of silver and zinc ingots pillaged from the Central Bank of Yugoslavia by the retreating German armies. Although most of the silver and all of the zinc were returned to the homeland, Topic, according to Breitenbach, kept for himself a significant number of silver ingots. He managed to spirit the hoard through the French Zone to Switzerland and into a Zurich bank.

By February of 1950, Breitenbach had almost fully unraveled what Topic had been doing. Just as he was about to confront the man directly, Topic vanished. At about the same time, the American activities at the Collecting Point came to an end. The first postwar elections were held in the West German Federal Republic, and the United States Military Government was disbanded.

Breitenbach remained in Germany, taking on a role in the "denazification" and reeducation of the German people. Yet his interest in Topic never waned. He learned that Wiltrud Mersmann had moved from Munich, and he tracked her to her parents' house near Bonn. One day, without warning, he went right up to the house and rang the doorbell. Mersmann was at home.

Gently and patiently he confronted the distraught woman with all that he had discovered about Topic and her. According to Breitenbach, "she admitted everything." But when Breitenbach asked her where he could find Topic, Mersmann swore she had no idea, saying that

Topic had walked out on her and had left her alone with their infant child. The baby began to cry. And Edgar Breitenbach decided to conclude his investigation of Wiltrud Mersmann and Ante Topic Mimara.

While Topic was working at the Collecting Point, his name had come to the attention of undercover operatives in the intelligence service of Federal West Germany, the Bundesnachrichtdienst. The BND, the most effective counterspy organization in Western Europe, had been founded by General Reinhard Gehlen, superspy and supersurvivor of the Abwehr, Hitler's military intelligence. Gehlen had been recruited after the war by American intelligence forces to establish an organization charged with internal security, counterespionage and external espionage for West Germany.

The "Org," as it came to be known, achieved a series of striking coups in smashing intelligence rings formed in West Germany by the Communist Bloc countries. In 1948, Gehlen's organization uncovered the existence of a spy network that had been established by Alexander Rankovich, chief of the Yugoslavian secret service and internal security. With assistance from the French Sûreté, in April 1949 the Yugoslavian espionage circuit with headquarters in Friedrichshafen was smashed.

Among those apprehended was a Yugoslav named Levec, who confessed he was the principal agent for Tito's intelligence service in French-occupied Germany. Levec, grilled at length, revealed the identity of his boss: "The head of the Yugoslav intelligence service in Germany is a certain Topic, alias Mimara, a museum custodian and member of the Yugoslav Restitution and Reparations Commission in the U.S. Zone."

The case was turned over to the Org. General Gehlen's agents stalked Mimara for six months, from August of 1949 to February 1950. Eventually, they were able to pick out five operatives working under him. Gehlen's Org handed over a dossier on Topic's "apparatus" to their U.S. liaison officers, and the Americans rounded up Topic and his gang.

After extensive interrogation by officers of the United States Military Intelligence, all members of the ring but one were expelled from Germany. The notable exception, a curious one, was Topic Mimara. He settled comfortably

in West Berlin and opened a modest art gallery. What he
did to merit this special treatment remains unknown.

He remained in Berlin for five relatively tranquil years,
broken only by a visit by the police on one occasion. Based
upon suspicions that he had illicitly acquired a number
of artworks, the Berlin police searched his gallery, but
they uncovered nothing illegal.

Then Topic suddenly departed and reappeared in Tangier in 1955. At that time the Moroccan city was a free
port, an international zone governed by a five-member
commission of the Allies. No sooner had Topic arrived
than he came to the attention of a young intelligence
officer at the American Consulate, Edwin Murray Jackson.

Jackson described Topic and his activities in Tangier
with gusto:

> In the mid-1950s, Tangier was a wild and exciting city
> where outlandish behaviour was normal. The city was an
> open money market. Everyone who was not pinned down
> flocked there to do business. Late in 1955, I happened
> to hear a particularly intriguing rumor on the sophisti-
> cated cocktail circuit. A certain Mimara had just sailed
> into the harbor with a boat loaded with art treasures.
> Helped by the Governor of Tangier, he had rented a
> luxurious apartment located in one of the best quarters
> of the city. It had five or six impressive salons, which
> Topic filled with paintings, sculpture and furniture he
> hoped to sell. There were some grand places in Tangier
> and this was one of them.
>
> As soon as Mimara had set up his apartment show-
> room, all sorts of tales began to make the rounds. One
> held that after the war a trainload of artworks looted
> by the Nazis had taken off from Germany bound for
> Yugoslavia with Topic Mimara in charge. The train
> never arrived in Yugoslavia. It ended up in Antwerp or
> Amsterdam. From there the stuff got to Tangier.
>
> I reported all this—the boat, the lavish apartment, the
> story about the train—to the State Department. Eventually,
> State reached people who had been at various Collecting
> Points in Germany and were familiar with the work of
> the Monuments and Fine Arts Commission. The Depart-
> ment sent me a list of works still missing from the
> Collecting Point and asked me to check up on Mimara's
> holdings. He was suspected of having gotten hold of
> some of those pieces.

One day I dropped in on Mimara's apartment. I didn't use my real name and, of course, I didn't reveal what I did in life. I passed myself off as a lover of art. I admit I am by no means an art expert, but I know something. I just looked the place over. I wasn't particularly impressed with what I saw. Mimara's collection looked to me like a random stew—paintings and statuary and loads of filigreed gold jewelry. My dictinct impression was that much of the stuff wasn't authentic. At the very least, it wasn't what Mimara claimed it to be. I brought a local art dealer with me. He had the same impression.

I went back a second time and revealed I was with the American Consulate and wanted to compare his collection with the State Department list of stolen goods. The man thought it was hilarious that anyone—particularly a member of the American Consulate—could possibly suspect him, "Ante Topic Mimara, an upstanding man of considerable international repute," of ever having art that wasn't his, or that wasn't bona fide. He was expansive and—well—jolly about it.

I compared my list with as many of his works as I could. I suppose my examination was inadequate, but I did my best. I wasn't able to match a single item on the list with the works of art in his apartment. At Topic Mimara's request I wrote up a brief report, saying I had found nothing. I signed it and gave him a copy. He really liked that.

Yet the rumors continued. Two years later, in 1957, the criminal investigating units of the West German police in Berlin and Wiesbaden received complaints about a certain "Popic," a resident of Tangier. The claims alleged that the man, a supposed art dealer who had once lived in the Berlin suburb of Charlottenburg, might have been the recipient of an extensive collection of oil paintings and objets d'art which had been stolen from museums in East Germany and Eastern Europe. The police requested that the German consulates in Rabat and Casablanca investigate "Popic" and advise them on the likelihood of extraditing him from Morocco.

The investigation by the German Consulate in Casablanca revealed that "Popic" was the same person as Maté Topic and Ante Topic Mimara, born on April 7, 1898, in Spalato, who had worked briefly with the Yugoslavan art mission at the Collecting Point in Munich.

Nothing was mentioned about espionage activities. German officials suggested that an art expert familiar with "the former and existing collections of the East German and other museums, which had been relieved of certain treasures allegedly in the possession of Popic Mimara, be sent at government expense to Tangier to seek out Popic and offer to purchase the illicit works of art." They also suggested an alternative ploy. If no true art expert could be found who was willing to travel to Morocco, a detective should be sent to play the role. The proposal was never carried out. Lack of money and interest on the part of West German officials about what was an East German issue caused the investigation to fade away.

But Topic Mimara's name did not long remain untarnished. In November 1960 a Czech lady, Mrs. Theresia Zscheyge, with the maiden name of Stanka, born on June 14, 1922, in the city of Brux, sent an official complaint to West German police. A certain art dealer named Ante Topic Mimara, living in Berlin and Tangier, had taken a number of old-master oil paintings from her on consignment, she claimed. He had assured her he would sell the pictures in the West at considerable profit for her. The paintings had thereupon been shipped to Topic. Mrs. Zscheyge contended that, after a year, she had received neither a report nor a payment. Once again, the West German police did not choose to pursue an Eastern complaint.

Late in 1974, I heard that Topic Mimara had died. I immediately wrote a letter of condolence to Topic's widow and tactfully pointed out that her late husband had intended me to have the information regarding the provenance of the cross.

I received no reply. I followed that letter with a half-dozen more. Still no reply. I sent a telegram and then tried to telephone Wiltrud Topic Mersmann at her late husband's *Schloss.* No response. It was just like old times. But this time, I reflected ruefully, the story had truly ended.

Then three years later I received the astonishing information that Topic Mimara had been spotted in the Inter-Continental Hotel in Zagreb, Yugoslavia. When I telephoned the hotel, I was informed that he had checked out a week before but had taken up residence in an apartment in the city. I called central information in Belgrade and within five minutes had obtained his telephone number. Within another minute, I could hear the phone ringing. A resonant voice responded in Croatian.

I could scarcely contain myself. "Is this my old friend Topic Mimara?" I asked in Italian. "Thomas Hoving here. Remember? The Cross? How are you?"

"*Vivo ancora,*" he responded and laughed. "I'm still alive."

I made arrangements to meet my old adversary within several months at his castle in Austria. On a crisp morning in mid-March 1978 my wife and I drove out of the old city of Salzburg up the narrow, curving road toward Topic Mimara's Schloss Neuhaus. We rang the bell on the stout wooden portal. A guardian appeared without a sound and, opening the massive gate, guided us through the courtyard to the house. We walked up two flights of stairs.

Topic was on the landing. He hadn't aged a day. His hair was dark, as was his ample beard except for a white slash precisely at the chin. He looked strong, although his shoulders seemed to sag a little more than before. Topic led us into a small chamber furnished with a marble-topped table surrounded by a couch and a pair of over-stuffed chairs. A large cupboard stood off to the left.

"Look at this! Greek. Seventh century B.C. Unique in the world," Topic exclaimed abruptly. He opened the cupboard and lifted out a crouching lion in solid bronze.

I groaned to myself. The sculpture was clearly modern.

"And look at this. I found this painting just last week." He handed me a set of Polaroid prints. They were photographs of a wretched copy of a well-known portrait by Leonardo da Vinci.

"Leonardo," Topic stated. "A lost original. Remarkable, is it not so?" Then he turned and reached into his cupboard. He wheeled around smoothly and placed another small bronze on the table. This one depicted a youth and obviously dated to the end of the nineteenth century.

"Alexander the Great," Topic announced proudly.

"By Lysippos, I suppose," I interrupted sarcastically, naming Alexander's personal sculptor.

"Yes. You are perceptive, as usual. You see this small

patch of gilding on Alexander's shoulder? Here? It is proof. One of the Roman historians relates how Emperor Nero acquired the world-famous portrait by Lysippos and then gilded it. So, here it is."

At that moment Frau Topic Mersmann entered the room, looking at me and my wife warily. She reached out her hand tentatively to shake ours. I told Topic Mimara and his wife I was writing a book about the ivory cross and wanted to ask a few questions about his career. He expressed himself as eager to help. Frau Topic Mersmann seemed to shrink away, smiling shyly at the same time.

"How did you get to the Collecting Point?" I asked, for starters. "And what were you doing there?"

Topic replied without blinking. "I worked for a while at the Yugoslav mission as a favor for my country. The Nazis had stolen thousands of works from Yugoslavia. A commission was sent to Munich in 1946. But the members performed poorly. In 1948 I was approached to lead the mission. I refused. I yearned to remain an independent collector, a quiet, unobserved person, the most private of private people. Also, I was fearful. Some members of the first mission had been suspected of stealing a quantity of works for themselves. I felt it would be just a matter of time before I would be blamed for what they had done. But my old friend Tito begged me in person. So I took the job."

"What about those silver bars some people say you found in a lake in Germany? Is it true you took them to Switzerland and put them into your bank?"

"People in the first commission stole the bars. I was blamed. You see, everyone was jealous because I was doing a good job. Poisonous words were spread about me."

"Someone you may know, Edgar Breitenbach, told me you retrieved many works of art from the Collecting Point which had never been in Yugoslavia."

"I knew Breitenbach. What he told you is false. Because of my intimate knowledge of art, I recognized works from Yugoslavia that had been placed in the wrong files in Munich. These, and only these, were returned, legitimately, to Yugoslavia. The American chief of the Collecting Point reviewed and approved all my claims."

"Mrs. Topic," I said gently, "Breitenbach told me he knew you too."

"Breitenbach took a dislike to me," Mersmann observed in a sharp voice. "I was suspicious of him. I believed he was in intelligence. In 1950 or 1951 he followed me all the way to my parents' house in Bonn and asked many questions. He accused me of helping to send objects from the Collecting Point to Yugoslavia. Nothing was wrong with what I did. I admitted everything to him, because in every instance the order was signed by American authorities higher than Breitenbach."

"All these stories about me were concocted by my jealous enemies," Topic interrupted. "I had given a third of my private collection to Yugoslavia to add to the pieces I had found at the Collecting Point. But certain powerful enemies in my homeland stole them. One of the most powerful men in the state, Alexander Rankovich, the chief of internal security, was part of the conspiracy. He took some of my art treasures for himself; others he gave away to such friends as Nasser and Sukarno. Tito was unaware of the facts. I tried to expose Rankovich. For that I was forced out of the Collecting Point. Later, Rankovich even tried to have me killed. Three times he sent assassins."

I gazed at him skeptically.

"Once was in Tangier, in 1955. I had not yet found my apartment. I was living in a hotel. One morning, on an impulse, I decided to shave off my beard. I don't know why. By that simple act my life was saved. And I did something else that day which also contributed to my salvation. Instead of taking the elevator down to the hotel lobby, I walked. On the bottom landing I happened to overhear two men talking in Croatian. 'Watch for him, watch for the beard. When he comes, we follow. Trail him. Shoot when you can. If we get separated, we shall meet again in Tunis.' Cautiously, I looked. Two dark men were sitting watching the elevator. Perhaps I was foolhardly, but I walked down the stairs and right by them. One of them looked into my eyes for a second, then turned away. Without the beard, I was saved."

"Why would Rankovich want to kill you?" I asked.

"For my collection, and because I tried to expose him. The second attempt was in 1956. I was staying in the Hotel Wolff in Munich. At three in the morning I was awakened by a soft rapping on my door. 'Who is it?' I called out. A voice said only, 'It is the police of the Criminal Division. Come out.' Then whoever it was tried to enter. But I had locked my door. I remained awake all night. In the morning I called the hall porter to come and see if there was anyone outside my room. There wasn't. And, curious thing, the clerk on duty throughout the night had seen no one."

"And the other time?"

"It was here, in the summer of 1963. At midnight one night I heard a knocking on the outer door. I roused myself, quietly went down and looked through the peephole. I recognized a certain Yugoslavian I had been friendly with in Berlin before the war. 'What do you want? I'm surprised to see you,' I said. He whispered that he was now a colonel in the Yugoslav police and had been sent to liquidate me. Quickly he warned me, 'Don't come out, don't come out.' I didn't. I never saw the man again."

"Do you think this kind of thing will happen again?"

"No. Alexander Rankovich was exposed and arrested by Tito in 1966. I could once more enter my country. The state is building a museum in Zagreb for my collection, which I have pledged to give to my country. The museum will open in two or three years."

"What are you planning to give to this museum?" I asked. "Your early Christian chalice? The blue-glass English reliquary? The statue of Saint Peter? The objects you have shown me today? Some people, you know, do not believe your treasures are what you say they are. They think you own a load of forgeries."

Topic was about to answer when Frau Topic Mersmann edged into the conversation. "My husband is a man not of today. He is of the nineteenth century. He is an amateur in the traditional sense of the word—a *lover* of the material in art. He has always collected purely from the heart, emotionally. Sometimes he is right, deeply right, in what he chooses; sometimes he is wrong, way wrong. But, to him, it doesn't matter. Experts and specialists can sometimes see when he is wrong. But sometimes experts cannot see when he is right."

"Signor Topic," I said, "I still find it a bit hard to believe that even a man like Rankovich would arrange to have you killed."

"He was evil."

"But didn't you once work for Rankovich? Isn't it true that in 1950 you were arrested by the Germans, General Gehlen's men, for being Tito's espionage chief in West Germany?"

Topic Mimara looked at me as if his gaze could kill. Then he threw his head back and roared with laughter.

"Splendid! Yes. Certainly, I, Topic, was the head of the Service." He paused, leaned forward and said, "I was head of Yugoslavian espionage—and I was also in the secret service of England and France and the United States. You know, in my time I have been accused of being the head of the Russian secret service in Germany! By the Yugoslavians! Ha! No, I was never expelled from Germany. That proves I did nothing wrong."

"Signor Topic, weren't you arrested by the French for blackmarket dealings and currency violations in 1946 or 1947 in Säckingen?"

"Ah. That was interesting. One day in the winter of 1947 a certain German woman came to my lodgings and told me her husband, a former German soldier, was being detained in a prison camp in the Soviet Union. Her husband had contrived to send her a considerable sum of Russian rubles. She wanted me, as a great favor, to exchange the money for Swiss francs. She was so pathetic, so obviously in need, I did what she asked. Amazingly enough, not an hour after she left, I heard dozens of whistles blowing. Suddenly the French Military Police burst into my rooms and arrested me. But you know, those French were really after my collection. Everyone has been after my collection—even you."

We talked on for several hours over lunch and through a spectacular rainstorm which passed over the *Schloss* like "The Ride of the Valkyrie." Ante Topic Mimara adroitly parried my every question. Had he been heir to a shipping and pharmaceutical fortune, as Harold Parsons had described him? Not at all. He had never been rich as a youth. His parents had been simple farmers. What had he done during the war? Had he lived quietly in Berlin until 1944 and then was arrested by the Nazis for political reasons. Friends helped him escape with his collection after the war. and he went to Säckingen. Why had he gone to Tangier? He liked the place. What about suspicions that his collection had come, in part, from the Collecting Point? He told me that an American consular official in Tangier, Edwin Murray Jackson, had signed an "affidavit" which cleared him of ever having taken works of art from the Collecting Point for himself. Although Mersmann looked anxious from time to time, Topic became more relaxed the more we talked. He was obviously enjoying himself.

"Isn't it time, finally," I asked, "to tell me where you found the cross? Look, it's been forty years since you discovered it. What harm could there be now? I need the information because it might help my continuing search for the missing block."

He gazed at me and smiled thinly.

"Come on, tell," I coaxed.

Topic leaned forward, started to speak, but abruptly fell silent.

"Was it Yugoslavia?" I asked softly.

"Never! I would never have taken anything out of my beloved country," he protested.

"Hungary?" I quickly asked.

"No." But his eyes flickered.

"Czechoslovakia?"

He shook his head slowly and then smiled again.

"Rumania?" I said in a whisper.

He raised his eyebrows. "Signor Hoving, you cannot expect me to reply to every step of your journey through the Eastern countries."

"Will you ever tell me?"

Topic Mimara smiled, and shrugged.

Sources

IN THE CASE of the ivory cross, I collected more than a work of art. Throughout the entire affair I retained every piece of correspondence and notes; I kept a scrupulous diary, day after day, recording conversations, the climate of the day and even the physical looks and reactions of the people I encountered. There are more than five hundred letters, notes and memoranda. The diary runs to several hundred pages. Inevitably, even with the most careful attempt to save documentation, a certain amount is lost. Some stories I have reconstructed to the best of my recollection. The anecdote about the vultures in the tree on the road from Mérida to Chichén Itzá is retold as it was told by the curator of Arms and Armor at the Metropolitan, Helmut Nickle, in his essay in my book *The Chase, The Capture,* published by the Metropolitan Museum in 1975. I have reconstructed from memory the whimsical notes handwritten by James Rorimer on my memorandum to him in which I explained the deal Topic Mimara was seeking. Two names have been changed because of the delicacy of the specific situation. One is "Willi" of the Zurich police. The other is the collector in Orléans, Guy Cranier. The rest is, to the best of my ability to remember and record, how it happened.

The information about Topic Mimara's encounters with the Sûreté and the BND is published in the excellent account of the career of General Reinhard Gehlen by Heinz Höhne and the late Hermann Zolling, *The General Was a Spy* (Coward, McCann and Geoghegan, 1972).

For the reader who wants to delve further into the scholarship surrounding the cross, the following will serve as a basic bibliography:

Beckwith, John, *The Adoration of the Magi in Whalebone.* London, 1966.

————,*Ivory Carvings in Early Medieval England,* London, 1972.

Hoffman, Konrad, "The Year 1200," *A Centennial Exhibition at the Metropolitan Museum of Art,* I, 1970.

Hoving, Thomas, "The Bury Saint Edmunds Cross," *The Metropolitan Museum of Art Bulletin,* XXII, 1964.

Longland, Sabrina, "The 'Bury St. Edmunds' Cross," *The Connoisseur,* 172, 1969.

————, "A Literary Aspect of the Bury St. Edmunds Cross," *Metropolitan Museum Journal,* 2, 1969.

————, "Pilate Answered: What I Have Written I Have Written," *The Metropolitan Museum of Art Bulletin,* XXXXVI. 1968.

Mersmann, Wiltrud, "Das Elfenbeinkreuz der Sammlung Topic Mimara," *Wallraf-Richartz-Jahrbuch,* 25, 1963.

Stone, Lawrence, "Sculpture in Britain: The Middle Ages," *The Pelican History of Art,* 2d ed., 1972.

Acknowledgments

To all those who were involved in the making of the adventure and the book, I owe profound thanks:

My colleagues in the British Museum, the most gracious competitors I have ever encountered: Sir Frank Francis, R.S.L. Bruce-Mitford and Peter Lasko.

Sir John Pope-Hennessy and John Beckwith who imparted to me the story of the Victoria and Albert Museum.

Peter Wilson and Timothy Clark of Sotheby & Co. for their invaluable recollections.

George Zarnetski for his learned opinion and vital words.

Hanns Swarzenski for his exciting tale and unflagging support.

My colleagues in Germany who provided treasured information: Erich Steingräber, Theodore Müller, Florentine Mütterich and Dr. Rike Wankmüller.

Richard H. Randall, Jr., an individual of wisdom and confidence.

My friends in the Medieval Department: Carmen Gómez-Moreno and Marj Baucom Spoerri.

Sherman Lee of the Cleveland Museum who graciously corrected some of my early mistakes.

Ante Topic Mimara and his wife Wiltrud Topic Mersmann for the interview of March 1978.

Giuseppe Cellini for the Roman information.

The late Edgar Breitenbach and Mrs. Breitenbach for witty and invaluable stories concerning the Collecting Point.

Gerald G. Stiebel for papers regarding the once missing Christ Before Pilate.

John Goldsmith Phillips for his stories of the London episode.

Edwin Murray Jackson for the Tangier recollections.

Henry Sayles Francis for his unique and key contribution in making available the extensive and splendid letters to him from Harold Woodbury Parsons.

Kurt Weitzmann for his guidance, support, trust, connoisseurship, scholarship and humanity over so many years.

Ashton Hawkins, Secretary of the Metropolitan Museum of Art, for permission to quote museum documents.

Alice E. Mayhew, Editor at Simon and Schuster, for her critical and friendly assistance in making the manuscript so much better.

In the preparation of the manuscript, Amy Miller, Jane Margaret Freeman and Marianne Lyden.

Philip Power for helpful criticism and keen advice.

John and Liz Allen for haven at Sugar Tree Farm during the early editing process.

Nancy Hoving for sage and gifted editing.

Robert Lescher, Author's Representative, without whose constant efforts through every phase of the creation, editing, and refinement of the many manuscripts, this book would never have been born.

THOMAS HOVING
New York, 1981

Index